CITIZEN PARTICIPATION
in NONPROFIT
GOVERNANCE

CITIZEN PARTICIPATION IN NONPROFIT GOVERNANCE

Sondra Z. Koff

Routledge
Taylor & Francis Group

LONDON AND NEW YORK

First published 2009 by Transaction Publishers

2 Park Square, Milton Park, Abingdon, Oxfordshire OX14 4RN
711 Third Avenue, New York, NY 10017

Routledge is an imprint of the Taylor & Francis Group, an informa business

First issued in paperback 2017

Library of Congress Catalog Number: 2009007533

Library of Congress Cataloging-in-Publication Data

Koff, Sondra Z.
    Citizen participation in non-profit governance / Sondra Z. Koff.
        p. cm.
    Includes bibliographical references and index.
    ISBN 978-1-4128-1042-5 (alk. paper)
        1. Nonprofit organizations--Management--Citizen participation.
    2. Boards of directors--Citizen participation. 3. Corporate governance--Citizen participation. I. Title.

HD62.6.K639 2009
658.4'22--dc22

                                                    2009007533

ISBN 13: 978-1-4128-1042-5 (hbk)
ISBN 13: 978-1-138-50816-3 (pbk)

For
Steve
A Committed Public Member who is sorely missed

and
Abigail, Atticus, Eleanora, Madelyn, and Zenyram
May they grow into
Committed Public Members

WITH LOVE

Contents

Preface

The idea for this research was born at a National Organization for Competency Assurance (NOCA) conference that I attended as a public member of the Healthcare Quality Certification Board. One session, at which I was present, consisted of a conversation with the late Ben Shimberg, a well-known authority on professional licensing and certification issues and a fierce advocate of public representation on regulatory boards. Many topics were discussed during that session, but I was particularly intrigued by the attendees' comments concerning public members on governing bodies. For the most part, the opinions expressed were negative in nature. On this subject I viewed the session primarily as an example of "public-member bashing." Being unable to attract the attention of the moderator, so I could have a say before time ran out, I vowed to further pursue this matter. This research endeavor was spurred by these remarks. I wondered how public members would react to these comments. How would other executive directors respond? Who are the public members? What are the precise problems related to their participation? How are these problems viewed by agency leaders? Do public members hold the same perspective? How might these problems be solved?

This work was long in the making. Unfortunately, progress was significantly delayed due to serious illness in the family and the resulting loss of my "sounding board" and always my first reader, Stephen P. Koff, a fellow political scientist and public member, who, even though he worked in another field, had a knack for posing challenging questions and advancing unique perspectives on issues. Even during his last days he wanted to discuss this research. Given his commitment to the public member role and his significant interest in the project, I had every reason to complete it.

I am most appreciative of the support and encouragement I received from several quarters. First and foremost, I thank those chief executive officers and public members who completed the survey instruments. Voluntary comments appended to them were most welcome and useful as were letters of encouragement from both constituencies. And even the few negative comments concerning the project were instructive. Bonnie Aubin was serving as the executive director of NOCA during the initial stages of this work. Her understanding of the research, support, and efforts on my behalf were singular and crucial to the completion of the project. Janice Moore, Associate Director of NOCA, enthusiastically provided valuable assistance for which I am grateful. The encouragement and support of my colleagues on the Healthcare Quality Certification Board and its executive director during my term of office, Jan Marone, must be recognized. Their understanding of the undertaking was immediate. Furthermore, my participation on other sub-national and national governing bodies as a public member has served to enhance my belief in the importance of this role. I am thankful to my colleagues on these boards and their chief executive officers for providing me with worthwhile, challenging, learning, and entertaining experiences along with much hard work. Acknowledgment is also gratefully made to an anonymous reviewer whose constructive criticism and helpful comments were much appreciated.

Hopefully, I have penned a volume of use to public members, agency personnel, and a wider audience as well. Although I have received aid from various sources, I assume full responsibility for its content.

Sondra Z. Koff

1

The Game and Its Background

Introduction

The performance, vitality, well-being, and effectiveness of a society, its government, and social institutions are related to communitarian involvement, associational development, and voluntarism, among other things. It is these ingredients that, in part, explain a social fabric permeated with trust and cooperation, or social capital, those "features of social life—networks, norms and trust—that enable participants to act together more effectively to pursue shared objectives" (Putnam, 1995, p. 664). In a broader interpretation social capital also consists of access as well as resources available to individuals and groups. Being the glue that cements linkages within various constituencies and across and beyond them, enhancing cooperation, and thus, allowing broader interests to be served, social capital is of great import. It is based on the premise that greater contact between people creates more trust and resulting social ties make individuals and groups more productive. The social and economic resources embodied in social networks are enhanced. In essence, these networks create value, the benefits of which serve a variety of purposes and reach beyond persons immediately involved. Moreover, the correlation between social trust and civic engagement is strong (Foley & Edwards, 1999; Putnam, 2000; Putnam & Feldstein, 2003).

Ever since colonial times Americans of all types have exhibited their propensity to form a wide variety of voluntary associations and their active voluntarism. Tocqueville's well-known picture of the United States had a prominent place for associational development and the citizens' capacity for participation. He observed: "In no country in the world has the principle of association been more successfully used or more unsparingly applied to a multitude of different objects, than in America" (Tocqueville, 1946, p. 126). He singled out the United States as the only

1

country in the world where the right of association had been used productively to secure all the advantages that civilization could bestow. For him "the science of association is the mother of science; the progress of all the rest depends upon the progress it has made" (Tocqueville, p. 381). Voluntary associations are ascribed a significant role in the development of social capital. Moreover, civil societies, consisting of a multitude of these groups that serve as counterparts to formal governmental institutions, are seen as necessary for robust and effective democratic performance (Wollebaek & Selle, 2002).

Voluntarism, another hallmark of American society, nurtures compassion, comradeship, self-confidence, and active public-spirited citizens, all important components of the national culture and fertilizer for social capital. Approximately 56 percent of the American population routinely volunteers and 90 percent makes financial contributions to a galaxy of causes on a regular basis (*Giving and Volunteering*, n.d.; O'Connell, 1997; Werther, Berman, & Berman, 2001). The United States is the only nation in which contributing and volunteering occur to such an extent. This participation, which also influences political behavior, is of great importance. Through volunteering people develop themselves, their communities, and the public good. Verba, Schlozman, and Brady (1995) underscore the significance of voluntarism to an understanding of America. They write:

> To understand voluntarism is to understand something important about Americans—how they express their civic and humanitarian concerns and how they pursue their self-interest, for they can do both through voluntary activity. To understand voluntarism is also to understand something important about America. Voluntary activity is not only about individuals—what they do and why they do it. More than in most democracies, voluntary activity in America shapes the allocation of economic, social and cultural benefits and contributes to the achievement of collective purposes (pp. 6-7).

There are different spheres of involvement as well as various degrees of participation. Society, like a car, needs four wheels to run. Each one symbolizes a sector that provides a channel for participation. An important wheel represents government, the public sector, the director of the social unit, and an important employer. A second wheel, consisting of for-profit organizations or business, because of its size and earning power, is an influential social force. The third wheel denotes the volunteer or nonprofit sector. It is composed of a myriad of diverse organizations that serve the public at large or the public good of a defined membership as opposed to the specific self-interests of a constituency. Many of these entities depend on volunteers to provide their services and/or to govern the organization. These associations influence heavily the direction of the societal car. The last wheel stands for the informal sector or units, such as the family, the neighborhood, and the community. Society, like a car, relies on all four wheels for performance (Van Til, 1995). Their individual output and their interaction are significant.

This work focuses on one of the wheels, the third one, the nonprofit sector. It examines an element of its governing structure, boards of directors, and, more specifically, their newest constituency, that of the public members, the name given to those citizens participating in governance as representatives of the public at large. The study is based on questionnaires administered to public members sitting on the boards of select nonprofit organizations and to the executive directors of these entities. Research objectives were fourfold: (1) to construct a demographic profile of the public member constituency, (2) to inventory the group's activities and opinions concerning various facets of board membership, (3) to catalogue the executive directors' perspectives on the public member role and experience, (4) to elicit problems related to citizen participation and strategies to help solve them. It is demonstrated that institutional climate and demography serve to limit the public members' role in nonprofit governance which is unfortunate, given the many advantages of citizen participation in this sector.

The sampling frame included the universe of units affiliated with the National Organization for Competency Assurance, a nonprofit membership association consisting of certification agencies, testing and consulting firms, as well as individuals involved in professional certification endeavors. It advocates excellence in competency assurance for people in all occupations and professions, and it serves the public interest by promoting adherence to standards that secure supreme competence in certification programs. It is the oldest and largest organization of its type. Its members represent over 150 professions and occupations, including 57 in the health care field and others, ranging from those affiliated with the construction and automotive industries to those identified with the financial world.

There is much variability in membership. This was reflected in the nature of the agencies responding to the questionnaire. They represented the following fields: health broadly defined, education, testing, finance, consumerism, engineering, the environment, safety and security, architecture, interior design, automotive services, insurance, housekeeping, photography, real estate, computers, personnel, consulting, public and private management, illustration, telecommunications, water, electricity, microbiology, lighting, construction, petroleum, landscaping, restaurants, glass, law, convention services, regulation, and crane operation. The list is long.

Two hundred nineteen executive directors of the member organizations were surveyed and the response rate was 77 percent with 168 useable questionnaires returned. A total of 203 public trustees sitting on members' boards of directors were contacted, generating a response rate of 75 percent with 153 useable instruments. Prior to their administration via e-mail where possible and, if not, by regular mail, the survey instruments, consisting of open- and close-ended questions, were subjected to a pretest.

All respondents were asked to identify the mission(s) of the agency with which they were affiliated. Ninety-five percent of the public members and 76 percent of the chief executive officers cited certification. Both constituencies noted that their organizations provided products and/or services to associations or other entities. This was the case for 16 percent of the executives and seven percent of the public members. Also, seven percent of the former and two percent of the latter reported that their units were affiliated with licensure. The "other" category was negligible in the case of the trustees (less than one percent) and for the executive directors it registered 13 percent and included professional, educational, advocacy, and accreditation activities, in that order of importance.

The concept of representation and the institutionalization of individual efforts have become so engrained in American life that the pattern of organizational control by a board of directors has been firmly established. These boards have provided a significant outlet for the spirit of immediate and direct social participation. Moreover, as government has come to rely more and more on organizations in the nonprofit sector, its success depends on the performance of these units, which, in turn, is determined, in part, by the talents of the boards of directors. Yet, in spite of their importance, there is a dearth of literature that focuses on board members, and, especially, on the newly arrived citizen participants, the public members (Hage, 1998; Herman & Renz, 2000; Houle, 1989; Kang & Cnaan, 1995; C. Oliver, 1999). This work is intended to help fill that void.

The public member cannot be understood in terms of the current balance of social relations. Social institutions, being historically rooted, one cannot study any element without studying its context. Present day phenomena have their roots in various stages and facets of the past. Thus, before pursuing the main focus of this work, the general nature of the third sector will be briefly explored so that the reader will be able to relate the major theme to a broader perspective.

The Third Sector: Its Nature and Characteristics

Activities of the public, private, and nonprofit sectors have never been mutually exclusive, even though historically they have been somewhat distinct. Their role, for the most part, mirrors their objectives and the social, economic, and political parameters within which they operate. Although nonprofit organizations exist in most countries of the world, it is generally acknowledged that their numbers, proportions, autonomy, and impact are greatest in the United States. This facet of society is known by various labels: the voluntary sector, the third sector, the independent sector, the not-for-profit sector, the nonprofit sector, the social sector, and the nongovernmental sector, among others. Cushioned between the marketplace and economic enterprise, on the one hand, and government and the state, on the other, organizations in this sector are great in scope and importance. In spite of this, they are often thought of as forming a sphere secondary to the private and public sectors (Brudney, 2001; Ferris & Graddy, 1989).

Manifesting differing organizational identities, degrees of visibility, power, and activities, as well as variance in scope, structure, and specific purposes, these nonprofits display common general objectives. First, as noted, they serve the public good. They undertake activities that the other two sectors, business and government, do not, are not doing well, or are not doing with adequate frequency. More specifically, nonprofits are formed for any of the following objectives: to perform responsibilities assigned to them by the state, to perform tasks of a public nature for which there is an unfulfilled demand, to influence the direction of policy in the state, the for-profit sector, or other nonprofit organizations (P.D. Hall, 1987; LeRoux, 2004).

The goals and functions of the sector have been divided into two categories. Although they overlap, one is primarily private and the other public. Focusing on individual wants, needs, and gratifications, the former includes activities that foster self-improvement, individual professionalism, personal services, and self-fulfillment through participation with others. The latter is based on the traditional American suspicion of big government and it centers on societal problems, the maintenance of the

American democratic value system, and the ideals of justice, liberty, and opportunity (Eisenberg, 1983). The principal categories of nonprofits are many. For example, they are concerned with community service and action, health, education and instruction, personal growth, self-development and improvement, arts, culture, communication and information dissemination, science, technology, and engineering; social welfare, self-help for the disadvantaged and minorities, political action, the environment and ecology, consumerism, international and transnational affairs, occupations and professions, expressive-leisure, religion, criminal justice, fund-raising and fund distribution, among other things. The list is long. In fact, Section 501(c) of the tax code catalogues more than twenty-five categories of nonprofits, the principal ones being charities, foundations, social welfare organizations, and professional and trade associations.

All groups in the third sector are private and do not operate for profit. A trait that distinguishes the nonprofit sector from the profit sphere is that associations in the former are prohibited from allotting profits or residual earnings to members or owners. These units do make profits, but they are not allowed to distribute these surpluses by issuing dividends or repurchasing shares of stock. Excess revenues are reinvested in the organization. In addition, the two sectors are distinguished on the basis of mission. In the for-profit sphere the objective is to grow market capitalization through products and services, whereas for the nonprofit arena it is, as noted, principally to serve the public interest and to deliver services to key constituencies. Depending on their legal status, voluntary associations are also concerned with empowerment of the people and advocacy for social change. These organizations, not being intent on maximizing financial gains, do not prioritize activities on the basis of potential to generate profit as in the private sector. Whereas financial performance is the key measure for the private sector, for nonprofit organizations this measure is balanced with others.

The social instruments utilized by the public, private, and independent sectors differ as well. The first relies on coercion based on law, custom, and a wide variety of financial inducements and incentives, such as taxes, grants, etc. The second employs the tool of exchange and the third, voluntarism. This last mechanism is vital to the life of nonprofit organizations. It means that they "are the vehicles by means of which people pursue together goals that are not primarily remunerative and they are not forced to pursue" (D.H. Smith, Baldwin, & White, 1988, p. 13). Also organizations in the third sector have traditionally been free from the usual instruments of accountability and popular control. Thus, they have enjoyed a great deal of discretion. Additional differences relate to size, leadership, board composition and structure, and what is expected of board members. The governing body of a nonprofit organization tends to be larger, its chief executive officer more autonomous, board members more diverse, and their turnover rate higher. In addition, board roles are less predictable as are the hours involved in service and most board members are usually not paid for their services (Bowen, Nygren, Turner, & Duffy 1994; Cole, 1981; Hodgkinson & McCarthy, 1992; Levitt, 1973; McFarland, 1999).

Most recently the traditional boundaries between the nonprofit and private business sectors have eroded and a blurred gray zone has emerged. Many organizations in the former, in an attempt to diversify and strengthen their financial bases, have undertaken earned income ventures which, growing rapidly, have become a, if not the, principal source of nonprofit revenues (Light, 2002; Young, 2003). For-profit firms, manifesting a sense of social responsibility, have assumed new social missions and engaged in philanthropy. They have developed missions and services that are almost interchangeable with those of voluntary associations. Also, they have partnered with voluntary organizations to address socioeconomic issues and have funded them as well. Consequently, multisector networks have developed. Traditional boundaries have become distorted with this overlap of sector roles. One commentator observes: "Nonprofits and for-profits have more opportunities to learn from each other than either might traditionally think, and both seem to be becoming more like the other" (Rosenblatt, 2000, p. 2).

In fact, each sector has transformed. Business has redefined performance. Government has reinterpreted its methods and objectives. Nonprofits have been straining to respond to an increased demand for service and nongovernmental social action. Organizations in the third sector that have created revenue generating enterprises have reported a positive impact on mission, services, and programs. Also, in addition to generating revenue, these ventures have produced valuable publicity, aid in retention of staff, enhanced prestige for parent organizations, and a way for staff to supplement income, to cite a few benefits (W.K. Kellogg Foundation, 2003). This new stance of the political economy resulted, in part, from increased pressure on nonprofits to show long-term financial sustainability, the emergence of a new generation of leaders wed to entrepreneurial and market values, and globalization.

Institutions have a number of effects on social life. Even though many of America's Founding Fathers were skeptical of voluntary associations, the third sector has been important to the nation's development. Its benefits and accomplishments, having been extensively documented, are well-known. Reflecting American pluralism, this institutional configuration meshes well with the political culture. In addition to providing vital services to a large number of people from diverse social strata, one of its formidable attributes is its role in the distribution of power. The authority of the state and its agents is tempered by the power of this constituency. Moreover, it distributes influence to a vast populace and, in addition, serves as a channel for these people to bring influence and demands to decision-making processes. Civil society, by giving citizens the means to control forces impacting their lives and to generate social capital, restricts the role of government in such a way that citizens become participants (Chrislip, 2002). This phenomenon highlights the significance of nonprofit organizations. In addition, the third sector provides a mechanism for pattern maintenance functions, the articulation of countervailing definitions of reality, self-fulfillment, extensive societal goal attainment, both operational and change-oriented; the creation and dissemination of new ideas, the initiation of social change, social integration, the affirmation of values, and protection of the public (Adler, 1988; Pearce, 1993; D.H. Smith, 1966). All of these elements underscore the import of citizen participation in the governance of associations in the third sector in the form of the figure of the public member.

The importance of nonprofits also derives from the fact that they offer an environment for innovation. Many phenomena of significance have issued from their confines and their contributions to broad-scale social and scientific advances have been widely recognized. Closely related is their tradition of independence and relative freedom from constraints that allows for innovation and criticism. Relying on this tradition, the third sector has also functioned, as indicated above, as a check on government and as a corrective to some of its deficiencies. Furthering active citizenship, political engagement, the development of social, civic, and organizational skills, as well as such civic virtues as charity, community, reciprocity, trustworthiness, active participation, and cooperation, nonprofits contribute to the health of public institutions and the functioning of democracy. They also serve as a coordinating hub in a wheel that unites the three sectors. They have coordinated efforts of business and government. In a sense, this sector reinforces the other two. Furthermore, given their intermediate position, third sector organizations have acted as mediators between the organized economic interests of the market and labor and the political interests and constituencies of state agencies. The social impact of the nonprofit sector has been and is immense (Commission on Private Philanthropy and Public Needs, 1983; Gardner, 1983; Nielsen, 1983; O'Connell, 1983; Seibel & Anheier, 1990; D.H. Smith, 1988). It can be viewed as a mechanism that links government, economy, and civil society. In terms of a power distributional perspective, it reflects the saliency and vibrancy of civil society and from a cultural point of view, the spirit of voluntarism, self-governance and the propensity to form associations. Its effects are both internal and external, influencing the larger polity as well as participants themselves.

The Third Sector: Its Development

In a comparison of nations the United States emerges as the one with the clearest concept of a distinguishable third sector (Salamon & Anheier, 1995). Modern associational forms of voluntary effort were stimulated by the Reformation and its concomitant movement toward freedom of association. In the United States the historical roots of the civic community date back to colonial times. The propensity to form associations devoted to the public interest found fertile ground in the New World. From this era a facet of American history has been based on voluntarism and civic engagement.

Social context, national development, history, and politics and government profoundly influence the institutional landscape. The settlers arrived in a country with a large territory, little structure, few built-in restraints, and much social mobility. Neighborliness, interdependence, and mutual aid were dictated by the harsh realities of life that compounded with the westward expansion of the nation. Folks joined together to support each other in common efforts and to further causes in which they believed. In undertaking these activities they were attempting to meet a pressing need, to alleviate unfulfilled social voids, to help special groups in the population, or to propagandize on behalf of social reform. Given that social institutions are born from repeated interactions among people, the seeds were planted for the development of the wide variety of nongovernmental organizations serving community purposes that pepper the American scene today. Max Lerner (1983) observes:

The permissiveness of the state, the openness of an open society, the newness of the surroundings, the need for interweaving people from diverse ethnic groups—or, conversely, of their huddling together inside the ethnic tent until they could be assimilated—these shaping forces were present from the start.What came later was the breaking up of the rural and small-town life of America and the massing in impersonal cities, bringing a dislocation that strengthened the impulse to join like-minded people (p. 86).

Even though the United States is considered a secular nation, the birth of voluntarism and its institutions was also colored by religious influences. Many of the religious groups provided for the needs of their followers within the doctrine and structure of their church. Initially, civic engagement impulses were accounted for by the Protestant ethic. Other religious imprints contributed by waves of immigrants from disparate lands added their stamp as well. Although the lessons were varied, the common message focused on goodness, traditions of help and service to others as duty and gratification, as well as the ultimate universal truth. Given religious freedom and the separation of church and state in America, it was possible to avoid certain conflicts, such as many of those that occurred in several European nations with a state religion. Religious diversity and the resulting competition between faiths generated a wide variety of associations. Religion was not only responsible for spreading values. It nurtured diverse local, state, and regional organizational models. Also, at the same time disparate membership organizations flourished nationally and locally alongside the religious ones. A multitude of new institutions, ranging from churches and ethnic associations to granges, became mechanisms for socialization and mutual activity (Hammack, 2001; O'Connell, 1983; Skocpol, 1999).

Also of prime importance to the establishment of the third sector is the American attitude toward government. From the earliest times citizens were generally suspicious of public power, perceiving it as a threat to liberty. This fear has been a fixture on the American political stage ever since, and it pervades the political arrangements that provided a favorable climate for the development of civic associations. The notion of a strong central government was unacceptable. Thus, the government that was established was limited in nature and power was dispersed. The political regime was designed to protect private rights from public meddling. Not having a strong pro-state tradition, voluntary nongovernmental organizations assumed on a broad scale many of the community responsibilities that governments exercised in other nations, especially those in Europe (Commission on Private Philanthropy and Public Needs,

1983; O'Connell, 1983). Max Lerner (1983) notes that "through these associations Americans avoid the excesses of both state worship and of complete individualism. It is in them, and not in the geographical locality, that the sense of community comes closest to being achieved" (p. 86). In terms of their function and utility these early institutions were of supreme importance. In addition to bringing people together, a significant factor, given the nation's strong and unique individualistic culture, nurturing social capital, they met the need of collective action problems and allowed for the achievement of group benefits through cooperation and exchange. Moreover, in addition to assuring commitments and providing focal points and enforcement mechanisms, they tempered uncertainty and enhanced possibilities for trade-offs (Thelen, n.d.). Thus, it is natural that they were endowed with a strong sense of community.

The shape and character of a nation's institutional structure are also influenced by its territorial distribution of power. It is generally acknowledged that the more centralized the structure, the less space for a coherent nonprofit sector. Conversely, the less centralized the structure, the greater the opportunity for a widespread and vibrant network of nonprofit associations. Given this tendency, the federalist division of power between the state and the national government in the United States has been important to the growth of the nonprofit sector. The individual states had prime responsibility for regulating nonprofits which, in part, contributed to their variety and lack of uniformity. As usually happens, group organization paralleled that of the state. Local associations were molded into federations and they reaped the benefits of this arrangement. The structure of the state served as an organizational model. In addition, regulatory mechanisms contribute to the nature of the organizational universe. Procedures for establishing nonprofit organizations were relatively uncomplicated and considerable powers were placed in the hands of their governing boards. Such practices, making it easier to establish certain kinds of associations, encouraged expansion in the sector.

Activities at the national level of government must not be overlooked. Interventions by all of its three branches stimulated organizational growth. Although it is common to make distinctions between the public, private, and nonprofit sectors, it must be remembered that the boundaries between them are not clearly demarcated. As noted above, there is overlap and collaboration among them is one of the hallmarks of the American political economy. Part of the nonprofit sector's history is its linkage to government. This relationship is not new. Recent empirical scholarship

challenges the widely held notion that classic American voluntary associations were small, local, and isolated from government (Skocpol,
Ganz, & Munson, 2000). Skocpol (1999) writes:

> For most of U.S. history, politics and government encouraged rather than stifled
> organized civil society. Competition and contention among politically active groups,
> representative institutions and competitive elections, and many kinds of national
> government initiatives—all were conducive to the emergence and growth of voluntary
> associations with active memberships (p. 33).

Since before the colonies united, there has been some form of mutual
dependency between the public and nonprofit arenas. Voluntary organizations were concerned with social problems before government. Thus,
when government assumed responsibility for solutions to these matters,
it was natural for it to involve the established nonprofits and to subsidize
them. Americans readily requested and took advantage of governmental
aid in the same way that government used voluntary associations to
implement many of its programs. Linkages between the nonprofit sector and government were principally cemented with subsidies. Government supplied these funds and voluntary agencies provided services,
creating a relationship labeled "cooperative autonomy." These financial
mechanisms were especially important to the well-being of the nonprofit
sector throughout the nineteenth and early twentieth centuries. Even
though government's role was important, it was subsidiary and minimal
in terms of impacting on the internal life of the voluntary associations,
whose large membership federations represented a force central to local communities as well as the nation (Adler, 1988; Loewenberg, 1992;
Skocpol et al., 2000).

Dating from the 1930s, government's role was no longer auxiliary. A
more equal partnership, known as "cooperative federalism" and "cooperative dependence," developed. The use of nonprofit organizations to
carry out public functions became more and more frequent and eventually
accepted policy in most parts of government. The scope of governmental
involvement with nonprofits expanded dramatically, especially immediately after World War II and since the 1960s. The kinds of services offered to government and the populace at large by these private nonprofit
agencies are varied and numerous. In part, America's uniqueness results
from the new stance of the political economy which features the heavy
load of public responsibility assumed by the third sector. This practice
has been labeled "the managed economy," "the contract state," or "the
pluralist state."

The linkages between nonprofit organizations and government are multifaceted. There is an elaborate network of these ties in virtually every policy sector. Economic bonds are of prime importance. For example, these associations are provided a special tax status in recognition of their collaboration with the public sector. Then, there are the other aforementioned financial bonds, such as direct and indirect subsidies, contracts, and grants, among others. Novel administrative arrangements, allowing the third sector to serve as the vehicle through which government fulfills some of its public responsibilities, have been established. Not-for-profits are generally perceived as alternatives to governmental bureaucracies and many of them often engage in public advocacy. In addition, government regulates these organizations on many matters, ranging from equal employment opportunity to fund-raising. Any discussion of the role of the nonprofit sector inevitably leads to an examination of its activity alongside that of government. The two arenas have been complementary expressions in the United States' experience and, being dynamic entities, both have been transformed. Government has drawn heavily on the energies of the third sector which, as a result, became more public in nature. Given these and other relationships with for-profit entities, the original hue of nonprofits, in general, has gradually faded (Ferris & Graddy, 1989; Lane, 1980; B.L.R. Smith, 1975).

The influence of legal systems on the character of the nonprofit sector must be recognized as well. In terms of the law, the major division is between countries organized on the basis of civil law and those, such as the United States, founded on the common law. In the latter, the third sector relies heavily on voluntarism and its organizations tend to be more competitive. As a result, they have greater resemblance to the private sector than government agencies. Moreover, they are more autonomous.

The notion of autonomy also relates to the institutional landscape that harbors the third sector. This ambience is of importance because the institutional composition of a society is identified with its style of innovativeness. It is generally acknowledged that in societies with little variation in the structure and culture of their organizations and well-developed institutional norms, habits, and rules that encourage conformity and rigidity, the institutional environment is such that it breeds little autonomy and flexibility. Innovativeness gasps for breath and innovations are few and far between. On the other hand, a weaker institutional environment nurtures heterogeneity on the organizational scene as well as greater autonomy and flexibility. Consequently, there is opportunity to be highly innovative (Hollingsworth, 2000). Being embedded in this type of environment, the American third sector has enjoyed a major advantage.

In addition, resources are critical to the health and growth of the nonprofit sector, meaning that it is also shaped by a nation's level of development. Governmental as well as nongovernmental resources are of importance. Again, governmental initiatives are concerned with grants, contracts, subsidies, and tax incentives, to cite a few, whereas nongovernmental means relate to the supply of surplus cash and time available to individuals and the private sector, principally corporations (Hodgkinson & McCarthy, 1992; Salamon & Anheier, 1995). In the United States, government, individual, and corporate largesse helped overtime to foster a significant nonprofit sector.

A community marked by a substantial amount of social capital equipped with norms of reciprocity and networks of civic engagement is more favorable to the expansion of voluntary efforts (Putnam, 1993). Having achieved this requisite, and with the roots of voluntary organizations firmly planted, due, in part, to the factors cited above, the American community stimulated growth in the third sector. These roots were institutionalized as a combination of top-down and bottom-up networks. Recent research substantiates an institutional and translocal conception of American civic voluntarism (Skocpol et al., 2000). Nonprofit organizations, aided always by developments in communications and media, grew steadily from the beginning of the nineteenth century, assuming continually greater importance on the local, regional, and national scenes. The growth was temporarily interrupted by the Depression during which nongovernmental action faded in significance indicating the close relationship between civic engagement and economic affluence. Most attention, as is well-known, was focused on the public sector and activities emanating from the nation's capitol until the early 1940s when nonprofit growth was rekindled. Throughout American history wars have fueled associational development and thus, in the post-World War II era expansion was spectacular and continued until the 1960s without significant controversy.

From that date there was a veritable explosion in association building. Even though growth was uneven and it periodically experienced exceptional economic strains, it was unprecedented in both scope and scale (Salamon, 1990). The American volunteer sector achieved a visibility and credibility unknown in its history. Civic engagement reached its zenith. It is noteworthy that in the ten-year period between 1987 and 1997 nonprofits augmented by 64 percent, whereas government bureaucracies increased at a little over five percent and business at approximately 26 percent. By the year 2000 nonprofit associations, numbering more than a million, accounted for approximately ten percent of the American workforce and nine percent of the Gross Domestic Product, whereas 40 years earlier, the percentages for both categories stood at two-and-a-half percent. In the European Union member states just under eight percent of salaried civil employees work in the nonprofit sector. Today well over six percent of all organizations in the United States are nonprofits (APSA, 2003; Hammack, 2001; Organisation for Economic Co-operation and Development, 2003; "What is the," n.d.).

This incredible enlargement resulted from a complex set of social changes that include the augmented affluence of American society, an increasingly educated and informed populace manifesting a new set of expectations, modification of the traditional family structure, the rise of the civil rights movement, the prevalence and extent of the AIDS crisis, the Great Society programs initiated during the presidency of Lyndon Johnson, as well as calls to service and involvement initially launched by the Reagan administration and reiterated by others. Most important was a transformation in the public's basic value priorities in general, accompanied by a more select reevaluation of more specific value systems by those, especially baby boomers, seeking more appropriate methods to experience success. Reference must also be made to the Vietnam conflict, Watergate, modifications in political institutions and governmental fragmentation, and rapid spatial mobility. The list is long. These factors, as well as others, influenced growth in and the dynamics of the third sector (Charles & De Maio, 1993; Hammack, 2001; Stepputat, 1995). The resulting conglomeration of nonprofit organizations has been responsible "for forging new bonds of community, a new commitment to active citizenship, to social responsibility, [and] to values" (Drucker, 1989, p. 93).

It should be noted that there is a debate on the nature of the expansion in the third sector in terms of its duration, the quantity and type of organizations, and the number and types of participants. Some scholars (Putnam, 2000; T.W. Smith, 1990) present arguments on behalf of a decline in civic involvement and mass membership organizations, resulting, in part, from pressures of time and funds, suburbanization, electronic entertainment, and generational change. Their claims have been challenged by others (Baumgartner & Walker, 1988; Brooks, 2006; Dalton, Scarrow, & Cain, 2003; Ladd, 1999; Warren, 2003). In any case, the third sector is a kaleidoscope of varied associations assuming diverse forms and working in many different ways.

The 1960s and 1970s were a critical period for nonprofit and other types of organizations. The environment was hostile and polemicized. Voluntary associations came under attack because it was revealed that the nonprofit network was riddled with bias. Regionalism penetrated its confines in that its associations were more prominent in the Northeast and the Great Lakes states than in other parts of the nation. This phenomenon can be explained by the fact that many associations, especially in the late nineteenth century, were launched from these more industrialized areas. A few took root and spread from the West, leaving the South unfertile (Skocpol, 1999). In addition, these entities manifested bias based on gender, income, and religion. They favored men, the wealthy, and the well-established, organized Protestants, Roman Catholics, and Jews as opposed to those people who were poor, not of the white race, female, and not identified with the main organized religious traditions, among others (Hammack, 2001). Such facts generated suspicion and alienation throughout the populace.

In addition, due to many of the factors accounting for expansion of the third sector cited above, linkages between citizens and government became strained as in other advanced industrialized democracies in which the citizenry became skeptical of political institutions, groups, and public figures. Although diffuse support for the values underlying democratic institutions did not erode significantly, confidence in these institutions and the people who managed them declined dramatically. There was a shift in the locus of power and responsibility from the legislative branch of government to the executive, and especially the bureaucracy. The latter assumed more numerous and more complex duties requiring utilization of highly specialized and professional personnel. The overwhelming size of administrative bodies, the nature of the general mandates assigned to them, and multiple opportunities for blocking change made the decision-making process appear unresponsive to citizen demands and to the public interest as interpreted by the citizenry.

Many observers were of the opinion that democratic customs were no longer central to the general operation of American government and particularly its bureaucracy. More specifically, there was a change in the perception of the use of discretion in public agencies. Along with greater discretion, these units also came to enjoy more rule-making power. The accelerated enlargement in the activities of government obliterated the notion of a defined, unitary public purpose. The appropriate role of bureaucracy, as well as the impact of its discretionary behavior on different interests, and its intrusion on individual rights became contentious subjects for public debate along with the dilemmas of how to incorporate new types of interests into a previously defined pattern of distribution and to reconcile the need to administer efficiently and professionally with the maintenance of democratic control. The theory of democracy was pitted against its practice and it was questioned whether government by experts was compatible with democracy (Collins, 1980; Eimicke, 1974). Many of the dissatisfactions with public bureaucracies were related to the third sector.

Moreover, even though the economy had flourished in the post-World War II era, a phenomenon which fostered expansion in the third sector, the basis for its enlargement was also questioned. Some observers felt it was based on indebtedness, speculation, and extravagant waste. With the increase in technology and organizational complexity, organizations of all types witnessed a parallel growth in the number and influence of experts. This occurrence initiated alarm because professionals, who made the "real" decisions, operated in these entities, as in government, so it was believed in many sectors, almost independently of the democratic process. Their capacity to supply superior decisions for the good of the entire community was doubted. The populace became generally more suspicious of the technical world and its elite. Surveys manifested the citizens' desire for an active role in affairs that at one time they were willing to leave to others. Previously, it was assumed that not only did consumers have little interest in policy deliberations, but also that they had little to contribute. Thus, the responsibility to guarantee that public needs were well-served fell to the experts. This assumption no longer prevailed. The basis of social, economic, and political decision-making was questioned. As a reaction to the belief that decision makers lose touch with common people and their problems, more responsive and benign behavior was demanded from them. Americans have always been skeptical about politics and politicians, but, in short, the nation was now experiencing legitimacy and participation crises that were seeded in the moralist and reformist culture of the sixties. Citizen attitudes towards authority changed. Individuals came to believe that they had a right to influence in multiple spheres the exercise of power that they no longer perceived as legitimate (Boyte, 1980; Ladd & Bowman, 1998; LaPal-ombara & Weiner, 1966; Levine, 1984; Levitt, 1973).

Initially the technological and citizen participation establishments travelled on parallel paths. It was only in the early 1970s with the growth of the environmental and consumer movements that they began to converge (DeSario & Langton, 1984). An awareness of the impacts of technology on daily life and the power of experts along with growing skepticism and mistrust of large institutions, both public and private, led to a demand for citizen participation in technological decision-making that eventually spilled over into other areas of endeavor. At the basis of this demand was the belief that decisions about their daily lives were becoming more and more removed from citizens because of the centralizing trends in government, the increased role of bureaucracy, and the remoteness of official decision makers that made it difficult for them to understand the needs of the public. Thus, it was deemed appropriate to participate in a more meaningful and different way in decision-making. It was argued that those affected by decisions should be able to exercise some influence over them to ensure acknowledgement of the public perspective. It was also made known that, for all practical purposes, the public at large as well as specific groups had been excluded from policy-making arenas to the detriment of democracy. This charge was echoed as well in many other nations in which citizens called for greater access, more transparency, and accountability.

From the perspective of government, the public, being an abstraction, was unavailable and thus, excluded. It was a unit to be recognized in theory, but not in practice. The prevailing view was that, being a representative democracy, in the United States it was only necessary to consult the public periodically via elections. Also, there being no practical way to link with the public in its entirety, it, in addition to being unavailable, was unreachable. Moreover, not having a common language and common objectives, the public was perceived as being incomprehensible and unintelligible. Last, in the eyes of government, the public was uninformed and lacking in the expertise required to make appropriate decisions (Mathews, 1984). Thus, it was generally excluded from all types of policy-making. Consumer involvement was proposed as the solution to this exclusion. New mechanisms were developed to link citizens with government and with diverse policy-making entities. Good governance and accountability to the citizenry in the public and third sectors were translated as transparency and efficiency with the citizen, acting as consumer of products and services, having the responsibility of guaranteeing the proper operation of decision-making bodies (Joseph, 2003).

More specifically, there were demands for greater direct client and consumer involvement in the decision-making processes of nonprofit organizations. It was also recommended that their boards of directors be more reflective of the public at large and that the public be accorded greater input into decision-making. These calls indicate that the public preferred new ways to be directly involved in the decision-making process. Opinion polls revealed that large majorities believed the locus of power in decision- making should be transferred from the professionals to the citizenry. Such a shift potentially reorients the process of decision-making by including more and new actors, increasing citizen control, and making outputs more sensitive to the public interest (Cole, 1981; Dalton et al., 2003). A new notion of participation prevailed.

Consumer Representation and the Public Member

The concept of consumer participation included direct recipients of benefits as well as members of the wider community. It was viewed as a critical means of protecting the public from arbitrary decisions emanating from entrenched professionals. Practically, the notion addressed the problem of equality in such a way that it aided people in challenging judgments, views, and plans. It helped them keep some control over decision-making impacting their lives. The call for citizen participation also represented a departure from the prevailing philosophy concerning who has the right to make what decisions in whose interests. This new approach, tempering professional dominance, favored a more democratic participatory type of decision-making. Policy-wise, it reflected the view that experts should not enjoy an informational advantage because of their technical expertise when it comes to the many value considerations central to resource allocation decisions. Stimulated, in part, by the Economic Opportunity Act of 1964 with its ambiguous prescription to obtain "maximum feasible participation" in the poverty program, demands for increased participation spread to every area of social concern.

The call for involvement of the public in decision-making identified with the participatory theory of democracy which is based on the premise that maximum participation is a prerequisite of democracy and an instrument of self-education (Richardson, 1983; White, 1988). This effort also continued to build on American political history which "can be seen as a process of democratizing a representative governmental structure"

(Kweit & Kweit, 1981, p. 4). Closely related is the so-called democratic wish that has accounted for many stellar happenings in American history. Serving as an ideology of reform and change anchored in the name of the people, it is wed to the notion of citizen participation because of its ability to produce better citizens and improved policy output. In addition to stressing the notion of community, it is also based on a consensus that assumes the people manifest an identifiable and distinct public interest. The expectation for the citizen participant, the public member, resembled the republican one of colonial times concerning the people's representative when it was expected that this figure would seek out and be the voice of the shared common interest (J.A. Morone, 1990).

Political systems are not likely to include previously excluded groups unless those groups coalesce their particular interests, develop group consciousness, and place demands on the body politic. Driven by groups in the third sector and the general alienation toward and disaffection of the American populace with the government, this was the route followed by the citizen movement, the label given to the potpourri of voluntary associations desiring change, in response to the perceived denial of their rights by a portion of the American community. Grass-roots citizen activism, armed with the "can-do spirit" and confidence in achieving a solution to problems, came into vogue, as evidenced by the galaxy of new social movements that swept across the nation in the last third of the twentieth century and the new role of interest groups in American politics. The amount of activism and voluntarism, involving myriad forms of protest, was vast. Participants, representing disparate and wide-ranging political and ideological forces, were hoping to heighten awareness about consumer rights and the need for greater public accountability in decision-making. Genesis of interest in citizen participation lies in the fact that it stemmed directly from pressures initiated by consumers themselves, who were demanding not only participation, but the right to participate in policy-making. Appealing to an implicit conviction that there is a broad public interest, the citizen movement aimed at increasing public access to and participation in policy-making machinery in multiple contexts, ranging from government agencies to nonprofit boards of directors, so that decisions would reflect this conviction. The third sector assumed a new stance emphasizing reform and social transformation. Its demands for institutionalization of the public member in diverse spheres of decision-making reflected its preference for reform from within through outside representatives, rather than through governing institutions. Government and many established organizations were perceived as a problem and having criticized their performance, the environment favored curbs and/or controls on their role (Ladd & Bowman, 1998; Levitt, 1973).

These efforts met a responsive chord. Government-sponsored citizen participation requirements and programs became one of the great megatrends of our time. Whereas in the past, the government response to participation crises afforded access to those demanding it, this response involved more. Not only were access and citizen participation granted. In many cases they were mandated. With an eye to improvement of the many decision-making processes in complex organizations that were empty of public accountability, a new type of decision-making of great utility and import, incorporating both citizens and experts, emerged in the public, private, and third sectors. As noted, it spread rapidly to many areas of social concern, in part, due to the fashionability and topicality of the notion. Consumers, having become "more demanding, more able, more numerous, and, not least, more organized," (Richardson, 1983, p. 114) were successful in their efforts to secure widespread introduction of citizen participation.

It was in this environment that the positive and most valuable figure of the public member, the symbol of citizen or lay participation, as well as a form of social capital involving the ways in which we connect with or relate to others, was born. Demonstrating their adaptability and flexibility, many nonprofit governing boards, identified with different fields of endeavor, chose to accept the birth of this new species and to add a new constituency, that of the public member, to their ranks. It is important to see how and in what ways these new participants have been incorporated into nonprofit institutions.

For this new type of citizen participation to be meaningful to both the participants and the organization, a precise statement as to a definition of the public member, the various dimensions of the concept, its relationship to the structure of the program in question, its practical ramifications, and the goals of such participation is required. A definition of the public member is an essential key to this statement. It has been said that "the idea of citizen participation is a little like eating spinach: no one is against it in principle because it is good for you" (Arnstein, 1971, p. 71). As at the time this observation was made, 38 years ago, beyond this general acceptance, there is today little consensus concerning what the term public member actually means, what it should mean, what it signifies, and what it should signify. There is a lack of clarity as to the goals of this participation in theory and practice. Is it an end in itself? Is it a means to other policy goals? Is it both? What specific purposes does it serve? Citizen participation is merely a strategy, a mechanism for the achievement of specific goals. It may be invoked for diverse purposes. It can be used as an administrative technique to protect the longevity of an organization, as an educational tool to transform attitudes, and as a means to define organizational goals and objectives (Burke, 1977; Charles & De Maio, 1993).

Unfortunately, the goals to be accomplished by adding a public member constituency to a board have not been clearly articulated nor have role, levels of participation, and decision-making domains for these representatives been detailed on a large scale. In addition, there is no common framework for describing the key dimensions of public member participation in diverse decision-making arenas. In wrestling with these matters, more confusion than agreement has emerged. Attempts to answer the questions raised above have generated more questions than crisp and clear answers. Thus, few of the aforementioned statements have been issued. It is important to answer these questions and to identify what motivates participation and what it is supposed to achieve. Responses will determine the appropriate approaches, methods, and procedures in public participation as well as criteria and measurements for evaluation. Participation must be organized in such a way as to be systematic, flexible, and productive (Brownlea, 1987; Hochbaum, 1977). Structure is determined by goals.

The public as a social category has been difficult to grasp. In part, the problem is nurtured by the fact that the public at large is a heterogeneous mass, encompassing three major subdivisions—the public en masse, the interest-differentiated public, and the public as individuals—each one manifesting unique behavior (Fagence, 1977). This has contributed to the difficulty of achieving a meaningful expression of public member as a citizen participant. The term public may be used substantively or empirically referring to all members of the community or society as a whole. In this sense, what is in the interests of all persons is assumed to be the public interest (Blitz, 2001). Victor Thompson stated: "In a democracy the owner is 'the public' and 'his' interest is called the 'public interest'" (cited in Eimicke, 1974, pp.16-17). There is only one public and one interest. But from an analytical or normative perspective, the term makes reference "to a particular sphere or domain of activity to which a particular significance or value is socially assigned" (Bèteille,

2003, p. 38). Thus, in this sense, not including and valuing the private as well as the public, the concept does not identify with society as a whole. Public members are representatives of the public, but what public or what publics? To whom are they accountable? Defining the public member is a crucial part of any strategy for identifying public member candidates and determining their behavior. Unfortunately, not enough attention has been focused on definition of the term and when it has been defined there is much variability. This diversity was reflected in public members' and executive directors' survey responses.

For those organizations most concerned with conflict of interest, public members are those individuals who do not make a living in a specific industry or are without personal or family financial ties to and interests in a specific field of endeavor. Interestingly enough, such an approach has often disqualified stellar candidates for certain board positions because they have had experience in the field. For example, a person having served on a hospital board of directors could be excluded from another board position in the health care sector because of this prior association. However, this experience could be an asset and not compromise objectivity.

For other entities, public members are those persons who do not possess expert knowledge in a specific professional area. Refuting this policy, one executive director in response to a survey question argued that public members "are most effective when they have a high level of personal knowledge/expertise of the regulated profession, and if their interest is primarily on public protection and consumer issues." Some public member survey participants fit this model. In one case a respondent, after having claimed to have represented the professional employer perspective in the field for many years, wisely penned the phrase: "Hardly the usual public member." And another public trustee reported a strong background in the profession affiliated with the board, but, not being active in it any longer, felt that he or she could bring history, knowledge, and now objectivity to the table. Even though the national membership organization which was used for administration of the surveys consists mostly of professional associations, it is not to be assumed that public members are necessarily individuals who are the nonprofessional members of the board. The cited cases are not singular. Evidently, the notion of public member can be quite subtly interpreted.

In another vein, a public member affiliated with a health care board in unsolicited comments astutely wrote:

> As a consultant with an extensive background in health care and credentialing, am I really representing the "public"? Is an academic specializing in health care issues really a public member . . . ? Perhaps experience and knowledge make one a better representative for the public, providing the ability to analyze and recommend directions. The question arises if an individual currently employed by any part of the health care industry, including education, should be considered the public member of a regulatory board.

Opposing this stance, another survey respondent sitting as a public member reported that in this position individual contribution resulted from 25 years experience in the field. Moreover, this person welcomed "the opportunity to share . . . expertise and experience with . . . fellow professionals." The appropriateness of holding a public member seat in these cited cases is open to question. And for some agencies, these representatives are individuals who do not provide services or are among those persons who are recipients of specific services. And again public members might be persons with residency in a specified area or with a specific income level. There are a variety of perspectives on this position.

Believing that in a sense everyone is a public participant some executive directors surveyed issued a call for a systematization of the public member concept. In one instance, the case of a nonprofit advocacy organization, anyone interested in the mission of the group can participate on the board. However, the certification body is organized as a standing committee of that board with its own bylaws and autonomous governors. Consumers of services also qualify as public members and hold positions on the board and all committees. At the same time there is a segment of public members who have to be professionally qualified to sit on the governing body. Thus, it was felt that traditional notions of the public member are not applicable to such a situation. Another executive director in an interesting twist wanted this representative to be redefined in a very broad sense to include major employers of certified individuals, i.e., those people who are financially damaged, if the public is harmed by the actions of the regulated professionals. Such a perspective provides a mechanism to make such trustees accountable for their actions.

As will be further demonstrated later in this work in the analysis of data collected in the surveys, there are still a variety of conceptions as to what the term public member actually means and should mean. Obviously, the definition selected influences the skills, resources, and constituencies that the representative brings to the board room. In addition, there are many diverse policies and practices that relate to the rubric of public member or citizen participation. To make the situation more complex, often the language used in discussions of this figure is most ambiguous. In the words of one of the early proponents of public members: "The idea was not as well conceived or as well implemented as it should have been" (Shimberg, 1994, p.121). Operationalization of the project in appropriate fashion requires development of consensus on basic questions raised in this section and, first and foremost, on a definition of the concept and the purpose of its realization.

It has been said that a good board member symbolizes the public interest, serves the public interest, and makes choices based on their contribution to or detraction from realization of the public interest (Cassinelli, 1958; Zwingle & Mayville, 1974). Obviously, such an affirmation is particularly cogent for the public member. But what exactly is the public interest? The term is equally as nebulous, elusive, and vague as that of the public member. The spinach analogy cited above is also applicable in this instance. Like the phrase, public member, public interest has generated an abundance of definitions of differing hues and scopes. It is a species of the common interest, but what species? It has been construed as commonly held values, as the wise or superior interest, as moral imperative, as an equilibrium of interests, as a process of adjustment and compromise reconciling divergent interests according to established rules, as a superior standard of goodness supported by specified values, as the ultimate ethical goal of political relationships, as a standard for evaluation that gives significance to the notion of rights and duties deducible from a general conception of human excellence, as myth, as symbol, and as an unknown quantity defying definition (Cassinelli, 1962; Fagence, 1977; Herring, 1968; Sorauf, 1957, 1962). It is not within the scope of this work to analyze each of these notions. Suffice it to say that each has been charged with serious and numerous shortcomings.

Schubert (1960) refers to "the cacophony of public interest." He comments:

> Most of the literature tends either to define the public interest as a universal, in terms so broad that it encompasses almost any type of specific decision, or else to particularize the concept, by identifying it with the most specific and discrete of policy norms and actions, to the extent that it has no general significance (p.11).

Although written several decades ago, this observation is still pertinent. Achievement of compromise between universalists and particularists has been difficult. The important fact is that scholars have not achieved consensus on a definition of the public interest. Equally important is that they also lack agreement on what it is that they are trying to define. Is it a goal, a policy, a means and procedure, a myth, or any combination of these? Like the term public member, public interest is widely used with various conceptualizations that share little common ground. In both cases, conceptual clarification is lacking.

The controversy concerning the meaning of the term public interest results, in part, from its dynamism and its elasticity. As in other cases, it is not a constant, but a pragmatic concept conforming to the mores of society at any moment in time. Given its relativity, it is of cardinal importance to realize that the public interest constantly necessitates reassessment and readjustment. What is regarded as the public interest in one setting may not be so regarded in another. Even though the notion is ambiguous, this does not deny its relevance or its significance. Redford affirmed: "The concept of the public interest is too comprehensive, too rich in variety and depth and too penetrating in our complex life to be either escaped or canalized in a definition" (cited in Eimicke, 1974, p. 56).

In spite of its ambiguity and operational dilemmas, the concept, a major facet of the democratic wish, is a significant factor in social life, in the ordering of human affairs, and, more specifically, in many dimensions of American life and in the development of American democratic theory. MacIver was of the opinion that "democracy itself is the final organization of the common interest" (MacIver, 1948, p. 220). Referring to public operations as well as the adequate satisfaction of individual desires, the public interest can be linked with all types of activities, individual as well as institutional. From a more limited perspective, it is affiliated with governmental decisions, lending legitimacy to them, among other things (Colm, 1962; Downs, 1962; Schubert, 1957). In the past, as in the present, it has had an important function in various types of decision-making. It is a mechanism that people can use to evaluate decisions and to share their judgments with one another. In addition, implying that there is a single common good for all, reference to the public interest can be invoked to co-opt or to placate people who must act against their own specific interests because of existing policy. Conclusions of recent research focusing on Western Europe and the United States support the influence of the concept on decision-making (Blitz, 2001).

Tribute is routinely paid to the public interest in all quarters and in both the written and spoken word. Its utility might derive from the fact that it is not a fixed term and that it can be used in seeking consensus as society undergoes change. The famed scholar and teacher Stephen K. Bailey (1962) has noted that the genius of the public interest lies in its persistent, perverse, and forceful intrusion on the daily discourse of rulers and ruled alike. It is this intrusion and not its lack of clarity that is of importance. In equally strong terms, Justice Frankfurter made reference to "that vague, impalpable but all-controlling consideration, the public interest" (cited in Colm, 1962, p.128). Especially pertinent to the public member is the fact that the public interest, as an "all-controlling consideration" and a device representing the broad versus the narrow or the more inclusive as opposed to the limited, serves as a constant reminder of all those so-called repressed interests that have been forgotten or slighted by myopic participants in the fray of decision-making.

Even though the noted difficulties related to the resolution of the legitimacy and participation crises were of consequence, barriers raised by these problems were not perceived as being insurmountable. It was generally acknowledged that with time these challenges would be met and with success. The introduction of citizen participation with public members, representing a kind of institutional bargain between professionals and consumers, was generally received with enthusiasm. Many supporters of the public member experiment pointed to the role such actors might play in reference to the unique structure of nonprofits noted earlier. Having no shareholders, a volunteer governing body and, in many cases, no members per se, plus being unable to distribute profits, a question arises as to who are the owners of these organizations. It has been argued that society as a whole can claim ownership because of the tax exemption enjoyed by these structures. At the same time, it has been asserted that, being legally responsible for all facets of organizational life, the governing body is the real owner. Whether it be one or the other, in theory, public members, because of their constituency, could be a very useful instrument for confronting this lack of ownership (S.R. Smith, 2003).

In addition, it was hoped that this new figure would significantly alter the trajectory of the decision-making system. It was believed that the new actors would afford institutions an opportunity to shift organizational priorities by creating more meaningful connections with the community, thus, generating a new collective conscience to produce different outcomes, those more appropriate to the constituencies affected. More accountability, transparency, efficiency, effectiveness, citizen control, better governance, and increased social capital, among other things, were all included in the positive evaluation of the public member project.

Optimism was based on a perceived shift toward a more democratic and participatory policy-making process and away from professional dominance. Countering the manner in which society was organized, and, more specifically, the way professionals had traditionally arranged themselves, the resulting redistribution of power, so it was believed, would provide the potential for ensuring fairer procedures and thus, better decisions for maximizing or, at least, enhancing interest satisfactions and making the notion of due process more meaningful. Hopefully, it would also decrease citizen alienation and thus, lead to improvements in attitudes as well as better service delivery. Public accountability was to be the prime reward of the new way of doing business. And, of course, decision makers, it was thought, would reap benefits from the increased legitimacy identified with their policies because of input by public members. In short, old institutions were to serve new ends with advantages for all players.

Having upset the equilibrium of many of its institutions with the addition of the public member constituency to many of its governing boards, the nonprofit sector assumed a new complexion. These structures, in theory, at least, became congruent with the imperatives of the new social and political environment. Institutional layering took place as some elements of a given set of institutions were partially renegotiated, while others were left in place (Thelen, n.d.). Third sector organizations had to change their perspective to clearly recognize that they were now accountable to a broader constituency than was once the case. Society at large and government at all levels were added to the list of members, employees, customers, and vendors. The current status of the third sector is indicated by the fact that, having operated outside the realm of harsh public scrutiny for a long time, it has come to attract the public eye and critical appraisal in much the same way as business and government (Bowen et al., 1994). Much of its significance results from the extent of its impact. Everyone is affected by its activities, some more, some less. It touches all our lives in one fashion or another.

The New Institutionalism

In the field of political science different perspectives for the analysis of political phenomena have been in vogue at different times. The traditional approach focused on the political structures that served as a framework for the political game and political exchange. Constitutions, laws, and other formal rules were considered of utmost importance because they defined the nature of the playing field, guided political behavior, and secured order in the political world. This approach was challenged and largely supplanted in the 1950s and early 1960s with the victory of the so-called behavioral revolution. Rather than concentrating on formal governmental structures, the behavioralist project gave much attention to informal distributions of power, attitudes, and the behavior of groups and individuals. The concept of institutions was substituted, for the most part, with a conception of political life that was noninstitutional. Socioeconomic and political structures were assigned lesser importance in the explanation of political outcomes and more importance was given to theory-building (March & Olsen, 1989; Searing, 1991; Thelen & Steinmo, 1992).

In the 1970s institutional perspectives made their reappearance in political science and the other social sciences. However, this return to institutional variables was labeled the new institutionalism because it contained subtle nuances that differentiated it from its ancestor. Stimulated by earlier works in economics, political science, and sociology, and extending a hand to political behavior, the new school of thought may be described "as blending elements of an old institutionalism into the noninstitutionalist styles of recent theories of politics" (March & Olsen, 1989, p. 2). The new institutionalism is much broader in scope than the old. It blends formal institutional structures with informal ones, such as routines, roles, conventions, norms, and reason. Thus, the resulting framework also includes political behavior. These institutions shape human action and control development.

The new institutionalism is not a unified body of thought. However, certain communalities among the various schools can be indicated. All of them assign a significant place to the notion of community and believe that human action is propelled by a logic of appropriateness contained in a structure of rules and notions of identities. Institutional change is perceived as being slow in nature and subject to multiple path-dependent equilibria. Furthermore, new institutionalists share a broad view of governance, believing that, in addition to manufacturing coalitions within given restraints, it also includes the formation of these constraints as well as the issuance of significant accounts of various phenomena to serve as the foundation for action (March & Olsen, 1995).

In its exploration of public members this study will rely on new institutionalism as set forth by March and Olsen (1984, 1989, 1995, 2005). For these scholars institutions are broadly defined. The term refers to formal structures as well as systems of law, social organizations, identities, and roles. Focus is on the endogenous nature and social construction of institutions. These are viewed as independent units consisting of structures, rules, and standard operating procedures that provide order and predictability. More specifically, institutions represent a "collection of rules and organized practices, embedded in structures of meaning and resources that are . . . relatively resilient to the idiosyncratic preferences and expectations of individuals and changing external circumstances" (March & Olsen, 2005, p. 4). Rules and practices indicate appropriate behaviors for political actors in particular circumstances. Critical to an understanding of institutions are the rules broadly interpreted, meaning "the routines, procedures, conventions, roles, strategies, [and] organizational forms . . . around which . . . activity is constructed" (March & Olsen, 1989, p. 22). It is these elements that are important to the definition and defense of values, norms, interests, beliefs, and identities. The approach adopted by March and Olsen is often labeled normative institutionalism precisely because of the significant role attributed to norms and values. Structures of meaning are an integral part of the identities, common purposes, and accounts that, in addition to legitimizing and providing a rationale for codes of behavior, also stimulate and direct that behavior. Capacity for action is furnished by structures of resources.

Institutions understood as such exercise a pervasive influence on human behavior. In that their rules define fundamental rights and responsibilities, they shape the manner in which issues are resolved. They empower some individuals and restrain others. They are the rules of the game. They determine who and what participate in various types of decision-making, the strategies and goals of the actors, the distribution of power, how information is processed and structured, what action is taken, who wins, and who loses. The list is impressive. Fashioning political behavior and policy outcomes, in essence, the role of institutions is paramount. They are critical to an understanding of reality. They structure the playing field, the game, and the outcome (Hall & Taylor, 1996; Hollingsworth, 2000; Searing, 1991; Thelen & Steinmo, 1992), and in the case of public members in negative fashion.

Survival and success are core goals of all institutions. Their achievement through the art of governing, according to March and Olsen (1995), relates to the development of identities, capabilities for appropriate political action, accounts of political events, and an adaptive structure. More specifically, governance "involves creating identities and preferences that define what is appropriate, right, desirable and acceptable, the rules by which citizens and officials are constituted" (March & Olsen, 1995, p. 246). People must be prepared for governance. Their political capabilities must be established. They must become thoroughly familiar with political institutions and their operation. Closely related are the creation and understanding of the cultures and rules that nurture completion of agreements. Roles must be created. Resources must be available and alternatives feasible so that the appropriate preferences are selected. Above all, elements must be couched in a system of meaning and an understanding of history (March & Olsen, 1995).

Governance is organized by the logic of appropriateness, a means of fashioning behavior of members of an institution, in this case, the public directors of a nonprofit governing body. This logic relates actions to specific circumstances in terms of their appropriateness within a conception of identity (March & Olsen, 1989). It dictates appropriate action for various situations. It specifies how a leader or any person, for that matter, acting in a specific capacity, is expected to behave. Individuals have to make decisions as to their course of action but, being inspired by institutional values, their preferences will always be within the boundaries established by these values and reflected in the logic of appropriateness. An outgrowth of this underlying logic is the development of a perspective on organizational life that offers members of an institution sense of purpose, meaning, focus, direction, identity, and belonging, all of which are related to trust, a major prop of the rules network. This logic serves as institutional glue. It promotes cohesion throughout the structure. If observed faithfully by organizational members, both individually and collectively, in the long run it fosters institutionalization. Chaos and ambiguity will automatically be decreased. Order, stability, and predictability will prevail along with flexibility and adaptability. The diverse scope and methods of institutionalization influence motivation as to what structures want to do and their capacity to do it.

Peters (2005) notes the logic of appropriateness' close relationship to role theory. Structures automatically establish behavioral expectations for people occupying institutional positions. They reinforce actions that are considered appropriate for the particular role and position and penalize those that are not. Some behaviors are appropriate to all members of an institution, whereas others are reserved for persons holding particular offices.

Possessing autonomy institutions also serve as instruments of change. Institutionalization means not only survival and success, but also growth and improvement over time. Changes in means and functions are important. Institutional features must be matched to exogenous social, economic, technological, and normative environmental requirements in a way that incorporates demands for change, functional imperatives, and normative concerns. Appropriate outcomes must be assured. This is a most difficult task, given that institutional forms, as noted, are path dependent.

Change basically results from "learning by doing," a process that allows for the identification of new circumstances that signal a need for modification. At a certain point, environmental changes create dislocations in a system, which, in turn, fashion new interests and means distributions, resulting in new coalitions, institutions, and outcomes. Institutional adjustments are not necessarily functional for the simple reason a misinterpretation of signals can produce dysfunctional results. However, March and Olsen (1995) claim that people, having multiple opportunities to tinker with their search for the right course of action, can learn from experience. In doing so, in the spirit of the aforementioned logic of appropriateness, the normative values of the institution serve as their guiding light, eliminating the need for an extensive calculation of outcomes (Peters, 2005). In spite of this logic, institutions, as noted above, are slow to change and they themselves impact this change by establishing elements of historical inefficiency. The process is a complicated one in which there are lags in terms of matching all the pieces of the puzzle. As a result, history becomes "a meander" (March & Olsen, 1995, 2005).

In the spirit of the new institutionalism, nonprofit boards of directors, like other institutions, such as legislative committees or governmental agencies, may be viewed as actors in the same manner that individuals are perceived as actors. They signify "arenas for contending social forces . . . collections of standard operating procedures and structures that define and defend values, norms, interests, identities, and beliefs" (March & Olsen, 1989, p. 17). Making choices "on the basis of some collective interest or intention (e.g., preferences, goals, purposes), alternatives and expectations" (March & Olsen, 1984, pp. 738-739), they are political actors in their own right. Determining the possibilities for participation, these units, the playing fields, are important to an analysis of the vital public member role. Although the benefits of public membership definitely outweigh the disadvantages, given the manner in which these institutions have operated, they have not been successful in empowering the public member constituency and thus, account for its failure to realize its potential.

In light of the value of the institutional structure in defining the context within which governance takes place and in explaining the role, goals, behavior, and power of any given actor in an entity, the next chapter will first generally discuss nonprofit boards of directors, the anchor of the institutional landscape for public members, and then attention will be focused on these new players in the context of these structures.

2

The Playing Field and the Public Member Team

Boards of Directors: Role and Responsibilities

Boards of directors are of supreme significance to the survival and performance of associations in the third sector. In fact, with the increasing scarcity of resources and the concomitant intensification of competition among organizations, these units are becoming more important. They can and do make a difference to a structure. "And while the topic of boards has been within the organizational literature for decades, their general importance for NPOs [nonprofit organizations] as distinct from for-profit and government organizations has not been stressed" (Hage, 1998, pp. 291-292). In light of the new institutionalism their significance is appreciated. Although nonprofit boards may be differentiated on the basis of the nature of their original mandate, their age, size, purpose, structure, caliber of board members, interest, and participation (O'Connell, 1985; Werther, et al., 2001), it is possible to address the subject of board functions in a general fashion. These roles will be discussed in terms of two diverse models.

Being answerable for governance and thus, bearing responsibility for all processes, routines, norms, rules, identities, shared meanings and cultures, units and relationships involved in an organization's operations and activities, among other things, boards of directors assume august, onerous, and comprehensive duties. They are the heart of the organization. In the words of one author: "The building begins with the board itself" (O'Connell, 1985, p. 57). This statement is most appropriate in terms of normative institutionalism. In the nonprofit sector this group, exercising a statutory and fiduciary trust role, holds an organization in trust for the public good (Freyd, 1988). As perceived by individual board members, the public good serves as the guide in decision-making. Given the notion of trust, governing boards are very often referred to as boards of trustees, rather than boards of directors. In this work these terms are used interchangeably.

More than a purely ethical matter, maintaining the trust requires governing boards to provide stability, continuity, and integrity to protect the organization's mission and to promote long-term values over short-term goals (Taylor, 1987). It is debatable whether this trusteeship relates only to the interests of the members or includes balancing these interests with others, especially those of the general public. A narrow interpretation of the nature of this trusteeship focuses solely on the members. The broader understanding includes the interests of the internal actors of a nonprofit, the members, staff, service beneficiaries, and vendors; as well as those of the external actors, the entire sector, society and governments, or the community at large (Connors, 1988; Gupta, 1989). Although there is no consensus on the extent of the trusteeship, the wider interpretation, given the events described in the last chapter, enjoys greater acceptance.

The prerogative to control and foster the institution lies with the board of directors. It is this unit that organizes the political life of a structure and how it does so makes a difference. The actors are driven by these decisions which in the long run affect the history of the sector (March & Olsen, 1989). As an instrument of governance, the nonprofit board is cushioned between the executive leadership of the association and its various stakeholders, those groups whose interests are related to it. First and foremost, its essential task, which has been given scant attention in the literature, and which is so important to the new institutionalists, is to govern on behalf of the stakeholders. Unfortunately, its report card in this area often leaves to be desired (Masaoka & Allison, October 28, 2004). As part of its governing function, the board determines the mission and course of the institution, and thereby, defines its values, objectives, and long-term strategies. In doing so, it must fashion policies and procedures that focus all actors on the production of the desired ends. It must address the rationale for the existence of the association, the recipients of its services, and significance of its results (Carver & Oliver, 2002). In theory, there has been a very clear distinction between governing, on the one hand, and managing, on the other. The board determines the ends of the organization and its policies, but it is not directly involved in their implementation. This is the responsibility of management, but within parameters established by the trustees. Harvard College President Abbott Lawrence Lowell once remarked: "Laymen should not attempt to direct experts about the method of obtaining results, but only indicate the results to be obtained" (Heilbron, 1973, p. 34). The board, then, as part of its support function upholds staff efforts.

The board determines the policies that govern all activities of the association. This is the first step toward organizational vitality. Focusing on issues critical to the institution, policies may be seen as risk management, as values and belief statements, as rules and norms, and as program improvement tools (Graff, 1995). They serve as guides to action in a fashion similar to the logic of appropriateness, which, it is hoped, will result in realization of organizational ends. These policies are basically statements of intent that generally do not emphasize details of administration. They establish a framework or basis for delegation to the executive leadership and clarification so that it can work with a strong sense of direction in unison with the board. In other words, the board via policy statements sets the institutional ship on course and defines the boundaries of delegation to the staff. Loopholes in these statements afford flexibility to management and it is its responsibility to fill them in as needed in order to achieve the determined ends. Thus, the board prescribes and proscribes. In terms of proscribing, it should be noted that it can delegate authority, for example, to the executive leadership, but not responsibility. Thus, in reality, very often this delegation involves the creation of imaginative mechanisms that allow board members to "keep their noses in" and "their fingers out" (Taylor, 1987).

In the real world of nonprofits it is not totally accurate to say that the board makes policy, while management puts it into practice. Staffs have ample opportunity to exert much influence on the policy-making function. Being involved in the day-to-day operations of all programs, information, counsel, and managerial skills that they offer are most useful to the policy makers. In addition, the latter provide much of the same to them (Block, 2001). This relationship can be beneficial and effective. However, as will be seen later, it has been an irritant to many public members.

Like most legislative bodies, a nonprofit governing board assumes a monitoring or oversight role. Although it does not formally perform the management function, a component of its supervisory duties is to guarantee that the association is being operated appropriately and efficiently on a day-to-day basis. Thus, as part of its governing responsibilities, the board is accountable to the stakeholders for the conduct and policies of the organization and it is also responsible for the general supervision of management. Ultimate responsibility for organization and administration lies with the board. Moreover, this unit has the power to hire and remove staff. It has been said that the most important act of any board is its appointment of a chief executive officer, given this figure's role in the organization. The board works closely with the executive leadership and staff. In this context the aforementioned policies that constrain or limit executive latitude assume significance (Carver & Oliver, 2002; Gupta, 1989; Heilbron, 1973; Houle, 1989; Louden, 1982).

Oversight is an extremely important and sensitive function. Monitoring requires that the board, without interfering in daily affairs, develop a sense of the organization's performance, including its legal and ethical dimensions. As part of its responsibility for institutional success, the board must constantly monitor and appraise the association's financial health and its programs in terms of achievement of goals and cost-efficient operation. In addition, it must monitor the performance of staff and ensure that the resources are available for it to carry out its duties. The board provides the operating requirements with respect to authorizing monies, creating requisite structures, and employing appropriate personnel, among other things. It must establish controls, financial and otherwise, to be used in an evaluation of the effectiveness and efficiency of operations and the realization of objectives. This involves reviewing managerial reports, predicting trends, forecasting, planning, and the like. Armed with data secured from these efforts, the board obtains the necessary information to hold itself accountable (Conger, Lawler, & Finegold, 2001; C. Oliver, 1999).

Questions of accountability and responsibility are critical. Responses to such inquiries as to whom is the board answerable, serve to define its purpose, functions, and status within and outside the organization. The board is generally the legal and accountable group responsible for all the association's actions and their results. Accountability refers to

> the requirement to explain and accept responsibility for carrying out an assigned mandate . . . . It involves taking into consideration the public trust in the exercise of responsibilities, providing detailed information about how responsibilities have been carried out . . . [and] accepting the responsibility for outcomes (Seel, Regel, & Meneghetti, 2001, p. 646).

As has been established, the governing board is accountable to the stakeholders. The scope of this accountability is determined on the basis of moral rather than legal ownership (Carver, 1990). In instances where state law mandates that nonprofits have a membership—i.e., a legal ownership—the board must decide if the moral ownership is a larger body extending beyond the confines of the formal membership. Governing bodies are responsible for the activities, results, and future of the organization. In essence, they are accountable for priorities, that is, for establishing the mission and policies of the organization, and for guaranteeing their congruency with social, economic, and political considerations; fiscal accountability or appropriate management of financial matters, and for effective organizational governance, and the quality, quantity, appropriateness, and satisfaction ratings of its various products.

Moreover, the board is accountable for its own performance, in addition to that of the institution. A recent study concludes that in the nonprofit sector board effectiveness has a strong correlation with organizational effectiveness (Herman & Renz, 2000). In that all authority rests with the board and can only be delegated by it, it totally controls exercise of authority. It is for this reason that "accountable boards are commanders, not advisers" (Carver & Oliver, 2002, p. xxii). All performance indicators reflect board activity and decision-making. Thus, this entity must accept responsibility for all types of performances, both internal and external, ranging from excellent to poor. Given that the public has become much more sophisticated, aware, and knowledgeable, the best way to justify its trust is to have a good report card. In any case, as on Harry Truman's desk, the sign on the boardroom door should read: "The buck stops here."

Given the events and trends described in chapter one, it is obvious that accountability is especially pertinent in this day and age. Its present significance stems from the growth of pluralism, professionalism, and consumerism. In practice, there are three basic types of accountability. One kind is known as explanatory accountability, meaning that the responsible party is required to give an account of designated matters. Only a simple explanation and nothing more is needed. Accountability with sanctions demands the same type of account after which it is possible to impose sanctions. Responsive accountability requires that the views of the accounted be given consideration (Leat, 1990).

Accountability also embraces legitimacy, an important stamp for any organization. It is possible to garner this in various ways. Having been provided an account of matters, leaders of the principal community organizations can endorse and support it. In this case, elite consensus supplies legitimacy. Another route is via rational analysis. Legitimacy is gained by a type of presentation in which the activities accomplished are presented in a framework that portrays them as rational, coherent, intellectual solutions to practical problems. Lastly, legitimacy may be claimed on the basis of system focus and flow. In this instance, legitimacy results from the fact that the system revolves around consumers of services and programs are designed, endorsed, or receive strong approval ratings from them (Leat, 1990). Obviously, a three-fold stamp of legitimacy represents the ideal.

Nonprofit boards have another function in common with many legislative bodies. Both perform a judicial role. Serving as an institution's final authority, governing boards are charged with acting as a court of appeal. They deal with internal disputes, for example, those pertaining to personnel matters, or with grievances forthcoming from their constituents, as well as complaints from consumers of their products. In addition, nonprofit boards act as buffers and bridges. As buffers, they protect the organization from inappropriate intrusions by other entities. Most of the members of a nonprofit board of directors come from the external community and they are usually identified with other groups as well. Thus, boards also function as bridges. In this capacity, serving "as boundary-spanning and control units" (Middleton, 1987, p. 141), they become important factors in the flow of information and resources across confines. In linking the internal and external environments and in creating organizational networks, they simultaneously channel societal interests to the institution and vice versa. This complex arrangement relates directly to a board's responsibility for updating the association's mission statement and policies. In carrying out this obligation decision makers have to continually search for and evaluate alternatives. Institutionalism and these networks are important in this frame of reference. March and Olsen (1984) note that the

> search for alternatives occurs in an organized context in which problems are not only looking for solutions, but solutions are looking for problems. Information about the consequences of alternatives is generated and communicated through organized institutions, so expectations depend on the structure of linkages within the system .
> . . . Guesses about future preferences are developed within institutions educated to defining and modifying values and the meanings of actions (p. 740).

It should be noted that congruency among all these roles is not perfect. There is much potential for tension and conflict between them, simply because each involves a different concept and style. Behavior appropriate to one is not necessarily befitting to another. For example, oversight is often difficult because as a function it can clash with that of policymaking. Many boards have had to address the conflict between these two principal roles. The question to be answered is: Can a governing board partner with management in developing programs for the organization and at the same time exercise independent oversight of staff? Boards of directors, in light of their interests and particular commitments, must make choices as to which functions will receive most attention and how the various roles to be performed will be integrated. This is the purpose of the logic of appropriateness. The actors must evaluate a situation, determine what role is being fulfilled, and their obligations in that role in that situation (March & Olsen, 1989).

In reality, the stage of an institution's development tends to dictate which functions and duties will be emphasized and how elites will be utilized. For example, younger organizations confront challenges different from those of established ones. In its initial phase a nonprofit board usually assumes a broad range of responsibilities of a leadership, managerial, and administrative nature. It is in a singular position of power which derives from the fact that, clothed in prestige, it is an important force in the development of the organization's mission, services, financial resources, and legitimacy, as well as the selection of its executive leadership and staff. Essentially the board, being concerned with internal and external orientations, is on the offensive. On the other hand, the staff, emphasizing implementation, occupies a secondary position. Its professional competence at this stage is of less importance than the obligation to get things done (Perlmutter, 1977).

However, as the institution matures and enters another phase of development, the board stresses diverse functions and modifies its role from that of a working board to a managerial one. Emphasis is placed on policy matters and administrative affairs are more and more left to the chief operating officer and staff. Internal concerns with a focus on quality of service become paramount. A particular significance is assigned to technical problems and thus, the lead rotates to the staff who acquires more autonomy. As the organization continues to age another transformation takes place. The managing board evolves into an advisory one, existing primarily to offer organizational guidance and direction as the association reassesses its position in the broader institutional landscape. The appropriate role of an institution's elites, both board members and professionals, is determined by its stage of development (Perlmutter, 1977; Werther et al., 2001). The new institutionalists' notion of change is important in this context.

Board role and effectiveness are interrelated and prime concerns for any governing body. As noted, there is a strong congruence between the competencies of effective boards and institutional indicators. Thus, this concern is understandable. The literature, both normative and empirical, reports a search for board roles that aid in the pursuit of better management techniques and other contributions to board and organizational effectiveness (Chait, Holland, & Taylor, 1993; Inglis, Alexander, & Weaver, 1999).

Recently in the nonprofit sector many dramatic changes have taken place. New organizational structures have been born in the form of entrepreneurial associations, interorganizational alliances, and multicorporate firms, such as nonprofits with subsidiaries. In the context of these changes small grassroots organizations have become more unique. Moreover, many nonprofit managers have become more oriented toward the leadership role, while many board members have identified more with management activities. Thus, the aforementioned policy governance model is no longer appropriate for all nonprofits. Arguing that governing has become "too complicated to reduce to simple aphorisms . . . like 'boards set policies which administrators implement' or 'boards establish ends and management determines means,'" (Chait, Ryan, & Taylor, 2005, p. 5), Chait et al. (2005), in a pathfinding study concerned with board effectiveness, recast governance in a new model labeled governance as leadership.

In this model governance is no longer fixed and unidimensional, as previously discussed, but contingent multidimensional practice consisting of three separate but equal and complimentary modes that link governance, represented by the volunteer board of directors, and leadership, symbolized by the organization's executives. Major actors are linked by appropriate work modes, the propellant of any structure.

The first mode, Type I or the fiduciary mode is fundamental to governance. Acting in this capacity trustees focus on financial affairs and their effectiveness, oversight, mission fidelity, compliance with legal requirements, and organizational interests. To take advantage of the leadership opportunities that fiduciary activities provide, trustees, in addition to the routine tasks, must probe the deeper implications of fiduciary issues and the fiduciary significance of other matters as well as evaluate the fit of programs and mission. Type I board activities represent only one facet of trusteeship. Broader horizons must be explored. Thus, boards of directors are also expected to operate in other modes.

The major objectives of the Type II mode of governance are to foster strategic thinking and to nurture a strategic partnership between the governing body and management. This mode focuses on the strategic activities that establish the organization's priorities and course as well as the deployment of resources. Strategizing and forging and digesting ideas, an organization attempts to relate its internal strengths and weaknesses to external opportunities and threats. Thinking is more important than planning. Proposals are not to reach the board's agenda prepackaged from staff, a prevalent and unfortunate practice that encourages board members to plan rather than strategize. Thus, in developing strategy importance is assigned to ideas not plans. Chait et al. (2005) write:

> Unless and until ideas, rather than plans, are the drive motors of strategy, the full range of trustees' talents will be vastly underutilized. As strategies are hatched and plans unfold, boards along with CEOs [chief executive officers], should be more akin to architects than general contractors or, worse, tradesmen. In order to fulfill this role, boards must work in a strategic, not fiduciary, mode (p. 68).

Of note is the fact that the board and management think, strategize, and work together in the pursuit of strategic priorities and drivers. The separate line of authority between board members and chief executive officers, so characteristic of Type I activities and the policy governance model, are much less clear in the Type II mode of governance. The realm and role of both sectors, the governing body and management, cannot be completely disentangled. The scenario is compared to that of partners in doubles tennis: "neither party . . . can afford to be particularly territorial or both will lose" (Chait et al., 2005, p. 69). Also, of importance in the Type II mode is that restrictions related to the board's role in implementation activities are cast aside. It is recognized that the governing body can be most useful and valuable in translating plans and ideas into action.

To date, Type I and II modes are the most practiced forms of nonprofit governance. However, being deemed incomplete and insufficient for maximizing the value and effectiveness of governance and boards of directors, Type III, the generative mode, is added to the classification. A novel mode, it is one in which governing bodies furnish a less well-known, but significant and critical source of organizational leadership. Type III activities, being affiliated with values, judgments, and insights, are vital to governing and determine the nature of Type I and II work. Thus, they are judged as "the most fertile soil for beds to flower as a source of leadership" (Chait et al., 2005, p. 9). These elements are the heart of normative institutionalism.

Generative thinking, producing a sense of what knowledge, information, and data mean, is essential to a governing body's performance. It affords an opportunity for a board to contemplate and interpret, possibly in new ways, the organization's past as a means for understanding options available for the future. Generative thinking is congruent with normative institutionalism's conception of governance. It involves shaping history, understanding it, and being able to learn from it. It reveals viable alternative courses and possibilities for action. Moreover, it can be invoked to control events and provide accountability (March & Olsen, 1995). Although generative work is essential to governing, very few boards engage in it. The key to its success and power is that both trustees and executives act in concert. Also of importance is the capacity for retrospective "sensemaking." Involving a different mind set, generative governance, going beyond fiduciary stewardship and strategic partnership, is deemed equivalent to leadership (Chait et al., 2005).

The governance as leadership model has redefined the nature of governance by adding the generative mode and a new perspective of the fiduciary and strategic ones. In this model the board assumes roles and relationships that differ from those in the policy governance model. Resting on different facets of governance and different assumptions about the nature of organizations and leadership, each of these modes assigns different responsibilities to governing board members. The trustees' task is to be able to respond to these different dimensions of organizational life, to become proficient in each mode, and above all, to recognize when and how to operate in which mode. Once again the logic of appropriateness is applicable. The board, perceived as a significant and generative source of leadership for the organization, must perform facilely in all modes of governance and be able to move swiftly from one to the other. "The better trustees do that, the more deeply the board will understand the purpose of governance. And the better the board understands governance, the better governed the organization will be" (Chait et al., 2005, p. 182). Governance as leadership will be achieved and the organization's value to the board members will be enhanced as will the board members' value to the organization.

The academic literature focusing on the crucial functions of governing boards reflects very different and particularistic views. Agency theorists are of the opinion that supervision of management's behavior and performance is of utmost significance. Resource dependence theorists, believing that the individual director's affiliations with other associations are critical to the generation of primary resources, take another tack. Legal scholars obviously focus on principles of law and stress the decision-makers' legal duties as overseers of the association. Responsibility for hiring and removing the top management, representation of the stakeholders' interests, and controlling for any infringement of the law are underscored. For the management experts, other obligations are of importance. They favor a board's advisory role to the executive leadership and promotion of the institution to a wide audience (Conger et al., 2001). Regardless of which perspective is deemed appropriate, it is evident that "responsible governance must be board-centric and board controlled" (Carver & Oliver, 2002, p. xxiii).

Board behavior, like political behavior, can be portrayed in terms of duties and obligations. In terms of carrying out their tasks, board members are expected to respect and invoke certain standards of conduct and attention. A consideration of these duties under common law usually focuses on the duties of diligence, loyalty, care, and obedience. Legal principles dictate that directors must manage a nonprofit organization with the same diligence and attention they would exercise in the case of a for-profit corporation. It is expected that decisions will be taken on an informed basis and that all board members will act in good faith. The duty of loyalty, representing a standard of faithfulness, requires decision makers to act in the best interests of the association at all times, not to take actions for personal benefit or the gain of another party at the expense of the association, and to avoid conflict of interest situations.

The level of competence that a board member is expected to demonstrate is set forth in the duty of care. This is commonly expressed as the care "that an ordinarily prudent person would exercise in a like position and under similar circumstances" ("What are the," n.d.). Board members are expected to perform their fiduciary responsibilities with the same sound judgment of any reasonable person. These stewards of the organization are supposed to demonstrate reasonable care in all of their activities. This standard applies to measures across the spectrum, ranging from monitoring the activities of the organization to use and maintenance of property. When board members become fully involved in policy-making, financial development, and evaluation, among other activities, they are exercising "due care" on behalf of the association. Moreover, it is expected that they will be fully prepared to carry out their responsibilities. It is anticipated that they will resist matters they believe to be inappropriate. The duty of obedience obliges directors to obey the law and it requires that their organizations do the same. It dictates that trustees perform their duties in light of the organization's mission and charter and according to all applicable legal instruments governing the third sector. Moreover, directors are to be held liable for any activities beyond the range of the law (Vargo, 1995). Federalism impacts on these duties in that some of these standards vary somewhat in state statutes and precedents. However, the spirit still remains.

Institutional Demography

For aeons political scientists have been wrestling with a fundamental and important question: Who governs? As noted above, nonprofit boards that carry out their responsibilities more fully enhance the performance of their organization and its effectiveness. In turn, how these duties are performed depends, in part, on board composition, and, in this case, on the public members. These representatives, along with their colleagues, being the players, assume credit for effectiveness or blame for the lack of it. They are responsible for the score of the game. In addition, governing boards symbolize and personify an organization to the public at large and to other entities. One criterion for evaluating an association is the caliber of its board members who come to the institution with certain resources and interests. Representing an organization, these people also become a basis for its legitimacy claims (Abzug & Galaskiewicz, 2001). Thus, institutional demography as it relates to board members, in general, and public members, in particular, is of consequence. A most important concern of any organization is the creation of its governing board.

Number of Public Members

The appropriate number of public members, if any, to include on a board of directors is an important question. The response often involves a trade-off because when public participation is injected, sometimes the professional or expert constituency is decreased in number. Of the agencies surveyed, only 40 percent included public members in their governing structure and only 23 percent of those not having this constituency expected to develop it within two years. Some executive directors commented that their organizations would be open to developing the public member role, if they could locate the appropriate person and if the concept could be implemented in such a way as to be of value. Some associations identified with the field of consumerism, such as the Citizen Advocacy Center, a service unit for public members on health care regulatory and governing bodies, have paid more attention to qualifications and credentials of public members than to their appropriate number ("Capitalizing on," 2001). It seems that, in general, this is not a high priority item for discussion. In fact, some authorities, claiming that the size of the board has a greater impact on how the unit works than on its level of performance, are of the opinion that board size is of lesser importance than might be imagined (Chait et al., 2005).

Public member representation goes from one extreme to another. Most nonprofit boards have only one representative and a few many more. Thirty-four percent of the responding organizations whose boards of directors included public members had more than one. Their constituencies ranged in size from two to 34. The majority of these had either two or three public members. One board boasted that its public member constituency accounts for 49 percent of the total board membership, the intent being to have it just under the professional representation. Believing that they make valuable members of the team, if provided with enough education, and because they do not bring all the professional biases to the table, one executive director surveyed was of the opinion that governing bodies should consist of a majority of public members. Other executive directors were very forthright in commenting that their governing board had only one public member for the purpose of meeting the standards for accreditation set forth by the National Commission for Certifying Agencies, the accreditation body of the National Organization for Competency Assurance. These standards provide that the structure of a certification organization seeking accreditation shall include at least one voting public member (National Commission for Certifying Agencies, 1995). The literature suggests no magic figure. It has been rightly argued that if a board is to include a public member constituency, it should consist of more than one person.

The rationale for this position is that this unit, requiring a background different from other board members, has a tremendous range of tasks to carry out. To complete these responsibilities alone is difficult. Also, if the public member constituency consists of only a single person, it is very easy for this individual to feel and become isolated and intimidated. Obviously, several public members might exert more influence on board proceedings than one. A governing body should have a reasonably large contingent of unaffiliated directors to provide objectivity, impartiality, multifaceted accountability, different points of view, diverse personal characteristics, and the muscle to demand superior institutional performance and a shift in the trajectory of the decision-making process. Without scientific validation and being based merely on intuition, some people assert that the more public members, the better. Arguments favoring more than one public member on a board are persuasive. But how many more remains unknown. Research on representative bureaucracies has concluded that group members have more chance of making decisions in their favor when their representation reaches a "critical mass," a minimal level of approximately 15 percent (LeRoux & Sneed, 2005). Whether this rule of thumb applies to the units in question is unknown. Research focusing on diverse types of boards with differing public member constituencies would aid in indicating the desirable magic number.

Studies have been done on independent outside directors in the corporate sector, figures somewhat similar to the public member. It was found that a majority of such directors does not necessarily produce superior organizational performance indicators. In fact, sometimes an inferior financial performance was the case ("Outside Directors," 2001). It would be interesting to see what findings would emerge from similar studies of the third sector. This also could be an interesting research endeavor that might offer information as to the appropriate number of outsiders or public members. However, it must be underscored that representation requires more than numbers.

Term of Office

An item of importance to institutional excellence is the term of office for directors. This excellence depends, in part, on the term of office for members of its governing board as well as on provisions for overlapping terms. The new institutionalists also remind us that the sense of identity is affected by tenure in office and turnover, the ratio of veterans to newcomers (March & Olsen, 2005). Some public members in their comments at the end of the survey noted difficulties in this area. A majority of the respondents (63 percent) had terms lasting at least three years. Two-year terms were the case for 32 percent of those surveyed and one-year terms were the least prevalent, being cited by five percent of the population. It was the shorter terms that were noted as problems. They make, according to those dissatisfied with them, the volunteer experience much more intense and stressful than it needs to be. Requiring an extended period of time to become familiar with an organization, there is not much or no time left for full participation. Moreover, board orientation and training must take place immediately upon appointment of new public members at a continuous and fast rhythm, if they and the board are to reap full benefit. One public member respondent succinctly wrote: "The term limits on the board impede achievement of strategic objectives since the orientation of new board members is a never-ending process." With these short terms of office, an important key is their renewability.

"Rotation off" provisions are significant as well. Without them "dead wood" can accumulate creating obstacles to productivity. A few executive directors in comments appended to the survey instrument asked outright how to get rid of their public member. Boards without term limits have to ensure that members remain engaged and enthusiastic year after year which is not an easy task. Term limits provide protection against less than desirable performance. On the other hand, they also force organizations to lose the talents of valuable board members, public and otherwise. Consequently, a reappointment process after a specific period of time off the board is beneficial and advisable.

Remuneration

Patterns concerning monetary matters fell overwhelmingly into one camp. Almost all respondents (98 percent) were reimbursed for expenses affiliated with public member responsibilities and 84 percent received no other compensation related to this position. These responses were not surprising. Voluntary activity usually receives only token financial compensation, reimbursement for expenses. However, in their comments a few of the public members surveyed noted that over and above their expenses they were given a per diem of approximately $250 per day. Others reported being paid on a per meeting basis. One public member was paid $50 for each two-hour meeting plus expenses. This respondent has served on this particular board for 13 years and intended to try for another similar appointment. In addition, reference was made to extra payments for committee assignments and every segment of six hours required for committee meeting preparation as well as readiness for general meetings. Non-monetary rewards for service that were mentioned in comments included laptop computers, e-mail accounts, and the like authorized for board business and other use. These payments are obviously used to keep board members engaged.

Other comments pertained to remuneration for participation. Noting that much time and effort are required for meaningful board member performance, some survey respondents suggested that people might not be willing to serve without remuneration. They noted that although most professionals receive their stipend even when they attend board meetings, this might not hold for all participants, especially certain types of public members. Consequently, an argument can be made to compensate directors over and above a per diem to recognize their expertise, service, time, and effort. On the other hand, one executive director provided comments rebutting this stance. This person wrote: "Rather than paying fees for their services, we give them a board position and allow them to reap the benefits and frills that come with it." In some cases, these perks are many. There is also the notion that any kind of payment is unnecessary, if the program is relevant to the public at large. Obviously, this subject relates to the problem of recruitment and it is a matter that all boards should address in connection with it. Drucker (1989) notes: "Nonprofits used to say: 'We don't pay volunteers so we can't demand much.' Now they say, 'Because we don't pay, we have to demand even more'"(p. 92). Some happy medium has to be found.

This search is not an easy one. The line between volunteering and paid work is not distinct. A gray area is involved. It is possible that voluntary activities, efforts that are not obligatory and not monetarily rewarded, advance personal objectives and careers. On the other hand, at the same time, people sometimes engage in volunteer programs that are extensions of their paid employment. For example, attorneys, as members of nonprofit boards of trustees, frequently furnish these units legal advice. Moreover, employees of third sector organizations often volunteer in other associations to advance the objectives sought through their paid employment. The distinction between volunteering and paid work is not always clear (Burns, Schlozman, & Verba, 2001).

Gender

Gender is a paramount social organizing principle. Traditionally the nonprofit sector has been gendered female, meaning that it identifies with hierarchical power relationships in which men dominate women. The large female workforce is controlled by an elite male power structure. This has caused many a confrontation originating in the women's movement and trade unions. The history of voluntarism indicates that over time there have been many more opportunities for females than for males (Odendahl & Youmans, 1994; O'Neill, 1994; Schindler-Rainman, 1988b). In the United States the nonprofit arena, unlike others, has principally relied on female employment. Shaiko (1997) in an excellent study reported that 75 percent of the labor force in the nonprofit sector is female compared with 50 percent of the total workforce. Based on data contained in the 2000 census, the female percentage of the nonprofit labor force stands at 67 percent, whereas that for the total workforce is 47 percent. The difference between the two rates is still substantial. Moreover, 50 percent of females in the nonprofit sector hold professional and managerial positions, decidedly more than in other sectors of the political economy. Female prominence, however, is only evident in certain types of associations, such as those identified with health care, education, training, counseling, library management, fundraising, and interior design, to cite a few.

Even though women are overrepresented in the staffing of nonprofits, they are not as successful in securing leadership posts. Shaiko (1997) found that they held only 18.7 percent of board positions. More recently, Gibelman (2000) and LeRoux and Sneed (2005) described a glass ceiling for women in nonprofit organizations, meaning a barrier that permits them to see the top of the organizational ladder, but prevents them from reaching it. In addition, although gender is not a significant variable, whether one volunteers or not, the third sector has traditionally been based on a primarily female volunteer force. Females tend to be more involved in all forms of volunteer activity than males. More than one-half of the volunteers are women (Bell, 1995; O'Connor & Johnson, 1989; O'Neill, 1994; Putnam, 2000). Although only three to four percent more women than men volunteer, men garner a lion's share of seats on boards of directors. Moreover, there is a variance of roles based on gender by board and types of boards. Females have tended to be directors of community-based nonprofits with small budgets, limited staff and activities, and little impact. Moreover, their compensation is significantly less than that of their male counterparts (Odendahl & Youmans, 1994; Wolfred & Peters, 2001).

Overtime females have achieved access to nonprofit and corporate boardrooms, recording more success in the third sector (Abzug & Galaskiewicz, 2001; Kang & Cnaan, 1995; Shaiko, 1996; Ward, 1997). Even though they have achieved more seats on nonprofit governing boards as of late, there is still a considerable disparity in representation as far as gender is concerned. This trend was reflected in the present study. Males accounted for 59 percent of the public members. This result confirms findings of surveys related to the gender gap and political activity. In general, men are more active than women, but the difference between them is usually quite small (Milbrath, 1965; Verba et al., 1995; Verba & Nie, 1972). However, in this study the difference was much larger. The gap, in general, is explained on the basis of life style and demands placed on people according to gender. Also the gender disparity in civic participation is rooted in the gender-differentiated experiences of major social institutions. The female deficit is significant which means this interest is and has been discounted. Recent research findings suggest that the gender composition of the environment has ramifications for female involvement in decision-making (Burns et al., 2001).

The paucity of women on nonprofit boards decreases the richness of the organization. Having had diverse experiences, behavior styles, and connections than men, they bring new and unique perspectives to the table. Although the trend has been for them to come from traditionally female professions, such as teaching, social work, secretarial work, and health care, such does not hold for an overwhelming majority of this sample. It is believed that being identified with these professions, females are exposed to different ideas, problems, and demands than men.

Having more women serving as members of governing boards as part of the justice and interest arguments is not the answer to representing them. Obviously, it is important, but other factors, such as the consequences of recruitment processes, mechanisms for the articulation of their interests, organizational constraints, the impact of prevailing norms, patriarchal and otherwise; and environmental circumstances, to cite a few, must be taken into consideration. As noted, representation requires more than numbers. They constitute only one of the variables that determine the degree to which an organization responds to the interests of a constituency. An augment in the representation of any group will help to increase its acceptability. However, this does not mean that the constituency will be more represented than previously. Other factors must be given thought. These must be considered as part of an effort to change the balance between participation and representation and in the context of a more participatory form of democracy (Phillips, 1991, 1998; Sapiro, 1981). These points are also pertinent to a discussion of the appropriate number of public members to be included on a board of directors.

Odendahl and Youmans (1994) suggest that perhaps the gender roles and activities lodged in the patriarchal family have penetrated the third sector. They note that its governing boards, consisting for the most part of males, carry out the father role of decision-making. Men hold positions of authority and to them females are subservient. The mother role is assumed by women who are concerned with the daily activities of care giving as illustrated by a galaxy of organizational routine tasks. Work in the home and the third sector receives less recognition than that in the for-profit or public arenas. The nonprofit arena, it is suggested, is frequently thought of as being compatible for females "because it often incorporates an extension of the nurturing work women have traditionally done in the home" (Odendahl & Youmans, p. 208). Furthermore, it is conjectured that as more women achieve leadership posts in this sector, they may be prone to take their traditionally subservient family status with them. This last statement is open to question.

Race and Ethnicity

A recent trend in terms of board composition is increased diversity (Ward, 1997). The status of women on third sector governing bodies has shown much better penetration than that of ethnic and racial minorities. As expected, an overwhelming majority of the respondents (93 percent) were Caucasian. They were followed by the Native American/Alaskan Native and African, African American, Black origin categories that accounted for two percent each of the sample. The Asian, Asian American, Pacific Islander grouping along with those of Hispanics and people of multiracial background registered one percent each. In contrast to programs with another focus, those studied have significantly less minority representation (Mogulof, 1970a). A more recent study (Abzug & Galaskiewicz, 2001) of nonprofit boards found increased minority representation. The investigators conclude: "Women and non-whites did achieve considerable gains . . . and . . . . were approaching proportional representation on boards as a whole" (p. 68). Results of another research endeavor concerned with minority representation indicate African American representation outstrips other minority categories (Kang & Cnaan, 1995). The same holds true for research carried out by the National Center for Nonprofit Boards and the Stanford University Graduate School of Business. They found that the average board consisted of 86 percent White/European, nine percent African American, three percent Hispanic/Latino, and one-and-a-half percent Asians (Rosenblatt, 2001).These findings do not apply to this work. Non-whites are not close to proportional representation and African Americans are equal to other minority categories, all of which are quite sparse in numbers. It is precisely these groups that are not well-endowed with the factors that nurture participation. In this survey as in others measuring participation (Verba et al., 1995), there is a gap on the basis of race and ethnicity. Also, it has been indicated that in the third sector race and ethnicity might differentiate the experience of females (O'Neill, 1994). Minority respondents to the survey did not include a significant number of females.

Age

Volunteering is related to age which as a predictor of civic engagement ranks second to education. The public member constituency is white-haired, a departure from the conventional wisdom in which participation rises gradually with age, reaching its zenith and leveling off in the forties and fifties and declining over 60 (Milbrath, 1965). According to the results of the survey, 43 percent of the sample was over 60 years old and 39 percent was in the 50-59 age bracket. The younger ranks were thin with representatives between 40 and 49 years old contributing 13 percent and those in their thirties, five percent. No one was under 30. There appears to be an increase in participation throughout the life cycle with civic engagement blossoming at middle age. One of the few studies focusing on board members, in this case, those involved in large human service organizations, found that the average age decreased so that these units included younger members (Kang & Cnaan, 1995). Such people were not visible in the public member survey.

Although civic participation has declined in the United States, this abatement does not apply to volunteering. The frequency with which Americans volunteer has increased and this expansion in activity has been affiliated with more mature persons. More specifically, people 60 and over have accounted for the entire increase in volunteers, almost doubling the rate of volunteering among seniors. Nowadays many people are retiring earlier. They are often healthier than cohorts in previous generations and they enjoy greater financial security. Such benefits account, in part, for their civic activity and the graying of civic America. For the general volunteer population the peak ages of activity are between 40 and 69 and there is also ample activity among younger persons, ages 25 to 40. According to a most recent study, members of this latter group, consisting of "generations X (those born between 1965 and 1975) and Y (those born afterwards)," contrary to belief, are more likely to volunteer than others. In comparison with general volunteers, public members are older. This is understandable in that often leaders are more mature. Moreover, nowadays middle-aged and older people have been organizationally more active than younger folks (Bell, 1995; Brooks, 2006; Goss, 1999; Putnam, 2000).

Marital Status

Although people who volunteer are more likely to be married, marital status appears to account for little difference in terms of level of activity

(Bell, 1995;   O'Connor & Johnson, 1989). Most of the respondents to the survey were married (76 percent) and the other categories related to marital status—single, divorced/separated, widow/widower—garnered eight percent each.

Education

Education is the strongest single predictor of participation in political activity. Providing skills and interests that bring people into civic life, higher levels of instruction mean more opportunities for participation, political and otherwise. Education has a strong consistent effect. It is as powerful in terms of voluntarism. It has been affirmed that as far as volunteering is concerned, education is the leading variable in an explanation of who offers their services. The evidence indicates that those having more education are more likely to volunteer and that formal volunteering increases as education increases. For example, it has been shown that an additional four years of education accounts for 45 percent more volunteering (O'Connor & Johnson, 1989; Pearce, 1993; Putnam, 2000).

The public members surveyed were a highly educated group. Fifty-seven percent earned graduate degrees. In this category 22 percent terminated their studies with a master's degree and 35 percent had a doctorate as a terminal degree. Twenty-seven percent of the sample held a baccalaureate degree and six percent an associate degree. The remaining ten percent acknowledged some credits in higher education. Thus, respondents surpassed elementary and secondary education, as one might expect. Those few studies that have discussed the socioeconomic status of governing board members found that the educational levels of directors increased significantly overtime, that a majority of consumer representatives were college graduates, and that there was a decrease in trustees with only a secondary education (Kang & Cnaan, 1995; K.H. Parkum, 1984). This is not surprising because since World War II higher education has increased the overall level of education in the population. More specifically, between 1960 and 1998 the percentage of American adults who earned a baccalaureate degree soared from eight to 24. And one in 12 citizens has undertaken graduate study (Putnam, 2000). It appears that this sample of public members is stellar in terms of level of education and that its formal knowledge bank is richer than most.

The group's high level of educational attainment is significant. Educational achievement is fundamental to the acquisition of other participatory factors, such as income, skills, and exposure to requests for activity. It "has implications not only for the kinds of resources individuals accumulate, but also for the kinds of citizens they become" (Verba et al., 1995, p. 514). In the general population, males are more likely than females to have advanced degrees (Burns et al., 2001). This trend, given the nature of higher education overtime, was reflected in the survey. Recognizing the relationship of education to participation, this fact may be used in an explanation of the gender gap on the governing boards surveyed.

Occupation

An overwhelming majority of the sample was professionally active. Retirees were not a significant part of the group, accounting for 25 percent, a percentage not much different from that of public members in the over 65 age category (22 percent). On the other hand, 84 percent of the female respondents were active in the workforce. It has been documented that as females entered the workforce and achieved professional equality, they have become more civically engaged. In fact, full-time employment has accounted for the increase in their civic activities. Putnam (2000) observes: "For some working women the increase in opportunity for involvement in community life has outweighed the decrease in time and they have swum against the society-wide current of community disengagement" (p. 202). Such holds for this female contingent.

In terms of occupation, the public members surveyed were distributed in two predominant camps: the professional and the managerial/administrative, accounting for 51 percent and 38 percent respectively of the sample. These categories were followed by clerical/sales (four percent), homemaker (three percent), skilled/operative (three percent) and laborer/service (one percent). Within the group of professionals, who are the people most likely to become civically engaged, attorneys and university faculty members prevailed, providing 38 percent of it. Given the litigious nature of American society and the legal character of board members' duties, attorneys are beneficial for any nonprofit organization. The link with academia is useful as well. The association, having access to substantive knowledge, garners intellectual capital, and for the academic, it combines the theoretical and practical aspects of learning. All persons in this professional category enhance the legitimacy claims of an organization. In the managerial/administrative contingent, given the responses provided, it appears that 41 percent of these representatives were affiliated with the business world, thus linking the for-profit and nonprofit sectors. This involvement is not out of the ordinary. In fact, it seems quite natural and logical to tap this source for public members, given the harsh economic times numerous nonprofits are experiencing. Many firms as a demonstration of their sense of social responsibility have required that their executives participate in national, regional, and local community organizations. Also, of note is the fact that often in pay and promotion decisions an executive is evaluated, in part, in terms of community activities. Organizations benefit from the personal and institutional financial contributions of these representatives. In addition, they are most useful because of their skills, knowledge, general competencies, fund-raising abilities, contacts, and aid with legitimacy claims, to cite a few talents.

More specifically, given the aforementioned tendency for many nonprofits to undertake income-earning ventures, these directors help associations respond to the need for business planning and resources. Often they are critical to such endeavors because many organizations have embarked on business undertakings without appropriate preparation. Lacking the expertise to apply business protocols to their income-earning enterprises, these endeavors have floundered or failed. Directors with business acumen can provide business capability expertise and assistance with targeted business analysis, market research, and strategic planning, critical ingredients for success. Organizations have indicated a need for business planning and assistance (Bowen et al., 1994; W.K. Kellogg Foundation, 2003). These public members provide the service.

Business representatives, according to results of empirical research, are of the opinion that their principal contribution to a governing board consists of their expertise and their unique managerial and business perspectives (Austin, 1998). A few public members surveyed seconded this conclusion in voluntary comments. Typical are the words of one respondent. "My background and life's work was management. Our Board [consists of health care personnel]. I have been able to inject a management dimension that was not present prior to my selection." Not only does the association benefit from these public member business leaders. For them there are skill enhancements, networking, new ideas and opportunities, invitations of various types, as well as access to information for purposes of career advancement. Such exemplifies the earlier noted fact that Americans through volunteering can satisfy their civic orientations as well as their own self-interest.

In spite of this positive evaluation with advantages for both business leaders and organizations, the literature issues some cautions. In the first place, it argues that management lessons cannot automatically be transferred to nonprofits, given fundamental differences between that sector and the private one, some of which have been noted earlier in this work. Moreover, people with a business background have a history of often being highly ineffective as members of nonprofit boards. Inappropriate values are frequently brought to the table because the differences between the profit and nonprofit sectors cause a lack of sensitivity to the organizational environment. In addition, often these leaders, like others, advance their own personal agenda during board business. It is easier in the nonprofit arena because the constraining focus on business and financial outcomes is absent. Also, of interest are early studies of executives in community service that concluded they tended to be followers and implementers, rather than leaders and innovators. They reacted to staff and their initiatives, rather than managing them. Moreover, they experienced difficult relations with staff because they felt their talents were underutilized (Bowen et al., 1994; Fenn, 1971; McFarland, 1999).

A broader call of caution must be issued concerning board members who are specifically recruited because of their technical expertise, whatever it might be. It is true that they are useful to an organization. However, there is the danger that such folks will become so involved in the organization's technical facets that they will do everything but govern. They will avoid Type II and Type III tasks, both of which are of significance. Working as technicians is of importance, but not sufficient to maximize trustees' value or that of governance. Chait et al. (2005) appropriately compare this type of board member to a component of a Swiss army-knife. It must be remembered that these trustees are first and foremost public members, not technicians.

Income

Not only does education account for the differences among people, especially activity disparities, but income is important as well. Being positively correlated with participation, it explains differences in the rate of engagement in political and other activities. The various types of participation are related to affluence. For example, there is a positive association between income and volunteering, but the relationship is not as consistent as is education (O'Connor & Johnson, 1989; Pearce, 1993; Verba et al., 1995; Verba, Schlozman, Brady, & Nie, 1993). Public members in the survey were asked to identify their present annual income before taxes and their total family income from all sources. As is often the case with questions related to income, the number of non-respondents was high, 29 percent and 25 percent respectively. Of those who answered the questions, just under a majority (49 percent) earned over $70,000 a year. Twenty-one percent had incomes between $50,000 and $69,999. The same percentage earned between $30,000 and $49,999 per year. Nine percent claimed an income of less than $30,000. Clearly in terms of individual wages, the public members are comfortable. The same is true of total family income from all sources. Well over a majority of the respondents (69 percent) had earnings of over $90,000. Twelve percent accumulated between $70,000 and $89,999 and 11 percent earned between $50,000-$69,999, leaving seven percent in the less than $50,000 category. In both cases the scales are quite heavy at the top. A study of consumer volunteers in health planning agencies indicates the same financial status for these representatives. For the most part, they are well-to-do (K.H. Parkum, 1984). Like education, income level is of consequence because the distribution of resources of all types to various groups is based, in part, on income. Public members definitely have ample access to these conveniences.

Size of Community

Public member participation also relates to community size and regional characteristics. Persons surveyed lived in communities of various size, ranging from small and rural to large metropolitan areas. Generally, people dwelling in larger cities tend to be less active than their counterparts from other surroundings. In fact, as communities increase in size and as the boundaries that separate them from other communities fade, participation declines and especially, in the center of society. Conversely, activity is enhanced and it flourishes in the periphery and particularly, in smaller and isolated areas. This trend also applies to voluntarism. People living in large metropolitan areas are less likely to volunteer than those hailing from other types of communities, especially smaller and mid-sized ones (O'Connell, 1985; J.E. Oliver, 2000; Putnam, 2000; Verba & Nie, 1972). Large metropolitan areas provided residence to 24 percent of the sample and 13 percent of the respondents lived in large-sized areas. The largest segment (35 percent) identified with mid-sized communities. Small/rural and small/non rural settings each were home for 14 percent of the respondents. Thus, it was the mid-sized communities that provided the lion's share of public members. This result confirms the cited "rule of thumb." However, contrary to it, the smaller settings, even combined, were not as productive. Still combined with the mid-sized communities, they surpassed the large metropolitan and urban areas. From the social capital perspective smaller is better. Social capital is definitely greater in smaller settings (Putnam et al., 2003).

J.E. Oliver (2000) investigated the effect of city size on participation in civic activities. He concluded that differences in behavior based on the size of the metropolitan area or rural settings are minimal. The effects of city size are practically nil. They are, for the most part, independent of the greater rural or metropolitan context. Rather, diversity in participation rates in different settings, according to him, results from individual demographic characteristics and differences in social context, social relations, and psychological orientation between residents of larger and smaller communities.

Region

Regionalism, an important ingredient of American life, is also reflected in voluntarism. O'Connell (1985) notes that people are most likely to volunteer if they live in the West and least likely, if they live in the South. In between these ends, going from most likely, are the Midwest and the East. Respondents to the survey were asked to identify their residence in terms of region. Given the responses, regionalism in this study has a different face as it relates to voluntarism and public members. The resulting continuum, being composed as follows, Midwest (38 percent), South (23 percent), East (20 percent), West (14 percent) and North (six percent), has a very diverse order. This ranking reflects, to a certain extent, Putnam's (2000) social capital "barometric map," although according to him, the pressure is lower in the last two cases.

Partisanship

Political party membership means different things depending on the country involved. Unique traits of the American political party system are its lack of a clearly defined membership concept and very loose membership requirements. Moreover, it is generally acknowledged that political party membership has been on the decline since the late 1970s, a manifestation of the general degeneration of the political party system. Thus, it was in a sense surprising to find that 58 percent of the public members surveyed responded in the affirmative to the question: "Do you belong to a political party?" In another sense, this response was not so surprising in that the respondents, given their age, could represent older people with more partisan orientations who are being and will continue to be replaced by members of younger generations uninterested in joining a political party.

Political behavior does not vary drastically according to gender. Men and women are not so different politically. In the United States they usually join the main political parties in approximately the same proportions (Greenberg & Page, 1993). In this case, 53 percent of those who held political party membership were males and 47 percent females. Partisanship relates to participation. Individuals, particularly those of a higher socioeconomic status, experience a boost in participation and especially in those activities requiring more time and effort.

Although they have become less strong, party loyalties or party attachments are important to citizen political behavior, in general, and more specifically, they are good predictors of how people vote. "Party identification is a long-term, affective, psychological identification with one's preferred political party" (Dalton, 1996, p. 199). This tendency to favor one party over another is comparable to identification with a social class, a particular religion, or any other social group. This allegiance endures overtime, strengthens with age, heavily influences other opinions, and tells us something about the individual's psychological involvement in partisan cleavages. Of importance is the fact that it is decidedly different from voting preference. Often strong party identifiers vote for their party, but many people also vote for candidates of one party, while expressing allegiance to another. Those who identify with the two major political parties in the United States tend to be more active than the population at large.

In an attempt to elicit the party attachments of the public members, participants in the survey were asked: "Generally speaking, do you usually think of yourself as a Republican, a Democrat, an Independent, or something else?" Of the respondents 41 percent thought of themselves as Republicans, 26 percent as Democrats, 26 percent as Independents, two percent as something else and four percent had no preference. Party identification has experienced a decline in recent times. Registering 75 percent around 1960, and falling to 65 percent in the late 1990s (Putnam, 2000), it was recorded at 64 percent in the 2002 General Social Survey. Thus, the 67 percent of the sample that identified with the major political parties is aligned with this benchmark. Other facets of these results contrast with national trends of party identification. Dating from the times of the New Deal, more Americans have thought of themselves as Democrats than Republicans. The gap between the two parties has varied overtime, but the Democrats have always prevailed. Of interest also is that the percentage of folks identifying themselves as Independents is equal to that of those claiming a Democratic orientation. The noted decline in the number of people who identify with political parties can account for the increase in the number of Independents. Moreover, these public members are different from other consumer counterparts. K.H. Parkum (1984) found the political affiliations of consumer volunteers in health planning organizations to be fairly evenly distributed. In this case balance is lacking. The predominance of Republican Party attachments can be explained on the basis of the income and occupation of the respondents and their social group. Often professional people with a high salary identify themselves as Republicans. Looking at partisanship in terms of gender, men are somewhat more Republican and women more Democratic in orientation (Ginsburg, Lowi, & Weir, 2003). In the survey men were more Republican than women. However, a majority of both males and females, 66 percent and 57 percent respectively, were Republicans.

Another variable affiliated with partisanship is age. It is currently acknowledged that people under 50 and over 65, tend to be fairly evenly distributed between the two major political parties, whereas those in the intermediate age group, 50 to 64, are much more likely to be Democrats. These tendencies were not reflected in the sample. The youngest cohort was predominantly Democratic and the remaining two overwhelmingly Republican. There is no scientific evidence that identification with a particular political party is affiliated with a designated age group. It just happens that usually when party loyalties are shaped, people in the same age bracket undergo similar experiences. Thus, people who are now between the ages of 50 and 64 matured politically during the era of the Cold War, the Vietnam hostilities, and the civil rights movement. More reacted affirmatively to the Democratic response to these events than the Republican one (Ginsburg et al., 2003). Such was not the case for this sample. Thus, it also differs from the general population in this respect.

Party attachments may also be viewed from the perspective of strength as well as direction. Those surveyed were asked to rate their identification with a particular political party as strong, not very strong, or not sure. Seventeen percent of the sample was not sure of the intensity of its partisanship. In terms of strength of party relationship strong Republicans outscored strong Democrats, 30 percent to 23 percent. The higher average socioeconomic standing of the strong Republicans may account for greater activity rates. In terms of not very strong attachments with a political party, Republicans again outscored Democrats. Twenty percent of the sample consisted of not very strong Republicans and ten percent of not very strong Democrats. Looking at both major political parties, strong party attachments prevailed over the not very strong ones (53 percent to 30 percent). Although, as mentioned above, it is generally believed that females are slightly more Democratic than males (Greenberg & Page, 1993), such was not reflected in this survey in terms of the public members' strength of party attachment.

Organizational Membership

Organizations have an important role in the transmission of voluntarism. As noted, the American scene is peppered with essential forms of social capital, notably networks consisting of a wide variety of associations. These voluntary units, having an impact on their members as individuals and, in turn, on collective endeavors, play an important part in a democratic political culture. Preventing the development of mass political movements and nourishing pro-social behavior, they aid in conflict resolution and in increasing citizen efficacy, participation, and influence. Membership impinges greatly on civic attitudes and sense of political empowerment. In turn, social interactions in this context also affect public policies, economic development, and public administration, among other things. Comparative studies of participation conclude that organizational affiliation is one of the most significant indicators of citizen activity. More specifically, persons who are members of organizations tend to have higher volunteer rates than nonmembers. In 1996, 73 percent of the membership of lay associations and 55 percent of that in religious organizations reported that they were volunteers as compared with 19 percent of other Americans (Brooks, 2005; Hooghe, 2003; Putnam, 2000).

Membership accounts for exceptionally high participation rates. As a predictor of political activity, it is even stronger than class identification. It is suggested that a rich associational life nurtures a rich political participant life. Although Americans are known for their high level of involvement in various channels of civic participation, this associational engagement is definitely related to socioeconomic status. Membership is not randomly distributed throughout the population. It displays an upper-class bias. Individuals of higher socioeconomic status are more likely to be members of organizations and in the company of other participants. This pattern is not unique to the United States. In all countries, as one moves up the socioeconomic ladder, there is a sharp increase in organizational membership (Almond & Verba, 1965; Ginsburg et al., 2003; Hodgkinson, 1995; Skocpol & Fiorina, 1999; Verba & Nie, 1972).

Civic activity, as noted, is widespread in the United States. Also, knowing that people active in the workforce and those with more education, the highest incomes, and most prestigious occupations, join more than others, and given the demographics of the sample, it was not surprising to find that 92 percent of the public members surveyed held memberships in voluntary associations. This figure compares with the 82 percent of Americans that are members of organizations. In other nations the corresponding percentages confirm the American propensity to join. For example, in France and Japan they register 39 and 36 percent respectively ("Americans Are Joiners," 2000). Like many consumer members of health planning organizations, (K.H. Parkum, 1984), this sample was quite active in other entities. However, being a more elite group, the sample's participation rate is much higher than those reported in other studies (Greenberg & Page, 1993; Reed & Selbee, 2000; Verba et al., 1995). Respondents to the survey were asked to list the organizations to which they belonged. Unfortunately, many, failing to indicate the full name of the associations as instructed, used acronyms. The result often was "alphabet soup." Thus, it was not possible to analyze affiliations in detailed fashion on the basis of type of organization as originally planned.

Early studies of involvement in American voluntary associations (Fagence, 1977) claimed that joiners preferred organizations of sympathetic political, recreational, and economic philosophy. Thus, those of higher socioeconomic status joined civic and service associations, leaving others to identify with more fraternal, social, and recreational groups. Such a distinction certainly does not apply to this sample. Their affiliations were with diverse types of groups and they failed to manifest such a pattern. In fact, their memberships were representative of bonding social capital, those affiliations connecting individuals possessing much in common, and bridging social capital, those identifications bringing together persons across a greater social distance, both of which are essential for a democratic society (Putnam et al., 2003).

Perusing the list of entities cited by respondents to the questionnaire, a wide variety was evident, including civic, service, political, fraternal, sports, military, neighborhood, recreational, ethnic, religious, business, professional, cultural, charitable, and public interest groups, among others. Trade union membership was almost completely lacking, being cited by only one person. This was interesting in light of the number of university professors and nurses completing the survey instrument. More citations might have been expected. In all, respondents cited 358 different organizations. Many retirees noted that they had been much more active in the past than they are now. They belonged to many fewer associations in retirement. One public member explained that upon retirement the family moved to a small town. Before, this person had a very high profile with activity in disparate major national and sub-national associations. With the new residence, however, there were very limited opportunities to become involved. This scenario probably applied to other respondents as well.

A useful indicator is the number of organizations to which an individual belongs. Involvement usually breeds further involvement and this tendency was evident in the sample. Most respondents held multiple memberships. Only seven percent belonged to only a single organization. The largest percentage (67 percent) identified with two to five groups. In the general population 19 percent reports belonging to four or more groups ("Americans Are Joiners," 2000). Those belonging to six to ten associations accounted for 20 percent of the sample. They were followed by those affiliated with 11-15 organizations (five percent) and then by those belonging to over 15 groups (one percent). As might be expected, the percentage of activists decreases as demands increase. On the average, each respondent belonged to five organizations. Organizational participation in the United States in terms of the number of people who hold membership and those who do so in multiple organizations tends to be much higher than in any other nation. Percentages pertaining to membership recorded in this survey outstrip by far those of other studies.

It must be remembered that in the Western world many voluntary associations are somehow related to an individual's livelihood. Thus, professionals join their professional associations and other individuals decide on their membership(s) often with an eye to increasing contacts. In essence, organizations become a part of the job so to speak and given this fact, explain, in part, the high percentages of multiple memberships. Professional responsibilities do motivate participation (Chesney, 1984; Pearce, 1993).

The number of organizations an individual belongs to is of importance because it has an impact on political competence, beliefs of being able to influence outcomes and actual capacities to do so, and social capital. Organizational membership, so it is believed, has a cumulative effect. If affiliation with one group enhances an individual's sense of competence, multiple affiliations are better, leading to even more competence. With multiple and overlapping memberships, participation pervades many arenas of community life and thus, social capital. A recent study (Wollebaek & Selle, 2002) underscores, however, the significance of multiple memberships, arguing that participation only has a cumulative effect when multiple memberships, preferably in organizations having diverse objectives, are held simultaneously. Thus, the authors issue a call for greater attention to multiple affiliations within associations.

Gender influences group membership, but exactly how and how much is not clear. Some scholars assert that females are somewhat less likely than males to identify with an organization and reference is made to a lower rate of organizational membership among women (Burns et al., 2001; Milbrath, 1965; Verba & Nie, 1972). On the other hand, it is argued that women who work belong to more groups (Putnam 2000). Then, it is also claimed that there is virtually no difference between the sexes in terms of relationships with voluntary associations (Verba et al., 1995). There is no agreement on the subject. In this survey the difference between the two sexes is greater than in other studies and in the case of public members' political party membership. As earlier in the twentieth century, males outjoined females. They outjoined them by 14 percent, but on the average each female belonged to more organizations than their male counterparts. In terms of the average number of associations each category belonged to, the difference between the sexes was not as great. Each male, on the average, held membership in four associations and each female was affiliated with five. Thus, as in other instances, there is no significant gender difference in the average number of organizations in which the individual is a member.

Organizational affiliation has also been examined in terms of partisanship and strength of party loyalty (Verba & Nie, 1972). Strong Republicans because of their superior socioeconomic status and their conservative political beliefs, it is affirmed, manifest a higher participation rate than strong Democrats. In this survey such was true. Ninety percent of the strong Republicans as opposed to 84 percent of the strong Democrats joined groups. However, once again, the difference in the average number of groups each belonged to was minimal: five for the strong Republicans and four for the strong Democrats. Moreover, it resulted that those with weaker partisan ties participated less. The not very strong Democrats had a participation rate of 75 percent and the same category of Republicans, 63 percent. The average number of organizations in which these persons held membership was the same for both political identifications: four.

It has been demonstrated that partisan identifiers are more active and that this activity reflects more than socioeconomic status (Verba & Nie, 1972). Data collected in this survey reveals that percentage-wise the nonpartisans were more active (85 percent to 79 percent) and, in terms of the average number of organizations joined per person, the partisans and nonpartisans alike claimed five. Thus, partisanship failed to account for increased activity.

People must decide whether to join an organization or not and then they must decide on the extent of their activity. One measure of civic skill is to identify the ways in which people have been active in organizations. Distinctions among members may be made on the basis of the quantity and type of their activity. Americans, who join organizations, are usually much more likely to be active within them than citizens of other nations. However, it must be recognized that not all members take an active role in an organization and they also assume diverse roles. There are different levels of participation involving various degrees of responsibility and repertoires of activity that coalesce into a hierarchy of involvement. Activities at the bottom of the scale require the least costs in terms of time, energy, and commitment and those at the top, being more demanding, the most (Arnstein, 1971; Milbrath, 1965).

Very often reference is made to "checkbook membership," meaning that the member pays dues by check and rarely, if at all, attends meetings or undertakes any activities. In essence, the individual only provides a name for the roll, some income, and little else. Membership involves meager individual commitment and no or minimal activity. Twenty-eight percent of the sample fell into this category at the bottom of the hierarchy. The rest of the respondents were definitely not "checkbook members." Their membership could be considered quite active. In addition to paying dues, they regularly participated in program meetings. This was the situation of the remainder of the respondents (73 percent). However, a portion of this constituency exerted even greater effort, assuming leadership responsibilities. Twenty-eight percent, served on or chaired committees or held office at the local or state levels of organizational structures and

14 percent, the so-called "gladiators," did the same on a national basis. Once again the percentage of participants decreases as one moves up the rungs of the participatory ladder. Usually fewer people are available for those responsibilities demanding more time, effort, and skill found on the steps near the top of the ladder. The size of the active membership constituency compares favorably, being slightly higher, given the sample's elite status, with results of other studies (Verba et al., 1995).

In a more recent work Putnam (2000) observes that as of the late 1980s only 21 percent of all organizational members have never served in a leadership capacity. This would mean the sample's service would be low in comparison. However, he continues and explains that between 1985 and 1994 active organizational involvement decreased by 45 percent. In this context the sample's participation record still compares favorably: 42 percent to 34 percent. The higher leadership rate in this study may be explained by the respondents' higher educational standing than that of the general population. College graduates are more than twice as likely to serve in an organizational leadership capacity. Here again education leaves its stamp. From the social capital perspective this active and involved membership contingent assumes a prime importance.

Relating to the amount of social interaction experienced, opportunities to participate in organizational decision-making and the general expression of individual perspectives, the degree to which a person is active in an organization has generally been considered important. Almond and Verba (1965) affirm that "organizations in which there is some opportunity for the individual to take an active part may be as significant for the development of democratic citizenship as are voluntary organizations in general" (p. 258). In an empirical study that examines the relationship between participation and social capital Wollebaek & Selle (2002) challenge the notion that active participation is crucial to the creation of social capital. For them the difference between active and passive participation or between active and "checkbook membership" as used here is absent or at most negligible. Affiliation is the critical act.

As in the case of group membership, the leadership contingent can be examined from the perspective of gender. Active participation in the form of assuming leadership responsibilities, usually varies on the basis of sex, among other variables, such as education, that relate to socioeconomic standing. Exactly 50 percent of the sample occupied leadership positions in diverse types of organizations. As very often happens, males, accounting for 59 percent of these respondents, were a dominant force in this more activist group. However, once again the average number of positions held by each of these leaders was roughly the same. Females, on the average, occupied three positions and males two. The bulk of positions for both sexes were at the local and/or state levels. Seventy-one percent of responsibilities assumed by females were in the periphery. For the males the percentage was 61. For places at the national center females registered 29 percent and males 39 percent. In terms of all positions available in local and state structures females, holding 51 percent of them, barely outpassed the male contingent. On the other hand, males occupied 60 percent of the positions in the national ranks. In terms of all positions occupied, 53 percent were held by males. Male leaders were definitely more prominent at the top organizational level and females barely so in lower parts of the hierarchy. As in other nations, men exhibited a higher rate of overall activity in organizational structures.

Age may also be related to this group of leaders. Putnam (2000) comments on persons 60 and older who have held leadership positions in local organizations. He reveals that these people provided 12 percent of the officers and committee members at the dawn of the 1970s. By the mid-1990s their contribution stood at 20 percent. The graying of leadership positions in the sample was much more marked, almost double. Persons over 60 filled 39 percent of the positions which again points to the increased activity of seniors.

Organizational affiliation is of utmost importance and widespread participation in voluntary structures, such as that demonstrated by this sample, provides many advantages beneficial to the growth and enrichment of democracy and democratic citizenship. Providing experiences with group relations and group goals, opportunities for communication and dialogue, the development of social and organizational skills, civic orientations, efficacy, interests, and mutual trust, among other things, they enhance social cooperation. Moreover, voluntary groups serve as socialization agents, although they vary in terms of their political and social environment and the amount of influence they exert over their members and others. Engaging in direct and indirect socialization, they are important mechanisms for social and political learning. Providing a framework for the development of primary relationships that impact on political and civic orientations and serving as reference points for members, they influence their outlooks, political and otherwise.

The dividing line between the political and the nonpolitical worlds is far from clear. Voluntary activity relates to politics in a variety of ways and is critical to an understanding of political participation (Dawson, Prewitt, & Dawson, 1977; Hodgkinson, 1995; Verba et al., 1995). Experiences, attitudes, skills, and basic perceptions of the social world developed in the third sector are easily transferred to the political arena. In fact, encouraging and developing participatory factors, among other things, voluntary associations can be viewed as a training ground and stimulant for political efforts. These groups, in essence, have a significance for the political world. Dawson et al. (1977) in reference to voluntary associations observe: "The more important the group is for the individual, and the more closely he or she is related to it, the more likely the group is to influence his or her political outlook" (p. 187). Given the fact that a large part of the sample consisted of active members and those who exercised leadership responsibilities in voluntary associations, one can appreciate the intensity and significance of the relationship. For Almond and Verba (1965) democracy benefits because voluntary associations train a participant "more likely to be close to the model of the democratic citizen" (p. 265).

Public Member Board Experience

The literature (Connors, 1988; Kang & Cnaan, 1995; Mogulof, 1970a) refers to interlocking boards of trustees, especially since the rapid growth in the number of nonprofits. An interesting finding in this study is that the respondents formed a relatively inexperienced group which was startling, given the vital role of citizen members. Fifty-six percent of them were not sitting and had not sat on other boards as a public member. Thus, more than a majority of the respondents had minimal experience and were sitting for the first time in this capacity. This left only a smaller seasoned group that had weathered many a storm. Seven percent had over ten years experience as public members, 20 percent between seven and ten years and 18 percent, four to six years. Prior experience is critical to effectiveness, especially when an organization appoints a public member for the first time. One such trustee explains: "You need to have strong experienced people in these positions to be 'trailblazers' when public members are added for the first time. Otherwise, the person will probably not add much value."

Reasons for Serving

What is it that predisposes individuals to volunteer? The answer is important because it can be used to explain why diverse groups of people have different rates of participation and it also aids in an explanation of the relationship between social and economic changes and variation in participation. There are a variety of motivations which, like the concept of voluntarism itself, has changed overtime. Thus, a plethora of reasons has been offered as to why people commit their resources, energies, and time to volunteer positions, such as that of a public member on a board of trustees. Researchers from various disciplines have studied these drives that feed, sustain, and direct individual behavior and a multiplicity of motives has been confirmed time and again. These studies have not focused exclusively on board membership in the third sector, but on voluntarism, in general. Only a minimal number has been concerned with boards of trustees.

The response to the question of what moves people to action depends on the perception of voluntarism at a given point in time. Being a dynamic and culturally sensitive concept, its definition has changed from one historical epoch to another. For example, it has been perceived principally as action originating from emotional commitment as opposed to a rational regard for choices. When the Progressive Movement was at its zenith with the ideal of pragmatism at its core, voluntarism was seen as an expression of commitment to pragmatic concerns. In other periods of history, it has been identified with missionary service inspired by religious dedication. Or it has been described, as noted, in terms of the pioneer spirit (Ilsley, 1990).

What the volunteer board experience can potentially contribute to the public member is just as important as what this person can possibly contribute to the nonprofit organization. Thus, participants in the survey were invited to set forth their reasons for becoming public members. In indicating why they volunteered, they were to designate all motives listed in the survey instrument that applied to their situation and to specify others not noted. Responses indicated that individuals are motivated to join boards of directors as public members for a variety of reasons, many of which have been cited in studies of voluntarism in general.

Participation is a goal-oriented activity in which people engage in order to gain some personal advantage. Thus, if they perceive a potential benefit for themselves, they are ready to participate. The most cited motive (66 percent) for involvement was a very simple one: "thought I would enjoy the experience." Persons selecting this reason were public members for the sake of enjoyment. Frequently, novice volunteers, such as those in the survey serving for the first time in a public member capacity, hope to derive fun, excitement, and a good time from the position. In this instance, feelings or forces from inside the self prompted the affirmative decision to accept a board position. The critical element in becoming a volunteer public member was self-actualization (Ilsley, 1990; Schindler-Rainman, 1988a).

Closely related was the second most important motivation for board service, personal enrichment. It was cited by 48 percent of the respondents, one of whom remarked: "I enjoy and benefit from contact with professionals who are not in my discipline. It enriches me personally and I learn from my fellow members." And another commented:

> This involvement as a public member has been very rewarding. My fellow board members are true dedicated professionals, but in a field [in which] I had no training . . . . This has been a great way for me to expand my knowledge of the profession and of nonprofits in general . . . . I am making contacts and friendships with talented people that I hope will continue in years after my board term.

Again, an inner orientation or one's own forces accounted for the decision to serve. In the same vein, the next motive in terms of importance (44 percent) was a desire for change and involvement. These first three motivations for serving are related in that they may be labeled inner-oriented. They were fostered by one's own inner feelings. Moreover, all three involve self-enhancement motives and psychological benefits: good feelings, opportunities for personal growth, camaraderie, and the development of new horizons. Research indicates that rewards, such as these, rather than others, are more likely to motivate general volunteers (Ilsley, 1990). These psychological benefits are an important element of voluntarism.

Needs theories have been used to analyze the various facets of voluntarism and to develop disparate types of programs for volunteers. One of the major proponents of this school of thought was Abraham Maslow (1943, 1954). Believing that needs serve as a basis for human motivation, he constructed a hierarchy consisting of five basic needs. Moving from the most fundamental to the most complex, the needs are physiological (need for food, water, and sleep), safety (need to be free from danger, order, predictability of the environment), belonging and love (need for affiliation and intimacy), esteem (need for respect and to be of value) and self-actualization (need to realize one's potential). Being convinced of the progression of these needs, Maslow argued that the lower-order needs must be satisfied first and then they must be responded to in ascending order. At different points in time one of the needs will be predominant and propel all activities. It, thus, behooves organizations to be aware of its affiliates' need level and to tailor programs to meet it. The responses noted so far to the question related to motivations for becoming a public member indicate that this constituency, to a large degree, was concerned with self-actualization or the realization of one's potential.

Needs theories, even though they aid in a comprehension of what inspires people to action, have been criticized because of difficulties in applying them to the real world. In a given setting often individuals will be experiencing different needs. If this is the case, it is difficult to identify the constituency's most important one. Also, even though one need tends to prevail, the interaction of all needs influences behavior. Thus, needs theory is of use, but alone does not sufficiently explain motivations (Peach & Murrell, 1995).

Another important element of voluntarism is issue engagement. Thirty-nine percent of the public members surveyed indicated that substantive interests played a major role in their decision to serve. For board members and volunteers alike, very often these interests motivate service (Meneghetti, 1995). And, of note is the fact that in other surveys, respondents that indicated they were moved to action by personal involvement with an issue, an organizational cause, an activity, or program, the percentages were more or less in the same range as in this study (Ilsley, 1990; O'Connell, 1985; Pearce, 1993). Normative institutionalists distinguish between aggregative and integrative elements. They would note that participation in this type of integrative institution, meaning one from which individuals gain much personal significance, as opposed to aggregative institutions whose affiliates depend on them for their livelihood, results from a commitment to the goals of the institution and the legitimacy of its claims. This type of institution expresses once again a logic of appropriateness (Peters, 2005). As in other instances cited, these cause or interest-oriented volunteers were guided to participation by their own forces or forces from inside the self.

For some volunteers an identity with the community at large and the public good is important. Altruism, as another motivator, also originates within the self. Indicating civic commitment and a belief in the importance and effectiveness of participation, a chief consideration of people so motivated is the welfare of others. A survey of 6,000 hospital trustees revealed that they served primarily for this reason. There was no close second (Panas, 1991). This orientation was cited by only 30 percent of the public member sample. These folks feel good about being involved, contributing, and believing they can make a difference. They want to be useful and feel a sense of responsibility toward the community at large. Having resources that they want to invoke in favor of the community, these people may be thought of as good citizens or humanitarians. Very often senior citizens or retirees are motivated in this manner. They view the volunteer role as highly salient and as a part of the senior lifestyle (D.B. Smith, 2004). Their utility comes from many years of professional experience and the accumulation of a wide variety of skills, both of which they offer with their services. Many respondents to the survey in personal comments indicated that they felt they had much to offer to a board of trustees in terms of expertise, experience, and skills. They viewed the invitation to serve as a public member as an opportunity to contribute to society in general, to improve the status quo, and to return to the community some of their knowledge. Often altruism goes hand in hand with repayment motives. Their activity perceived as a kind of payback was fostered by a concern for others and by a confidence in their efficacy and ability to make a difference.

Not all motivations for volunteering originate in the self as in the instances cited above. Different forces that nurture voluntarism derive from relations with other people. These are the interpersonal and group member forces that inspire action. Very often those in the general volunteer population initially participate because someone invited them or they had a relative, colleague, or acquaintance involved in the activity. In fact, for general volunteers such reasons have been among the most important and most common for involvement. The most significant factor leading to participation is being asked (Daniels, 1988; Hodgkinson, 1995; O'Connell, 1985; Putnam, 2000; Schervish, 1995). As in the political arena, people are more likely to take part, if they are recruited. Personal contact stimulates interest and provides information, which, in turn, increases the likelihood of participation. The activity, being spurred by a request, results from somebody else's expectations or desires. For participants in the survey these reasons were much less compelling than in other studies involving general volunteers and board members (Widmer, 1985), registering 25 percent as compared with 44 percent.

Instrumental theory is also related to voluntarism and is especially pertinent for the business and professional constituencies. It asserts that people will act only if they are convinced that their actions will lead to highly valued outcomes or advantages. This theory applied to the sample. Some respondents (30 percent) became public members because of the opportunities for business, professional, and social contacts. Others (21 percent) were mobilized because they realized the utility of the visibility, prestige, and recognition affiliated with the public member board position. Still others (18 percent) believed that this volunteer service would enhance their job status and be useful for career purposes. A small group (six percent) noted the opportunity to travel, and to receive rewards in the form of laptops and the like, and five percent stressed economic and financial benefits.

People often seek connections for the benefit of their own interests. They engage in activities that provide benefits specifically for themselves as well as for others. In other words, a giving hand is also a getting hand (Brooks, 2006). It is well-known that jobs are often awarded to individuals on the basis of networking and not necessarily because of their expertise and knowledge. It is social rather than human capital (education and experience) that is important in this context. This is quite relevant in this day and age, given the lack of stability throughout the entire labor hierarchy. From an economic perspective these weaker and casual social ties are more important than solidified long-term ones. They definitely sport a monetary value (Putnam, 2000).

Voluntary comments offered by public member respondents clearly confirmed that board positions served as an instrument to seek valuable rewards of various types. Typical are the following statements. "As a result of that experience, one of my clients is [name of the organization]." Or "A great experience for me, will certainly go on my resume, likely to help in my long-term career path, and thus, has made me more likely to volunteer for other board work." A valued goal for many professionals who volunteer is to be viewed by others in a positive manner. Echoing this outcome are the words of one participant in the survey: "I enjoy the title of 'a get things done guy.'" Several other comments were similar in nature.

Closely related is McClelland's learned needs theory (Meneghetti, 1995; Peach & Murrell, 1995) which is concerned with the impact of learned, culturally based needs on behavior. Although he focused on three needs: affiliation, power, and achievement, it was the last one that he emphasized. Achievers are self-starters, driven to excellence and improvement, ready for a challenge, and willing to assume responsibility for outcomes, both positive and negative. Nine percent of the survey respondents cited a desire for excellence, improvement of the status quo, and the achievement of the highest possible standards for the profession as reasons for their volunteer board service.

The need for power relates to the desire to exert influence and authority over others. One way to meet this need is to achieve prestige, recognition, and visibility. As noted earlier, some respondents became public members precisely for this purpose. Others (six percent) accepted the board position because they wanted to influence the direction of an important organization. In this sense, influence could also be perceived in a negative sense, meaning control. The need for affiliation has essentially been dealt with earlier in another context. In terms of their propensity to join multiple organizations and to become public members, participants in the survey certainly manifested their desire to engage in diverse social relationships.

It was very surprising to find that only a mere six percent of the public members joined their board because they were convinced of the significance of a voice for the public. Such reflects the failure to define and project the purpose and important role of the public member. Very few respondents paid tribute to the value of the public perspective and the desire to hold an organization accountable for its activities. And none referred to a sense of civic duty. This is puzzling in light of the fact that middle-class society has traditionally emphasized the development of conscience and duty. An important value has been duty to society. But such was not evident in this survey. On the other hand, other studies, some completed as long as over three decades ago, concluded that a majority of consumer members was motivated by the notion of citizen duty (Chesney, 1982; Parkum & Parkum, 1973). The lack of reference to this element in the present study can be explained by the change in valued goals that accompanied civic disengagement in advanced industrialized societies.

Another variable having an importance for volunteering, in general, is whether a person has taken advantage of the services offered by a nonprofit (O'Connor & Johnson, 1989). In the case of this sample, service usage motivated three percent of respondents who received a service in the form of treatments and thus, wanted to be involved in the organization. Board membership as a public member was the result. Similar percentages accounted for public members who were serving because they were fulfilling service requirements for their profession or they just happened to be available.

Religion has served as a bridge to civic engagement. More specifically, voluntarism and altruism have traditionally been identified with it. In fact, Brooks (2006) claims that religion is the number one characteristic that predicts who volunteers and who does not. Very often people volunteered and still do, but to a lesser extent, because of religious concerns, commitment, and convictions (O'Connell, 1985; D.B. Smith, 2004; Wuthnow, 1999). Religiosity competes with education as a significant correlate of civic engagement. With religion being important in American society, Americans are more likely to be religious than citizens of other nations. This fact might account for the higher level of volunteering and joining of groups in the United States than in other advanced industrialized societies.

One question asked of survey participants was: "Do you consider yourself religious?" Even though over the past three decades or so, the number of people exhibiting confidence in organized religion has decreased considerably, and citizens are generally of the opinion that religion has a lesser impact on daily life (Ladd & Bowman, 1998), 68 percent of the public members responded in the affirmative. They considered themselves religious. This response is also understandable in light of the age of the sample. Older folks are attracted more by religion than younger ones. Twenty-eight percent answered the question in the negative, leaving four percent that did not know. A most recent study carried out by the Sociology Department at Baylor University and the Baylor Institute for Studies of Religion, concerned with the spiritual life of Americans, reported that only about 11 percent are not identified with a congregation, denomination, or faith group. Of those not having a religious affiliation, 60 percent claimed to believe in God or a higher power ("Americans are more," 2006). The results of this survey indicate that people, in general, are more religious than the public members surveyed.

In spite of the overwhelming affirmative response to the survey question, a mere two percent attributed religious concerns or spiritual motives to their board positions. Other research focusing on citizens participating in local government agencies as volunteers also found that these matters were not of great importance (Sundeen, 1990). These findings compare with a 1987 Gallup poll in which 28 percent of the respondents linked religious concerns to their volunteering (Pearce, 1993). The decreased impact of religion on volunteering is evident. In fact, Wolfe (1998) argues that religious belief does not correlate strongly with altruistic behavior. The relationship between the two tends to be weak.

There is a diversity in the level and type of social capital and civic engagement among the major faiths (Wuthnow, 1999). The Protestant denominations encouraged a broad civic orientation. However, they have experienced a decline as a result of an intense competition with evangelical and fundamentalist churches, which advocate a different focus, an inner one aimed at individual piety and social capital nested in their own units. Religion's ability to mobilize civic engagement is definitely experiencing a transformation.

The social capital perspective emphasizes the socialization of individuals into civic engagement. Participatory factors are accumulated throughout the life cycle, beginning at a tender age in the confines of the family, a paramount socialization agent whose influence on participation is very high. In spite of this, it is noteworthy that no respondent made reference to the family as a unit or individual family members as having an impact on their decision to serve. Through prescription, discussion, and role modeling, parents pass on outlooks and evaluations to their offspring that increase with age in frequency and in crystallization. Participating in community affairs and underscoring their importance, parents foster positive attitudes toward civic involvement among their children. Here the interpersonal and group member forces are at work. More specifically, the family transmits a set of social identifications and feelings through which the maturing individual establishes relationships with the social world. The impact of the family as a socialization agent is especially important during the early formative years. Research efforts have confirmed the impact of family life on voluntarism and civic orientations. Role modeling, particularly on the part of the parents, was found to be especially potent. Board members have frequently been raised in families where a positive civic orientation and voluntarism were central to daily life. It has been confirmed that those with parents active in the third sector are more likely to be so themselves. In addition, role models external to the family and experiences and events from the pre-adult years exert their influence as well (Duca, 1986; Hodgkinson, 1995; Schervish, 1995; Sears & Valentino, 1997).

Recognizing the importance of intergenerational transmission and parental legacy encompassed in the "persistence" perspective which asserts that basic outlooks are acquired at a very young age and persist throughout life, survey respondents were asked to evaluate their family's community interest when they were growing up and that of their present family. The possible ratings were low, average, and high. The largest segment of those surveyed (46 percent) were raised in a family manifesting an average interest in community affairs. Thirty-three percent had a family demonstrating high interest and 21 percent came from homes with low interest. The responses concerning the level of interest of the present family were very different. A high interest in the community was claimed by over a majority of respondents (58 percent) who were followed by those with an average interest (38 percent), leaving a very small group (four percent) with low civic orientations. The lack of similarity in the evaluations confirms that across-the-board family transmission of social outlooks does not always happen. Other socialization agents intervene as individuals progress throughout the life cycle. Moreover, certain conditions, such as the homogeneity of the family unit, the existence and articulation of social outlooks by parents, the consistency of parental perspectives, and the nature of the relationship between the offspring and parents, affect the family transmission of social attitudes (Alwin & Krosnick, 1991; Dawson et al., 1977). In addition, it must be remembered that participatory orientations and resources are primarily acquired through education. It might be that respondents to the survey, being a highly educated group, have more education than their parents, given the widespread and rapid growth of higher educational opportunities in the post-World War II era. Consequently, the level of community interest in the present family is higher.

Volunteering, being an act of the spirit involving freedom of choice, is an undertaking that is not obligatory and also, as noted, is usually not financially remunerated. Recognizing this, a pertinent question arises as to the motives for serving in a volunteer capacity and more specifically, in this case, as a public member on a nonprofit board of directors. What is it that stimulates people to offer their services in this manner? Data collected in this survey concerning the backgrounds of the public members involved clearly indicate that they are prepared and predisposed to participate. They are achievers in terms of education, profession, and income. Moreover, they have had an extensive group experience with a civic orientation. In addition, they have acquired the appropriate resources and attitudes.

Volunteers have different reasons for their commitment. An examination of these reveals the participants' value structure and the significance of the volunteer experience to them. The public members surveyed recognized more than one incentive for their involvement. Although the forces propelling them to volunteer were multiple and wide-ranging, they relate to the two fundamental human inclinations from which voluntarism originated. The first, the self-regarding inclination, nurtured by forces from within the self, is concerned with the creative human powers, self-enhancement motives, and self-actualization. The individual's own forces, such as sense of relevance, values, and feelings, dictated the guidelines for decisions concerning whether to volunteer or not. An examination of the reasons offered for becoming a public member indicates that respondents assigned most importance to the self-actualization possibilities affiliated with the volunteer experience. The self-regarding inclination was significant.

Freedom of spirit also allows an individual to identify with a realm beyond the self and thus, to focus on the second fundamental human inclination, the other-regarding tendency or altruistic human powers and virtues (Story, 1992). These other-regarding aspects are also related to the interpersonal and group member forces. They were evident in the data collected, but to a much lesser extent. They are concerned with the relevance of action to the community, the notion of service, concern, an orientation toward the highest human standard or good, and repayment, among other things. Other research endeavors, such as that of Chesney (1984), concluded that public members on regulatory boards served out of a sense of citizen duty. This orientation was not prevalent, much less evident, in the present survey. In this study the self-actualizers prevailed over the servers who are more concerned with the impact of action and action and its social relevance. Respondents were not generally oriented toward a social problem world. Representing diverse priorities for different people, both of these human inclinations were reflected in the sample, but in distinct ways. Situational forces were involved as well, but only to a minimal degree. Those respondents who referred to an opportunity to travel, professional service requirements, receipt of per diems, laptops, and other rewards as reasons for serving were moved by these forces.

The volunteer experience may also be looked at from the perspective of the amount of autonomy allotted to the individual (Schindler-Rainman, 1988a). A good many of the responses offered by participants in the survey suggest, that for them, autonomy was of great importance. It appeared that excitement and a flair for pleasure, fun, the new, the unexpected, change of pace, freedom, and novelty, among other things, were attractive to them. In fact, in comments public members adopted these words in reasoning why they accepted their board positions. Thus, a large segment of respondents were autonomy oriented as opposed to being interdependent or dependent. A structural dependence seemed least attractive to them.

Data collected in the survey also suggest that the incentives for volunteering are much more varied and more numerous than they once were. As society has changed, so have the motivations for involvement. It is possible to classify the incentives for participation as a public member on a nonprofit board of directors on the basis of the forces involved in the acceptance of a position, as noted above. However, it must be recognized that the public member can identify with more than one category at a time and can overtime go from one to another. This makes it difficult to pinpoint motivations precisely. Moreover, it is difficult to evaluate the strength of the volunteer's sense of commitment and motives (Ilsley, 1990).

Voluntarism, being an expression of commitment, volunteers have also been distinguished on the basis of the objects of their commitments. They have been labeled volunteer-centered (manifesting a loyalty to colleagues in their group), organization-centered (focusing on a specific association), client-centered (being dedicated to a particular segment of the population), or social-vision centered (being committed to the realization of an ideal). A sprinkling of responses from participants in the survey referenced some of these orientations, but they were so sparse that they were meaningless. It appears that the public members did not have these specified types of commitments. The strength of any commitment they might have had was tenuous. Failing to clearly articulate the nature of their commitment and demonstrating an orientation lacking such focus, it is difficult to precisely determine what exactly voluntarism means to them.

Representation

Participation is a strategy to create goals, establish priorities, and select the appropriate resources for goal achievement. The ideal democratic order presupposes full participation on the part of all members of the community. However, obviously, everyone is not able to be involved. Thus, people need representatives because they cannot be present themselves. Structures and practices incorporating some kind of representation are necessary in any large and articulated society. Institutions and people, other than legislatures and elected representatives, such as nonprofit governing boards and their members, serve representative functions. It is the notion of representation that connects these various actors with representative roles. Questions of representation have been central to the theory and practice of politics for aeons. Representation may be construed as a mechanism for the articulation of needs, opinions, desires, and visions, as well as a method for obtaining consensus and a certain amount of consumer satisfaction. It is a strategy for realizing predetermined and preferred ends (Fagence, 1977). Nonprofit boards of directors are representative institutions. The issues with which they are concerned and the manner in which they are resolved depend on their members, especially their demographic attributes, among other considerations.

The ancient Greeks, having no such concept, the idea of representation began to develop with the Romans. Although they made reference to representation, the meaning was very different from the one with which we are familiar. It stood for bringing into presence something that previously was absent and it referred to inanimate objects, rather than people or the Roman state and its institutions. It was in the Middle Ages that the notion began to develop as we understand it today. It penetrated Christian religious literature in which the Pope and cardinals were portrayed as representing the persons of Christ and the Apostles. They were viewed as their images. In this period the term was also planted in the political arena. However, it was only in the seventeenth century that the modern notion of representation appeared. At this time it was related to agency, acting for other people and democratic entities. As the concept has evolved, it has come to pervade most institutions central to daily life (Abzug & Galaskiewicz, 2001; Pitkin, 1967, 1969).

Representation may be viewed as acting for other people and therefore, the focus is on behavior, substance, or role. However, it may also be perceived as standing for something that is absent without taking into account activity. The former perspective will be developed in another context later in the discussion. When representation is viewed as "standing for" rather than "acting on behalf of," it is labeled descriptive representation. In this case, a person can stand for another provided they resemble each other. An individual is considered to be fit for being a representative because of personal attributes that are typical of a particular constituency. Representation is dependent on the representative's features and appearance. There must be a correspondence relating to selected elements which might include religion, socioeconomic status, race, education, and group membership, among others. These characteristics are of significance because the representative, resembling or reflecting the characteristics of members of a larger unit, has the right to stand for them. In essence, the person denotes them. Thus, representation is concerned with the resemblance of existential attributes on the part of representatives and those whom they represent. It should be noted, however, that Pitkin (1967) is quick to point out that "the best descriptive representative is not necessarily the best representative for activity or government" (p. 88). Socially descriptive representation has been utilized by theorists, such as Simon Sterne and John Stuart Mill, in connection with advocacy of proportional representation.

From this perspective in terms of decision-making institutions, such as nonprofit boards of trustees, what is of utmost significance is their composition. They must be composed in such a way as to reflect accurately the larger constituency. To become representative entities, institutions must meet this prerequisite. Decision-making bodies literally serve as mirrors for the larger population for which they stand. Obviously, it is a challenge to accurately reflect in an institution the characteristics of those who are formally represented. Thus, descriptive representation often refers to the extent of correspondence between the representatives and the larger unit they portray (Nordlinger, 1968; Pitkin, 1969). Significance is assigned to the profile of the decision makers because it is assumed that it, in part, determines policy output.

Descriptive representation has been evaluated positively, especially in terms of its benefits for deprived groups. Representatives of these units serve as role models and their constituents thus profit from seeing fellow group members in positions of authority. Not only is institutional loyalty fostered, but a larger commitment and identity are nurtured as well. In terms of decision-making the quality of deliberation is enhanced and such group representation also provides a channel for the articulation of perspectives, interests, and issues, many of which have been traditionally ignored in the confines of the institutional agenda. Legitimacy is promoted, the benefits of participation bear fruit for other sectors, mistrust is tempered, and past and continuing injustices toward certain constituencies are alleviated (Dovi, 2002; Mansbridge, 1999).

Socially descriptive representation does not stress accountability. In no way are representatives held accountable to those for whom they act. They, merely reflecting the social fabric, have no standards concerned with their actions as representatives. They represent their constituencies' attributes as opposed to their attitudes and preferences. Attitudes cannot be inferred from attributes and many cleavages are cross cutting in that they transcend class, race, ethnicity, community, and other strata. The problem only becomes magnified, given the minimal number of public members, most often only one, on many directorates. Morone and

Marmor (1981) argue that "opinion polls measure public views more accurately than does descriptive representation" (p. 31). Because any member of a group is as qualified a representative as any other, they, thus, describe this type of representation as pernicious and as an invitation to tokenism.

Although descriptive representatives are important to the policy-making process, the criteria for their selection have received little attention. A broad perspective of descriptive representation has been deemed useful. Focus on the profile of the representatives is necessary because of the requirement to reflect the constituency at large. Emphasis on broad representativeness reduces the focus on selection and accountability. It has been suggested that the nature of the relationship between the representative and the subgroup involved also be given consideration. Dovi (2002) proposes that a descriptive representative should enjoy a mutual relationship with a constituency, meaning that the group and the representative should recognize each other in a particular manner. Both should partake in an interactive relationship. Such reciprocal recognition would encourage dual efforts and allow for their coordination.

The construction of this relationship is more difficult than it appears. The mutual affiliation ideally requires that both parties assign the same meaning to group membership and that they achieve a consensus as to the goals and aims of the descriptive representative. It is the degree of congruence between the perspectives pertaining to aims that is of significance because they serve as a guide for policy preferences. It is this relationship that blurs the aforementioned distinction between the representative as "acting for" and representative as "standing for," or between how a representative acts and what a representative looks like. It is the sense of group membership and shared aims that compose the foundation of mutual relationships. Descriptive representatives who enjoy such a relationship with their constituents, according to Dovi (2002), are the preferred ones. They are armed with the instrument that affords a group a stake in the decision-making process and an opportunity to influence its agenda and output. As will be discussed later, it is this relationship and the notion of constituency that create problems for public members.

Selection and Recruitment

Representation may also be viewed from another perspective, a procedural one that refers to the manner by which representatives are nominated and selected. In this instance, representation, indicating the system by which representatives are chosen, is concerned only with selection. It makes no assumptions about the representatives' behavior or traits. However, as in other notions of representation, it is assumed that the existence of periodic elections makes representatives responsive to their constituencies (Nordlinger, 1968; Peterson, 1970).

In cases where public participation in the form of the public member has been institutionalized and, for that matter, in all instances where representative systems are used, there should be a formalized system of representation and a selection process to designate the desired number of board representatives for a specified term of office. The decision as to what procedures are to be used in appointment and recruitment is a delicate one. All electoral arrangements are skewed in one way or another. The system selected affects the characteristics of the people chosen, which, in turn, heavily influences the way in which an institution functions and its external relationships, among other things. It dictates the basic thrust of the institution and in the long-run its performance. Taylor (1987) reports that variations in board quality among states, within states, and overtime, derive from the appointment process. There is no best way to select public members, just as no electoral system is the best. It all depends on the nature of the organization, its objectives, and its clientele. Each unit has to determine what it believes to be the most appropriate method.

A vital ingredient of a strong, effective, and powerful board is the selection of suitable members. People are selected for board membership principally through appointment by an outside authority, or by the existing directorate, or through election, either by the general public or members of an association; or self-selection. Many nonprofit boards are self-perpetuating. In the organizations surveyed most public members (61 percent) came to the board of directors via the appointment process, including political appointments; and 36 percent were elected. The remaining slots were filled by a combination of these methods.

It is generally acknowledged that selection by election establishes accountability on the part of the representative to a constituency. The electoral mandate creates a relationship. Consequently, voluntarism or self-selection, a practice used less than others, has been criticized for leading to a lack of accountability. In this instance, there are no sanctions to be imposed on the representative. Elections allow the electors to decide when the representative leaves office. Volunteering often leaves this choice, for the most part, to the representative. In notes appended to the questionnaire some executive directors, as indicated above, asked for advice on how to get rid of volunteer representatives. It is difficult to create a representative structure on the basis of voluntarism. Moreover, volunteers also leave themselves open to challenges of legitimacy from professionals as well as from other public members (Chesney, 1982; Metsch & Veney, 1977).

A few executive directors in personal comments bemoaned pressure even with the use of secret ballots to elect "insider" candidates. As one of these agency leaders explained:

> I would appreciate any help you can provide in identifying public members, particularly in that I want to move away from board-recommended public members. Even with private written ballot elections, there is pressure to elect an individual nominated by a board member, rather than one from an outside source.

Such pressure was not uncommon in agencies surveyed. An examination of the methods used to identify public member candidates offers an explanation for this situation. Executive directors were asked how the agency identifies candidates for public member seats. Responses indicated that a variety of strategies are utilized and some organizations mentioned several. A small group of associations (ten percent), given their nature, had candidates identified and selected by governmental organs. The previously cited executive director's comments are cogent in that for the rest, board members were the most prevalent source (84 percent) for suggestions. They were followed by other like organizations (39 percent), key stakeholder groups (32 percent), advertisements in newsletters and professional journals (29 percent), nominating committee (14 percent), membership or certificants (14 percent), staff and/or chief executive (11 percent), and former board members (seven percent). Thus, all these sources, with the exception perhaps of other like organizations and the printed word, are important components of the agency institutional landscape not likely to produce richness in terms of diversity.

The general selection process used by many boards is parochial and insulated in nature and encourages the homogeneity found in this study in terms of public member representation. Boards tend to reinforce themselves. This self-perpetuation relates to individuals as well as to the representation of categories (O'Connell, 1985). Moreover, although it is the easiest way to find candidates, this heavy reliance on board members as a source for nominations is a hazardous practice, especially, if they serve as the sole point of reference. This was the case for a group of agencies in the sample. It is generally acknowledged that nominees for board positions tend to resemble those making the nominations in terms of socioeconomic status, age, occupation, geographical location, interests, and the like (Taylor, 1987). People usually suggest the names of those persons they know and to whom they relate well. Empirical studies have demonstrated that people of a high socioeconomic status tend to recruit those of similar background. Interpersonal bonds are important in terms of recruitment and also in creating strong social control mechanisms. As for a portion of this sample, in the political world, recruitment networks are rooted in personal ties as well (Pearce, 1993; Verba et al., 1995). This might be considered beneficial from the perspective of board harmony and unity. In fact, comments offered in the survey by an executive director confirmed this benefit. This person wrote:

> It is helpful if a board member has previous experience with a candidate. One of our public members was on the [name of board] board with a board member, so they had worked together on a different issue, but knew each other well. It has been a most successful association for us.

These words exemplify the fact that the selection process is self-perpetuating. Frequently, only those people who "fit in" are tapped for membership to the detriment of more strategic considerations of organizational needs. Often, it is precisely because of this wish to avoid tension and conflict that boards do not always carry out their governance responsibilities (Masaoka & Allison, October 28, 2004).

Moreover, this homogeneity can be detrimental from other points of view. Representation is limited along with the diversity of ideas, the nature of resulting dialogue, and, in the long-run, opportunities available to the association. Furthermore, Gupta (1989) observes that boards including people of different styles and backgrounds generate better solutions to problems and more innovative ideas. It is also of significance that generative work and governance flourish on the diversity of multiple perspectives and dialogue. It is these elements that provide the power and shape a large part of what takes place in an organization. Executives might find it convenient to have all trustees think mostly alike. This might suffice for fiduciary matters, but overall and in the long- run, pluralism is central to a board's success and effectiveness.

> Generative work thrives on deliberations among participants with different perspectives and different frames for noticing different cues and clues. The more hypotheses and angles of vision, the more likely perceptive reformulations and keen insights will materialize . . . generative work benefits from the interplay of ideas (Chait et al., 2005, pp. 99-100).

Normative institutionalists would applaud this statement.

Selection and recruitment of board members are most significant for a governing body can be no better than its members. Members of high performance boards have an abundance of knowledge in many areas, information related to the organization and its environment, power allowing for exertion of influence on all facets of the decision-making process, rewards motivating performance, and opportunity and time to fulfill responsibilities. These elements aid significantly in effective organizational management. Board composition strongly determines the quantity and quality of attributes present in the institutional structure and, in turn, the functions it performs and how they are carried out. In addition, it is closely related to the kinds of power a board possesses and how they are exercised. Ideally, the institution should reflect personal power, based on the traits of its members; expert power, concerned with their knowledge and information; and position power related to their formal authority. In that personal and expert power can be exercised independently of the individual's formal authority and situation, combined with position power, the image internal and external to the organization can be formidable (Conger et al., 2001).

In light of the prominence of the board of directors, the general lack of focus on the recruitment function by executive directors is startling. More specifically, one study indicated that these officials spend less than two percent of their time on matters pertaining to recruitment, a function of momentous proportions (Panas, 1991). The building of a stellar board must be viewed as part of an organization's ministry, if it is to come near to achieving its ideal or real potential. This neglect of the recruitment and selection processes seems to be widespread. They have been described as "at worst haphazard and at best casual" (Taylor, 1987, p. 20). The same evaluation still applies. Given this situation, it is not surprising that many governing boards and their organizations fail to act in an appropriate manner and to realize their potential. Proactive recruiting methods should be firmly in place in all organizations. These processes should be given careful attention. They must be planned with a great deal of thought.

Each organization should meticulously evaluate its needs in terms of board members and, especially public members, with emphasis on basic traits required of participants, categories of representation, special resources, skills of a social, intellectual, economic, political, and functional nature; values, and range of social group memberships (i.e., race, gender, age, profession, socioeconomic status) desired. These are all important considerations. As noted above, the professional abilities that members bring to a board are often unexpectedly tapped. Most, if not all, directors are asked to perform as consultants to the organization at one time or another. Possessing a needed professional talent, whether it be legal, accounting, engineering, public relations, investments, or whatever, board members are useful to the agency in terms of response time and cost, being on the scene and less expensive than purchasing that needed skill on the market. However, once again these talents must be used sparingly and not be assigned top priority. Furthermore, it is important to have the appropriate mix of talents represented on a board because of the wide range of responsibilities to be covered and the diverse behaviors required, especially in light of governance as leadership. This mix of intellectual, management, and personal capital must be blended in relation to the organization's mission statement, its program, and its institutional landscape.

In addition to talents and attributes, other factors must be given consideration as well. For example, types of roles within third sector organizations, including leadership roles, such as board members, relate to individual life styles. Each role attracts a different model. Pairing a particular style with a specific role allows for recruitment strategies to be given a special focus (Heidrich, 1990). Utilizing this approach, problems of retention might be somewhat lessened, but, unfortunately, not eliminated. They represent a thorn in the side of an organization, because constant turnover in board membership creates obstacles to performance.

Until the advent of strategic planning and market-based competition, nonprofit organizations in creating their governing bodies focused primarily on certain desirable traits, such as social status. As these new activities evolved in the sector, more stress was put on pertinent expertise and competencies along with demographic diversity. However, more recent changes in the nonprofit world bring to the surface new forms of work capital important to board competition. More specifically, intellectual capital is furnished by the common or shared knowledge or "organizational intelligence" of the trustees. It represents "a shared sense of the nature of the work and enough common knowledge to do the work together" (Chait et al., 2005, p. 143). In reality, what the board thinks, its "collective mind" is nurtured by what the board knows, its "collective brainpower." Reputational capital, so important to any structure, commences with the selection of board members. Trustee reputation and name recognition can be utilized in diverse ways to portray specific images to particular audiences.

As noted in the introductory chapter, boards of directors are political actors in their own right. Thus, political capital, the influence and leverage that trustees acquire and use in performing their responsibilities, relates to their activities internal and external to the organization. The political capital brought to the board via the recruitment process contributes significantly to a nonprofit's rate of return. Governing bodies to function in superlative fashion also require a strong sense of mutual obligation, a propensity for critical inquiry, and a sense of diligence, accountability, and productivity. These elements are furnished by "social capital that stresses personal responsibility, collective industry, and improved performance" (Chait et al., 2005, p. 157).

Board selection is not only about recruiting individuals. In that governing bodies are working groups, the team concept pervades these structures. Thus, it must be remembered that, in spite of the significance of descriptive representation, it is also important to reach out to people possessing broad vistas and a collaborative spirit. A difficult assignment, the appropriate mix must be conceptualized in terms of team members as well (Conger et al., 2001; O'Connell, 1997).

This asset mix, consisting of intellectual, reputational, political, and social capital, is most valuable in terms of the possibilities for producing a high rate of return to an organization. This approach to the recruitment of board members assigns emphasis to quality of mind, a capacity to endure ambiguity, an enthusiasm for organizational puzzles and challenges, as well as a receptiveness to new ideas, an ability to thrive on intense discourse, and a commitment to team play. Chait et al. (2005) note that while the aforementioned methods focusing on trustees' personal, professional, and financial backgrounds may still be useful in the recruitment process, "these new criteria deserve equal or greater weight . . . . Otherwise, the organization may find itself with a board that plays many, indeed *any*, useful roles, other than the most important one: to contribute leadership through the practice of governance" (p. 178). Regardless of which recruitment approach is used, in no organization should the recruitment of board members, public and otherwise, be haphazard. Utilizing careful nomination and selection procedures, a wide range of valuable traits, a richness of diversity, and a wealth of experience can be lodged in a board of directors.

Recruitment and selection of stellar board members are arduous and significant tasks. One respondent to the executive directors' survey in comments underscored this importance by affirming: "It is extremely important to select public members carefully. We solicit nominations from a variety of sources, but we are also very thorough in looking at candidates." These tasks were cited as severe problems for a substantial portion of executive directors surveyed (33 percent). Many baby boomers are retiring, leaving board positions vacant and the third sector is increasing in size by about 3,000 to 4,000 new institutions each month ("The age of nonprofits," 2003). Competition has always been and is becoming more fierce. Moreover, the pool of candidates is not as large as it might or should be. Supposedly, Woody Allen once remarked: "Getting good board members is just about as tough as getting a plumber on a weekend" (Panas, 1991, p. 147). A vital facet of the public member experience, recruitment, has proven to be an elusive task.

Even though the third sector, as noted, generally supported the notion of public participation, its organizations were not quick to come forward with names of candidates to fill the new public member positions. As a result, in many cases, recruitment and selection fell and continues to fall into the hands of political patronage machines that often serve as vehicles for appointment. Moreover, sometimes those responsible for the appointment process fail to understand the public member concept. They do not have a clear notion of the role involved and the qualifications needed. As an aid to recruitment, each organization should have available a statement delineating the role, domain, and level of participation of the public member, as well as other trustees. The last element is of particular importance. De Maio and Charles (1993) observe:

> The level of participation in . . . decision making is the extent to which individuals have control over the decision-making process. There is a significant difference between listening to the views of lay individuals on the one hand and shifting full decision-making authority and responsibility to lay individuals on the other. The level of decision-making involvement is key to defining what is meant by participation and the processes established to structure it (p. 893).

This comment is especially relevant.

Not only would such a statement be useful for organizational recruitment, but it would also serve to answer questions related to training, support, and evaluation of these board representatives. In addition, it would provide public member candidates with a notion of what is expected of them. Whether people will get involved and want to get involved depends on what involvement actually means. People, depending on their orientation, have very different expectations concerning the role of directors. Confusion reigns as to exact roles and responsibilities. Such a statement would clarify several issues. It seems that most of the documents concerned with public member requirements take a negative approach in that they deal with what a public member cannot be. They tend to focus on exclusion criteria and slight almost completely qualities that public member candidates should possess and the nature of their duties ("Capitalizing on," 2001). Rather than a negative approach, a positive one would be most useful.

Qualifications and credentials of these representatives have served as a source of debate. Perhaps, this is a reason why statements pertaining to the public member role and requisite qualities have been less than crisp and not all-inclusive and positive in character. Basically two schools of thought have emerged. Equating the public member role with the judicial function, and thus, valuing good judgment and wisdom derived from personal experience as keys to the decision-making process, one camp stresses individual experience and the credentials of public member candidates. On the other hand, the other camp, believing that links with a constituency make it legitimate for the public member to speak on behalf of a part of the public, assigns prime importance to a candidate's affiliation with a particular constituency or a network of groups over and above all other considerations (*Public Representation*, 1995).

Each board of directors must find consensus on these issues. Careful thought must be given to answering a few questions. How diverse should a governing board be? How should the public member constituency be represented? Which of its dimensions should be included on the board? In what ways do public members differ from other directors? What are public members expected to do? To whom should public members be accountable? Is accountability possible? What attributes do public members need? How important are advocacy, boardsmanship, communication, leadership, lobbying, negotiating, and public relations skills; identification with a constituency, personal experiences, personal and demographic qualities, and other relevant criteria? What kind of consumer orientation should public members have? Are organizational structures congruent with the expectations that are to govern public member behavior? Answers to these questions, as well as others, must be agreed upon and, most important, they must serve as a guide for boards of directors in search of public member candidates.

Earlier in this work reference was made to the various phases of organizational development and the changing role of the governing board in each stage as well as diverse modes of governance. Every element signals diverse requisites for board members. The qualities that make a board member good in one might limit this person in another. Recognition of this fact and utilization of an evolutionary model of agency development, in some instances, can facilitate the selective recruitment of appropriate board members based on developmental circumstances. One survey respondent, an executive director, wrote:

> The most appropriate distribution of public members is variable by organization as well as by time in the business. If you are starting out, an objective person on the board can help you weed through the policy arguments, but they may be looked down upon due to their disconnection to the daily workings of the organization. As things get rolling, their input could be valuable to make sure there is industry and nonindustry representation in discussions on vision and direction.

In any case, it has been demonstrated that the effectiveness of governing boards, in part, is attributed to the utilization of a profile in recruiting new members along with written selection criteria (Herman & Renz, 2000). If a board is to serve as a resource to its organization, it must have the needed capital represented in its ranks. To do so the necessary tools must be available and, moreover, they must be related to terms of office, as discussed earlier.

A well-thought-out statement as to the requisites of governing body members is critical. March and Olsen (1995) in their discussion of new institutionalism allude to the significance of the expertise and capacities needed for decision-making. They write:

> Acting appropriately . . . require[s] not only a will to do so but also an ability. Capabilities define potentials to affect politics, to exercise rights and to influence . . . . Democratic governance must accept responsibility not only for responding to the distribution of capabilities . . . but also for modifying that distribution to make it more consistent with the requirements of democratic identities (p. 46).

Voluntarism overtime has experienced ups and downs that are reflected in the pool of public member candidates. This source has never been deemed sufficient and it is currently under strain. Due to this fact, arguments have been posited against the establishment of stringent public member qualifications. One such representative argues in typical fashion:

> It is very difficult to find public members and setting qualifications may reduce that pool further. I am concerned that soon the pool of public members will be the same people who know the governor and the legislators—the "ol' boy network." However,

the role of the consumer member is to bring a fresh point of view to issues. If you start qualifying people, you may end up with people who all have the same point of view, or all come from urban areas ("Capitalizing on," 2001, p. 24).

It might be easier to find retired people anxious to enter the public member world than appropriate people in diverse age categories who are employed. However, questions have been raised concerning the civic engagement of the so-called baby boomers, those persons born between 1946 and 1964, some of whom will soon be eligible for retirement. A recent report (*Reinventing Aging*, 2004) notes that this generation has been less active civically and the link between age and retirement is eroding. Thus, organizations will have to rethink their needs and approaches in order to generate a sufficient volunteer capacity including leadership. Earlier it was noted that many public members in the sample agreed to serve for reasons related to their careers. Although employers have been willing to grant leave for board activities, they are now becoming more reluctant to do so. Some firms actually limit the number of boards on which their executives can sit. Often it is only one or even none. This is a cross-cultural phenomenon. It might be that in the future governing bodies in the third sector will have fewer representatives from the corporate world. Economists note that such practices limiting civic engagement create negative externalities or unrequited social costs. Putnam (2000) also makes reference to the declining importance of the workplace as a recruiting ground for board membership, in spite of the declarations of an overwhelming majority of its elite that allude to encouragement to serve. Evidently, their opinions are one thing in theory and another in practice.

In response to this limitation, it has been suggested that the benefits of board membership in terms of financial return to the firm should be underscored, rather than the virtues of participation, such as commitment to the organization's values and objectives, and an effort to discard the barbarian image and status, among others. A study conducted in Britain at the University of Leeds demonstrated that firms that allow their employees to participate in other organizations per employee benefit from 9,000 pounds ($16,560) worth of free training in team building, project management, and the like ("The Voluntary State," 2004). This suggestion should not be taken lightly.

It should also be noted that the connection of the professions to public life has become tenuous. Professionalism has been led away from its original and ideal interest in protecting and bettering society. Professional associations have demonstrated less interest in civic engagement and in contributions to public life. In the last three decades or so they have developed specialized and bureaucratic units to deal with civic and community improvement. As a result, many professionals feel that their civic obligations are "taken care of" and that they are free of any burden. Professionalism has been transformed into an ideology focusing on market and skills as revealed in the reasons given for becoming a public member. Thus, Brint and Levy (1999) warn: "Insofar as the professions are perceived to be a major vehicle for the 'new volunteerism' . . . in American society, they are likely to prove a poor form of transportation" (p. 199).

Board responsibilities are also becoming more burdensome for all trustees, regardless of governance model. There are more of them and they take longer to complete. Time required to perform them has almost doubled. Extra demands on time, in part, have resulted from an increased emphasis on the ever important accountability function. Policy-making has also required more attention with many nonprofits facing more competition and often less than favorable economic circumstances. A prominent feature of our litigious society, legal liability, often presents an annoyance along with extensive training requirements in some fields. The time commitment was always great, but it is greater now than in the past. Many offers of board positions are declined on the basis of lack of time. The attractiveness of board membership is definitely decreasing ("Outside Directors," 2001; "The Voluntary State," 2004).

The challenge of identifying talented public member candidates remains large. The serious nature of this challenge and the fact that not enough thought has been paid to it were recognized by the Citizen Advocacy Center, a nonprofit association hoping to enhance the public interest "by providing research, training, technical support, and networking opportunities to help public members make their contributions informed, effective, and significant" (*Public Representation*, 1995, preface). It has engaged in various activities to address the flawed system for identifying and placing public members as well as other relevant matters. As possible solutions to the problem at hand it has offered the consortium model, organization talent banks, and the court nominee model (*Public Representation*).

The first arrangement, the consortium model, an adaptation of the methodology utilized by the Food and Drug Administration for recruitment and selection purposes, is based on a complex of state-wide coalitions of consumer organizations. Each component is responsible for providing upon request names of candidates in its jurisdiction for public member positions. In addition, it is responsible for serving as a resource and accountability mechanism for public members in office. An advantage of this arrangement is that a public member would have a constituency for accountability purposes as well as a point of reference to use for "testing the waters." Recognizing the amount of work required to implement this model, it was suggested that it be piloted in a few states and then evaluated. Also with an eye to reducing the workload, it was thought that perhaps it would be more practical to persuade existing groups and coalitions to add quality assurance and consumer protection activities to their programs that would naturally lend themselves to encompassing the appointment and support of public members.

Organization talent banks, being less complicated, are at the opposite end of the spectrum from the consortium model. As is obvious from the name, in this instance, each organization would develop its own pool of candidates. Acting alone, there is the possibility that the resulting suggestions for public members could be more parochial in nature than those forthcoming from the consortium model. The court nominee model is already in use in the legal field. It consists of a review panel established by the Bar Association for the purpose of evaluating nominees for judgeships. The model would simply be applied to public member candidates with an organization or organizations designated for appointment of the review panel.

Although these frameworks were designed with the health care field in mind, all of them could be applied to any field or combination of fields of endeavor. The structures have been conceptualized, but they have not been piloted in broad or narrow form, due to a lack of finances, interest, and support. However, recognizing the significance of recruitment efforts, their development warrants serious attention on the part of all organizational stakeholders.

Board recruitment should be an on-going process rather than a sporadic effort to fill a particular vacancy. This is true for all board constituencies. Each organization should have a list of potential candidates for all board positions that is continually updated. Names should be regularly added and deleted. The ultimate objective is to be able to fill a board vacancy with a prime candidate on a timely basis.

The search for the ideal board member, "a man or woman with the versatility of Leonardo da Vinci, the financial acumen of Bernard Baruch, and the scholarly bent of Erasmus" (O'Connell, 1985, p. 25) is difficult. There are multiple sources for identifying potential public members. The list that follows is not meant to be exhaustive by any means. One obvious direction in which to look is to other organizations, like and otherwise. All three sectors in the political economy—public, for-profit, and not-for-profit—are fertile sources. In each case, there are people, meeting the designated requisites, who would be willing to participate as public members or who have served these organizations and, for one reason or another, it is time for them to move on to other pursuits. As public members, they can bring a wealth of experience and knowledge to a board. Even younger, less experienced nonprofit leaders, public officials, and members of the corporate and general workworlds are prime targets. People who hold local, state, regional, and national leadership positions in a desired field of endeavor are important points of reference as are present and past office holders and others who have run for office. Persons affiliated with the media, radio, television, and the printed word, can be used. A perusal of media reports on a specific subject can help to identify leaders in the areas needed. Religious, trade union, professional, and community leaders; academia, and retirees are other fruitful sources for public members. If these people are not available as possible candidates, having regular exposure to lots of people, they can serve as referees and "linkers" by indicating who might be approached. Internet has created new opportunities and facilitated the process for identifying candidates for board positions. For example, the express purpose of one web site, boardnetUSA, is to link nonprofit boards and potential leaders with the hope of providing a more efficient recruitment process and achieving a more knowledgeable and diverse leadership and thus, enhanced board governance.

The tasks of identifying a potential pool of board leaders, public members and otherwise, and an appropriate arrangement for their selection, as noted above, are not easy ones, but they are doable. The costs of a serious recruitment program are low in comparison to those of the dysfunctions caused by many of the existing ones. Proactive recruiting and selection initiatives are critical. They deserve major effort because as Drucker (1990) reasons:

> People decisions are the ultimate—perhaps the only—control of an organization. People determine the performance capacity of an organization. No organization can do better than the people it has .... The yield from the human resource really determines the organization's performance .... The quality of these human decisions largely

determines whether the organization is being run seriously, whether its mission, its values and its objectives are real and meaningful to people rather than just public relations and rhetoric (p. 145).

In summary, data presented in this chapter clearly underscore the survey respondents' propensity to participate as public members. The Civic Voluntarism Model (Verba et al., 1995) portrays participation as a function of individual resources, such as time, money, and organizational and communication skills; engagement, and mobilization. Public members surveyed enjoyed all of these advantages in varying degrees. This constituency, like that of all active citizens, is distinguished in its demographic attributes from nonparticipants.

The institutional demography of these public members presents a very parochial picture. This is a matter of concern. The portrait that evolves from a review of these demographics is one that represents an imbalanced world. It mostly includes people of mature age, a high level of educational achievement, higher status occupations, and higher incomes. Hailing from heterogeneous communities in terms of size and diverse regions of the nation, and demonstrating diversity with respect to organizational affiliations, these people form a gendered world with almost no divergence in terms of race and ethnicity. They are activists, joiners, and partisans, who fall, for the most part, into one political camp. In short, representing a specific segment of the population, they compose a lopsided world.

Given the relationship between socioeconomic status and participation, this conclusion is not surprising, nor is it limited to the United States (Reed & Selbee, 2000). Social status nurtures a participant population different from the population at large. Citizens of high socioeconomic status possess the tools and wherewithal for participation. Other factors, such as partisanship and affiliation with voluntary associations, increase the disparity. Like other institutional representatives, public members are atypical of the population as a whole. They definitely do not serve as descriptive representatives. They are the result of the American process of participation that tends to produce representatives who are nonrepresentative in the descriptive sense of the term. They fail to reflect the demographics of the social fabric. In addition, those in this sample also differ from the general volunteer community. Even though the affluent are overrepresented in it, participation has widened in terms of type and especially, age, gender, and economic status (Chesney, 1982; O'Connell, 1985; Putnam, 2000; Schlozman, Verba, & Brady, 1999).

Although the conclusions related to the socially descriptive characteristics of this sample have been documented in other studies, especially
those concerned with public representation on health planning boards,
there is evidence that some select nonprofit boards of directors are dominated by a diversity of gender, racial, and religious identities. On the
other hand, it has also been found that local neighborhood boards have
included an Afro-American constituency that exceeds the percentage
of that population in the community receiving services of a particular
program (Checkoway, 1982; Mogulof, 1970a). These last two situations
are few and far between.

It should be recalled that the public member was introduced to broaden
participation in the decision-making process, to increase the representativeness and responsiveness of institutions, to enhance the citizens'
sense of efficacy, and to serve as an important check on bureaucratic
indiscretions, all worthy objectives. Essentially, this figure was established as a mechanism of control. How this control is exercised depends
on who exercises it. Based on the results of this survey, it is being carried out by a very narrow social stratum. Participation might have been
broadened numerically, but certainly not to the fullest extent and not in
terms of other factors. In essence, this means that input has been and is
forthcoming from the more advantaged members of society which, in
turn, determines its nature and the response it receives. The nonprofits
studied manifest many of the same characteristics of other representative
institutions, political and otherwise. With the introduction of the public
member, nonprofits had a golden opportunity to revamp their representative system and their organizations in imaginative ways. They failed to
take advantage of it.

All citizens are not created equal. As far as public member presence
is concerned, many types have been excluded from the table. Will this
constituency's input reflect the interests of the participants only, exclud-
ing that of the citizenry as a whole? Does this mean that only certain
perspectives are articulated in board decision-making processes contrary
to the spirit of the governance as leadership model? The homogeneous
nature of this public member constituency in terms of socioeconomic
status and its paucity of diversity could produce negative consequences,
if it has not already. It could create a formidable homogeneity of outlook,
but that is the subject for another study. Moreover, camaraderie among
board members could strengthen this similarity, making it even more
difficult to penetrate. The question then becomes: Is there a difference
between the perspectives of participants and nonparticipants? It has been

suggested that even though activists are not accurately descriptively representative, this does not mean that there is a policy gap between them and nonactivists. In reference to voters and nonvoters, it has been determined and generally acknowledged that demographic disparities do exist between these two camps. On the other hand, the difference of opinions on issues between the two constituencies is so small as to be of little consequence. However, at the same time, it has been determined that when demographic characteristics are relevant to policy issues or disagreements, such disparities in participation could be of consequence. The social characteristics of activists contain implicit information, especially when they are pertinent to policy. When a constituency is active and articulate, it achieves a certain visibility. It becomes a reference point for decision makers and they are sensitive to its scrutiny. They anticipate its reactions and preferences. Consequently, the difference in opinions between participants and nonparticipants is of consequence and, in addition, demographic characteristics are of importance as well. They cannot be slighted. It does matter who speaks. Verba et al. (1993) thoughtfully argue:

> If those who take part and those who do not were similar on all politically relevant dimensions, then substandard inequalities in participation would pose no threat to the democratic principle of equal protection of interests . . . this is hardly the case. Those whose preferences and needs become visible to policymakers th[r]ough their activity are unrepresentative of those who are more quiescent in ways that are of great political significance: although similar in their attitudes, they differ in their personal circumstances and dependence upon government benefits, in their priorities for government action, and in what they say when they get involved. In short, it does matter who participates (p. 314).

Although written in reference to the governmental arena, this commentary is applicable to other institutions, such as those in the nonprofit sector and their boards of trustees. The disadvantaged in terms of demographic traits express unique sets of concerns, needs, and opinions with priorities and communications that are diverse from those of the advantaged (Schlozman et al., 1999). The nature of the message that is articulated and its voice, plus the reception it receives, depend on the attributes of the composers, who, in this case, are not descriptively representative, and their relation to the society at large.

This chapter has set forth the institutional framework, the nonprofit governing board, in which the policy-making game is played. In addition to discussing the playing field, it has examined the profiles of and the procedures for recruiting and selecting some members of the team, the public members. The next chapter will concentrate on how they actually participate in the game.

3

Playing Ball: Batting Averages

The Participatory Experience

The terms civic engagement, citizen involvement, and public participation refer to a variety of mechanisms that allow the individual access to decision-making arenas. These devices may be viewed as a continuum of authority, power, and control held by public members, on the one hand, and professional providers of services, on the other. One end of the continuum is lodged in token citizen participation and the other in total citizen control. As acknowledged earlier, there are different types of participation and any redistribution of decision-making control to the public depends on the quantity and types of activities with which its representatives are involved. Meaningful participation is linked, among other things, with specific duties performed and also the characteristics of the citizen participation structures. The power of the various actors is defined by the institutional context in which the decision-making game is played. Internal organizational arrangements affect the distribution of power and preferences and the administration of control.

Voting Rights

Many diverse activities are related to the decision-making process and participation may encompass any one or all of them. There are many different points and capacities in which public representatives may be involved. The way in which the board is structured determines the nature of the input into the decision-making process. One method to register an opinion and exert some leverage is the vote. Surprisingly, not all public members surveyed enjoyed voting rights. More specifically, five percent of the contingent was not allowed to cast ballots at board meetings which is difficult to understand. The percentage is small, but, at the same time, impressive. In voluntary comments one member of this constituency rightly reasoned: "To have a public member with voting privileges is a clear statement of the value the 'Board' places on the consumer." And the denial of these privileges is also a clear statement. Not possessing the right to vote clearly limits the participatory experience.

Committee Membership

Most governing institutions, like boards of directors, usually cannot operate successfully as committees of the whole. They experience a great deal of pressure resulting from the large amount of work to be completed and increasing complexity and specialization. Thus, hoping to be more efficient in carrying out their responsibilities and to provide a sounder basis for action, among other things, they often devise a committee structure for the performance of special tasks that tends to resemble the institution's administrative organization. Often, much of the board's work is done in this context. Survey results indicate that public members experienced less formal discrimination in this area. Only two percent of the organizations surveyed officially excluded them from committee membership. However, there is a difference between form and fact.

Committee assignments have been a problem for some public members. Many did not cite committee membership in their survey responses and some only sat on a subcommittee. One respondent commented: "Because I am a non [health-care professional] on a [health-care] board, they could not think 'outside of the box' and recognize that I could provide input in areas other than financing and being the public member." Only a minuscule number (three to be exact) reported sitting on an executive committee and a few indicated membership on ethics, disciplinary, and marketing committees, among others. Their service, for the most part, was not on the most prestigious units. Evidently, board members of lower status, such as public members, are affiliated with structures deemed equivalent to their status.

Committee service is important because work of significance is done in this setting and also, it can serve as preparation for leadership positions. Exclusion from committee membership and limited participation on these structures automatically has an adverse effect on the diversity of opinions expressed within the institution, the pool of outlets for the expression of these opinions, and opportunities for public members to be heard. Institutional dialogue is pauperized and the sense of purpose, direction, and belonging to an institution for the public members involved, elements of significance to the new institutionalists, are tarnished. These restrictions are difficult to accept as they were for many respondents. The participatory experience is automatically skewed away from democratic tenets due to these institutional factors.

Leadership

In part, organizational influence is based on the positions and titles assigned to individual trustees. Also, the impact of the latter on governing board output is partially determined by the distribution of these official positions. Recognizing that an organizational role is an instrument in the exertion of authority, executive directors were asked if public members were eligible for officer positions on their governing boards. Discrepancy in practice is greater when looking at board leadership. In 36 percent of the cases, public members were denied access to the organizational elite in that they were not allowed to hold any office. In several instances, where they were eligible for leadership positions, eligibility was qualified. The top position or board chair was not open to public members. Such practices obviously place limitations on their exercise of power. The head of the governing board, serving as its agent, enjoys the sanction of the board and consolidates legitimacy and authority based on the force of the bylaws of the organization and the stakeholders. Individual trustees not functioning in a leadership capacity must leave their mark in other ways. Their task is that much harder and it is even more difficult for the public member constituency, given the noted obstacles to full participation.

In situations where the door to leadership positions was open to public members, often it was open only in theory. As in other cases, there is a difference between theory and practice or between form and fact. In an overwhelming majority of cases (69 percent) public members were not counted among the organization's leaders. And it is noteworthy that, in several instances, when they held office it was as parliamentarian. This office evidently was reserved for a member of this constituency on an ad hoc basis. In other instances, public members served as subcommittee chairs or a scant number (four) chaired a committee. The lack of public member leadership posts is interesting in light of a fact noted earlier. Many of these trustees have served as officers of organizations in which they hold membership. The talent bank is not being fully tapped.

All trustees are not equal in terms of access to leadership posts. This is significant because, from the new institutionalist perspective, for the individual, holding an office dictates this person's institutional duties and ties to other actors and thus, it impinges on a definition of self-interest. It also influences the likely direction of any power exerted in the decision-making process. For the group the level of its incorporation into the organizational elite is a key to defining its participation means, the distribution of power and control within the institution, and, specifically, the amount of power it has over policy outcomes.

The situation at hand was bemoaned by an executive director who wrote: "Public members are what you make of them. If you consider them simply an outside opinion and do not give them full rights as a member, then you miss their capacity to act as a plumbline." The writer continued with a plea to "let them serve on committees, vote in sessions, everything." It is interesting that such a call was issued by a chief executive officer.

Constituency

The potential effect of the public member is, in part, determined by the mandated role of the board and its members. Trustees, and especially public members, often have diverse and unclear notions of their proper role that make it difficult for them to adopt an appropriate decision-making perspective. It is generally acknowledged that directors of nonprofits represent the membership or the corporation's owners (Connors, 1988; Schutz, 1983). But having assumed a board position, who exactly does the public member represent? Survey participants in an open-ended question were asked: "How would you define the constituency you represent on the board of directors?" A majority (53 percent) claimed to be the voice of the users of professional services. Fewer (44 percent) indicated they spoke for the general public. The definite distinction between representing consumers of services, on the one hand, and the public, on the other, was somewhat surprising. But perhaps most astonishing was the 24 percent of respondents who believed that they represented the professional providers of services involved and their board as well as the smaller percentage (nine percent) that thought it had no constituency. There was definitely uncertainty on the part of the respondents as to whom the public member represents. The existence of confusion as to the nature of the constituency is also evidenced by the fact that this question had a very high no-response rate (23 percent). These results, with the exception of the importance assigned to users of services, confirm those of Schneider (1986) who concludes that public members tend to identify their role in terms of the public as opposed to professional interest.

This lack of clarity is a major preoccupation because each board member must select an approach to board participation. For the public member, given the existing ambiguity as to constituency, this role perspective is ill-defined. Does the public member adopt that of the user of professional services or one aligned with a broader public policy? The former, being narrower in scope, focuses on a decision's impact on parochial or limited interests, such as those of an individual, a family, or a specific constituency or interest group. On the other hand, the public policy perspective, being concerned with a public or community good, is much more cosmopolitan, involving broader vistas. Each approach connotes diverse attitudinal assumptions and expectations that the public member brings to the table. The lack of a well-defined notion of constituency is of concern. Given its relationship to the adoption of a role perspective, "the result can be mismatched expectations, conflict over roles, and failure to achieve goals, however, defined" (Charles & De Maio, 1993, p. 891). Moreover, it is generally acknowledged that effective public representatives require a constituency to support their activities.

Understanding of Role

Very often boards become compromised. This situation can be prevented or tempered, if, among other things, all constituencies represented have an understanding of their own role in addition to that of others. Executive directors surveyed were asked if public members understand their role and the public member participants were queried as to whether they and their board colleagues had the same perception of the public member role. Agency personnel were overwhelmingly convinced that these representatives understood their role. Ninety-one percent responded in the affirmative. The response from the public member constituency was less enthusiastic. One-quarter of the group thought that their board colleagues had ideas diverse from theirs. In fact, one respondent affirmed: "They want to see us as just one more body to do work, but our role is different from others." Congruency of perspective is a requisite to superior board performance. Common frustrations of leaders of nonprofits relate to poor board performance and often this results from a failure of directors to understand their role on the governing body.

Orientation

According to the new institutionalism, preferences and meanings are fostered through a combination of education, indoctrination, and experience (March & Olsen, 1984). Preferences and meanings related to the public member role require preparedness and, in part, they are developed through participation in an organization's orientation program. Recruiting and selecting quality people for board membership are not enough. They must then be socialized and trained for participation. Information must be acquired. Confidence must be gained. New skills must be learned. Old ones must be further developed or forgotten. Initial participation must be facilitated. Selection, recruitment, and orientation are all related in that they provide the foundation for superior board performance.

If a candidate accepts a board position, it is assumed that this person expects to be successful in the venture. Most neophytes receive no preparation prior to their appointment. For the most part, they are unfamiliar with the organizational culture, mission, programs, structure, and policies; the role of the governing board, its structures and processes, its relation to the total operation, and expectations affiliated with the scope and mandate of their role as a board member, to cite some elements. Lacking this information, they do not always understand their responsibilities in the framework of the total structure. The problem is complicated by the fact that many board members are not furnished with a complete orientation and continuing education programs once they become part of governance. Another complication is that much of the knowledge about board membership falls into the category of conventional wisdom. It has not been scientifically tested nor empirically based. Consequently, trustees are forced to rely on hand-me-down information, the less formal elements referred to by the new institutionalists, rather than a solid body of knowledge (Chait et al., 1993).

All board members, regardless of the constituency they represent, should have to participate in an orientation program before taking a seat at the board table. Unfortunately, many are often left "to sink or swim" and to learn the "ins and outs" of board membership by observation and osmosis which are not the most effective methods to enhance the pace of participation, in general, and especially, the development of meaningful engagement. This was not the formal case for the situation at hand. Of the agencies surveyed, 76 percent provided an orientation program for public members. In a few instances, the agency prepared materials for the public member and then assigned this person a buddy to whom specific questions could be directed. Obviously, this is a less than desirable practice.

Thirty percent of the public trustees deemed the orientation to their board responsibilities inadequate. It was interesting that even several public members who thought their program was adequate, in penned comments, indicated it was barely so. Many respondents requested better orientation sessions. More specifically, some noted that their personal contribution to the organization would have been more meaningful, if they had a more satisfactory orientation. Also, of interest is the fact that several executive directors as well expressed concerns about their efforts in this area. A few admitted that their programs were poor and others claimed it was difficult to know if the information provided was sufficient. Obviously, some type of evaluation is always needed. Under these conditions it is very easy for trustees, and especially, the public constituency, who, theoretically, is farther removed from the specific field involved, to become disengaged, or maybe never engaged, and disillusioned.

Given the significance of induction programs, it is surprising to learn that agency chief executive officers have spent only two percent or less of their time on director development (Panas, 1991). In light of this fact the negative comments concerning orientation from both constituencies surveyed are partially explained. Orientation and continuing education should have a high priority on an institution's agenda.

Board Responsibilities

As noted, there are different types of citizen participation, the character and intensity of which vary from organization to organization, depending on their purpose, environment, structure, and policies, among other elements. Public participation can mean very different things. However, in all cases, an important facet is the simple interaction of public representatives with policy makers from diverse constituencies. Moreover, it is critical to establish board activities in which public members are expected to engage. The key to making any board member effective is involvement in appropriate duties so that a sense of contribution results. Furthermore, successful directorates are those whose members are actively involved in organizational affairs. It is noteworthy that a few organizations assigned no specific tasks to the public member constituency. In a critical and constructive vein, one executive director commented: "Public member participation would improve if a specific board role was assigned—for example, seeking funding, being a link to citizen advocacy groups, etc." Recognizing the importance of involvement, information was solicited from executive directors and public members as to the latter's board activities.

There was a difference of perception between the two samples. The outstanding contrasts related to public speaking, publications, and disciplinary and legal issues. The executive directors gave much more weight to the public members' participation in these areas. For example, public speaking was cited by 45 percent of the agency respondents and only 17 percent of the public members. The results pertaining to this particular activity were interesting in light of voluntary comments offered by many agency executives. The basic thrust of these opinions was that representation of the organization is a leadership, and not a public member responsibility. Thus, this group of respondents was hesitant to let these directors make presentations focusing on the organization to the public or to any other association.

Yet, civic capital, an important part of social capital, must flourish. The education of public opinion is a constant and continuous duty of public representatives. To enlarge its knowledge base the public needs information about organizations, their purposes, and their programs so that it is aware of various options and informed decision-making can take place. And what better opportunity is there than to receive this information from a member of your own constituency? Public education is a prime responsibility of public directors who should serve as communicators regarding organizational purposes and activities as any other trustee. Nonprofit boards are intertwined with many publics. Houle (1989) rightly reasons:

> By its very nature, the board is the central instrument for interpreting the program of an institution to the people outside it whose support is essential or desirable. A board member is usually chosen because she represents some facet of the community or constituency. This fact puts her at once into the position of explaining and supporting the program to those whom she represents (p. 167).

Given the nature of the organizational affiliations of the public members surveyed, each board potentially becomes a part of a wealthy network. Failure to utilize public members in this sphere is to lose a golden opportunity.

Involvement with disciplinary and legal issues was cited by 73 percent of the executive directors and 55 percent of the public members. As far as publications were concerned, being noted by 25 percent of the chief executive officers and 19 percent of the public members, the spread was eight percentage points. Public members thought they were more involved in ethical matters than the executives did. However, this is as should be expected. Again, the spread was not large. Eighty-three percent of the public trustees cited these issues as opposed to 77 percent of the agency executives.

There was more congruency between the two perspectives concerning policy-making, selected by 90 percent of the public trustees and 95 percent of agency personnel; oversight and application of principles of fairness, cited by 85 percent of the governing board respondents and 83 percent of the nonprofit leaders; and marketing indicated by 32 percent of the chief executives and 28 percent of the public members.

From the perspectives of both constituencies the most cited activities related to the policy-making and control functions. Included under these rubrics are several critical board duties, such as choosing the executive director, evaluation of this officer's performance and that of the association, strategic planning, policy-making, and ensuring compliance with legal mandates, good governance practices, and effective procedures; among other things. In spite of their significance and good intentions on the part of their members, governing boards often cannot respond adequately and appropriately to the demands placed on them. In reality, they are able to deal with only a handful of the issues that confront them. Thus, the governing function is not always fulfilled appropriately. Very few boards are described as macrogoverning. This situation serves to highlight the value and importance of orientation programs. Often, board members, and particularly, public members, are unfamiliar with nonprofit management and governance and the field involved. Time pressures, lack of independent information, and aversion to conflict are other elements that hinder realization of the governing function (Masaoka & Allison, October 28, 2004; November 19, 2004).

The role of public members as it relates to the governing and control functions is very delicate. Studies undertaken in Great Britain suggest that many independent or outside directors, as they are labeled, perceive a conflict between the two roles. Stressing the control function tends to fissure relations between the outsiders and the professionals in the field, whereas the strategy development or policy-making function is based on close collaboration ("Outside Directors," 2001). Do public members advise the leadership on strategy or is their principal responsibility to monitor it? Is their role that of a colleague or a police person? Ideally, they would play both roles, that of guard dog and loyal member of the team, simultaneously and with equal agility. Unfortunately, however, this rarely occurs. Happening only occasionally in the best-run structures, this is not always possible. It has the best chances of occurring in the governance as leadership model. Frequently, public members, wishing to feel at ease, have chosen to be loyal members of the pack which pleases the constituencies internal to the organization who much prefer, as one might imagine, directors who do not get in their way. Yet, a primary function of public members is to monitor an organization's leadership and its performance. There are certain essential tasks and questions that are only in the province of these directors. Therefore, as noted earlier in a public member comment, they require a different stance from that of their colleagues. Independence, being an attitude of mind, is important and a cornerstone of the public member's role.

Although collegiality and social bonds are important to effective board operations, the perils of collegiality are noteworthy as well. It has been observed that "'boardroom atmosphere' means that collegiality trumps independence" ("Board Directors," p. 17). However, it might be that social ties make it that much easier for the public member constituency, especially, if it consists of only one person, to ask the right questions. Perhaps they enhance the watchdog function so that this contingent "can speak softly and carry a big stick."

It was noted that governing boards serve as bridges. In the spirit of the new institutionalism, organizations, like any system, are lodged in an environment. For nations it is said that politics does not stop at the water's edge. For organizations activities do not end at their confines. Intraorganizational decisions impact extraorganizational events. Being related to the world outside itself and the organization it governs, every board has to deal with special publics. Thus, networks are developed and having extensive formal and informal interactions, they become complex enterprises. These interorganizational linkages are significant because of their influence on goal setting, programs, organizational complexity, and autonomy (Gittell, 1983). Moreover, they aid an association in its efforts related to constituency development. They are useful in identifying various constituents, such as users of services, friends of the organization, advocates, volunteers, the appropriate special interest groups, and strategic partners. These relationships between boards and other entities are of three types: governmental, i.e., those involving linkages with various levels of government; nongovernmental, i.e., those relating to a galaxy of units in the private and nonprofit sectors; and those unique ones having ties with so-called "parent" organizations, i.e., certification boards connected to a professional association. All these relationships have an international dimension as well.

Needed resources and information are located in a number of provider organizations, other associations, and government agencies, all of which share some common goals and have diverse objectives. To realize their overlapping interests they engage in interorganizational relationships. It is generally acknowledged that interdependence is beneficial, but the identity and distinctiveness of each unit must also be maintained (Cohen, 1982). Engagement in boundary-spanning work is of the highest significance to the success of nonprofits, in general, and two of its major components. For new institutionalists, such as March and Olsen (1995), these external contacts allow for the capture of the knowledge of others and they fuel the collective intelligence. For others, they drive generative thinking. The evaluations are similar. The boardroom environment is generally hostile to these elements because "it isolates trustees from cues and clues, features only information that is already framed [and] makes debate about the frames off limits" (Chait et al., 2005, p. 111). Working at the boundary and beyond, trustees are exposed to new and alternative frames and are provided valuable opportunities for generative deliberation and the distribution of reputational capital to advance the organization's success. Moreover, information gained from these contacts can be used to manufacture the internal organizational changes necessary to meet environmental requisites. The capacity to represent a governing body at the boundaries of an organization is "more critical than a determination to represent a constituency to the board" (Chait et al., 2005, pp. 177-178).

Public members can aid in the management of interdependencies and identities among groups. Given their background, especially, in this case, their multitudinous memberships, and board role, these trustees can facilitate the balancing of interorganizational interests and enhance cooperative benefits to society. They can be particularly useful in building these external relationships. This task requires a great deal of time, but it can be very productive in terms of the benefits reaped.

Being positioned as part of the organization and as part of the environment, a governing board becomes an instrument for each sector to utilize. It can include representatives from important constituencies and have as a principal board function, the responsibility of mediating its relationships with these elements. Including among its ranks persons from organizations important to it, a board can establish and fortify via these representatives some of the external resources the association needs. In this case, constituencies are carried on the back of specific trustees, such as public members. The galaxy of organizations to which the public members surveyed belonged are important in this context. At the same time, it must be remembered that trustees and the groups that they represent can also use the governing institution for their own purposes as was witnessed in the reasons offered for agreeing to serve as a public member. As noted, frequently the objective was to achieve prestige and status or to make contacts. It works both ways.

Agency representatives felt that public members were valuable to the organization in terms of forging relationships with external groups and individuals. Eighty-two percent acknowledged these directors' utility in this sector. This was interesting in light of the revealed tendency to not want to allow public members to present the organization to other structures and to the public in general. Also, in spite of this noted utility from the perspectives of the executive directors and public members surveyed, it results that the largest part of the public members' activities focused on responsibilities internal to the organization and only to a limited sector of these. Those activities that afford external exposure and linkages were given much less emphasis. Public members were definitely not linked to the broad panorama of nonprofit life and its system of governance. Their exposure was limited.

Contributions of Public Members

Regardless of the activities involved, 95 percent of the public members surveyed felt they personally contributed to the efforts of the governing board in one way or another. According to the responses, there were various reasons for positive contributions. For 41 percent of the public members they were based on active participation, meaning attending most meetings, participating in conference calls, providing input via committee membership, holding leadership positions, even though very few in number; or being an initiator of a particular policy or policies. Professional and/or other experiences were important to 38 percent of the respondents as witnessed in other instances. This group, for the most part, felt it contributed to board output because of a background in another profession and/or other volunteer activities. These experiences allow a person to bring to directorates certain skills and expertise that complement those of board colleagues. However, a few of the respondents based their value on expertise in the industry with which the board is affiliated. Some even reported between 25 and 30 years of experience in the field, as noted above.

Contributions to board activities, according to 30 percent of the sample, resulted from an outside perspective. Being external to the board's constituency, the public member provides a perspective different from that of the other trustees. In the words of one public member: "I contribute by asking questions from a perspective different than the other board members." Several members of this constituency penned similar comments. The question becomes: What is the nature of this perspective? What makes it different? Definitive characteristics did not emerge from the responses. It is useful to have some members who are knowledgeable of the profession, and the issues, but have the ability, as one respondent claimed, "to be more objective and be thinking of the organization as a whole and the interest of the public."

For a small percentage (five percent) the fact that they were viewed as the same as any other member was important to their contribution. In this sense the public member is no different than any other board member. This "narrow consensus" approach reflects the notion that the various constituencies represented on a governing body are impartial. Focus is on the creation of consensus, rather than the reflection of diverse points of view, an element so important to the development of the "collective mind" and the cornerstone of the governance as leadership model. Moreover, this perspective could be construed to mean that public members are not essential because anyone can represent the public orientation (Barger & Hadden, 1984; *Public Representation*, 1995). Eleven percent were of the opinion that their contribution was sporadic and minor in nature. Often, this situation was regretted and attributed to no or poor orientation. Five percent felt they made no contribution whatsoever, due mainly to inexperience, personality, and a lack of understanding of how to use a public member. As one respondent remarked: "This is the first year they've had public members, so they don't 'get it' yet." The need for an understanding of the concept surfaces once again.

Fulfillment of the Public Member Role

As noted throughout this work, there exists in many realms an ambiguity concerning the public member's role. More specifically, as demonstrated, there is no real agreement among these trustees about their mission and the goals of their participation on governing boards. Frequently, the only agreed-on goal is participation itself. Moreover, these folks can become involved in the decision-making process in a variety of ways, depending on which status or role they adopt. They bring diverse role perspectives and orientations to the decision-making context. In order to solicit information concerning their role and their success in carrying it out, public members surveyed were asked: "Given your unique role on a board, do you feel you are fulfilling the public member's role?" They were then requested to explain their answer. Ninety percent of the respondents answered in the affirmative, leaving ten percent for the negative camp.

Various reasons were given for their responses, but principally they fell into four major categories. Twenty-two percent of those queried made reference to the public interest. They felt they were meeting their responsibilities because they were working to foster the public interest and to safeguard the public. In doing so, they were bringing the average person's concerns to the table and were analyzing issues from the public perspective and in terms of how the public might think. Typical of this orientation is the response of one public member who affirmed: "I approach each question and each decision with 'what is in the interest of the public?'" The critical questions still remain. What does it mean to represent the public interest? What does it mean to be informed about the public interest? What is the interest of the public? How does one act in the interest of the public? From what is the public being safeguarded and how? Responses skirted these questions. In no case was public interest specified which perhaps demonstrates the poignancy of Bailey's (1962) views on the subject expressed earlier.

Guidelines have been suggested for those attempting to serve the public interest in decision-making. For example, other things being equal, decisions should promote users of services, rather than producers. Long-term as opposed to short-term thinking should prevail and output should be oriented toward the future rather than the present. In all decisions individuals should be viewed as equals (Griffith, 1962). Trustees, giving such emphasis to the public interest, exercise the "broad-divergent" role which captures the notion that the public and an industry have diverse constituencies and interests. Thus, public members must highlight any differences and in decision-making must articulate the thinking of the public. Policy output must represent the public interest, that alternative which most deserves enactment because "it is the highest standard of . . . action [and] the measure of the greatest wisdom or morality" (Sorauf, 1957, p. 616). Much clarification is still required, even with these guidelines.

An equal percentage of respondents, 22 percent, felt that they were fulfilling the public member role because being of a background that is different from other board constituencies, they offered the view of an outsider. Many made reference to a nonindustry view and outside perspective, but not necessarily that of the general public. There are diverse types of outside perspectives. These range from self-interested and parochial approaches to problem solving, on the one hand, to a broader approach, promoting a public as opposed to a parochial interest, on the other. Such a distinction was not manifested in the comments of participants in the survey. Some responses signaled a parochial orientation.

One public member explained: "I bring a lay person's perspective which can be used positively to challenge other board members whose professional or political affiliations sometimes color their judgement." Or in the words of another respondent:

> I think I make a valuable contribution that others cannot. The organization's staff doesn't always appreciate my contribution. They want me to pitch in like all other members and just help shoulder the workload instead of giving them an external and not always docile perspective on what they are doing and its effectiveness.

And still another remarked: "I view all issues from a business perspective as the non [name of a professional] on the board. Other board members view from a professional perspective." In addition to indicating the role of the public member and a failure to fully understand it and the lack of consensus as to its nature, these comments also point out a thorn in the side of many affiliates of this contingent, relations with staff. Respondents referring to a nonindustry point of view, recognizing their diversity, assumed a "narrow-divergent" approach to the public member's role. In the interests of the decision-making process, under certain conditions, according to this perspective, it is necessary to diverge from the consensus (Barger & Hadden, 1984).

A different type of participation was reflected in other responses. It was much less vigorous and more passive in orientation, reacting rather than acting. Twenty-one percent of the respondents mentioned that they fulfilled the public member role because they did whatever they were asked to do. They carried out the duties assigned to them and attended most, if not all, meetings. In most cases their responsibilities were within their professional expertise, as referred to earlier. Respondents made reference to spending major portions of their time on filing briefs and other legal activities, designing satisfaction surveys, the creation of databases and web sites, and undertaking efforts related to marketing, as well as examination development, and helping with financial matters, to cite a few activities. In this case, initiative and activism were not perceived as part of the public member's role. Ideally, however, public members would demonstrate initiative. These are all useful and important responsibilities, but only to a certain point. What about the public member role? What about the larger picture? Such heavy reliance on public members as such misses their purpose. Both parties, the institution and the public member, are at fault: the former for continuous requests of this nature and the latter for automatic compliance with institutional requests without questioning.

Boardsmanship talents were important to some respondents. Twenty-one percent referred to facilitation skills, objectivity, becoming familiar with functions of the board and issues that will or need to be addressed by the governing body, responding in a timely manner, being well-prepared for meetings, and a willingness to ask questions when appropriate. Of interest is the comment of one public member respondent who wrote:

> I've been particularly successful in pulling separate factions—i.e., professional and public members—together. Councils and boards are to be responsible to their clients (public or otherwise) and therefore, must leave [their] personal agenda behind when they "come to the table."

A few respondents in this category volunteered that members of the board listened to them and they had positive feedback concerning their efforts.

Other responses to this question were of much less importance. Fifteen percent of those surveyed claimed they fulfilled the public member role because they represented the consumers of services provided, but they did not detail how so. Public service, volunteer community experiences along with those of governing boards, and being a chief executive officer of a nonprofit satisfied the role for nine percent of the constituency. An equal percentage made reference to professional advocacy which was surprising. These respondents were of the opinion that success in their board positions related to being an advocate for the profession concerned as well as its board.

Next in terms of importance were eight percent of the constituency who felt that their public member role was carried out because they possessed the appropriate knowledge to contribute to policy decisions. Given that their work and their knowledge kept them in regular contact with the constituency served by the board, they claimed a comprehension of its focus as well as public needs. In other words, they had their feet in both camps. According to some definitions of the public member, these people would be ineligible for such board positions. For a very small group of respondents, four percent, personal prestige and status or reputational capital were important to fulfilling the public member role. One member of this contingent explained that he or she provided visibility and served as a credibility factor and a confidence builder for the governing body because of his or her personal reputation. The significance of personal authority and influence was recognized in the comments of one executive director who wrote:

> Finally, as we look for a board for our new endeavors in certification and industry-wide training, we look for individuals that will give us clout as an organization, not necessarily expertise in the field of certification. If we had to, we would get one of both—an industry giant and a certification expert.

As evidenced by these results, there are a variety of interpretations as to what the public member role is and how it is successfully fulfilled. According to normative institutionalists, individuals, in acting, must pick and choose among an array of influences and assign meaning to their institutional commitments which are fashioned, for the most part, by their relationship with the unit and its socialization efforts (Peters, 2005). The public member role varies with the characteristics of the institution, the power of the individual, and the board function being performed at a given moment, among other things. However, such nuances were not recognized in the responses.

The public member role was not related to major models of governing board functions or to the representative role. It was construed in very narrow fashion and, in fact, most board functions were completely overlooked. Responses indicated again a vague commitment and lack of focus. Moreover, few answers, as noted, manifested activism and dynamism, such as that revealed in the following comment by one of the survey respondents. "My role is to represent and protect the public and consumers. I regularly register my opinion and regularly work with other public members to lobby professional board members on issues important to the public and consumers." Few respondents were in possession of the activist view of their role envisioned by those who sowed the concept of public representation. References to initiative, imagination, networking, education, organization, lobbying, as in the above citation, activism, advocacy, and the like, were scant. Individuals often engage in many a struggle to become involved in decision-making and being victorious, fail to engage themselves with vigor. Normative institutionalists note that sometimes mechanisms, having origins in the democratic wish, result in the co-optation of challengers to the status quo (March & Olsen, 1989). This could be the case in this instance.

For those who claimed they were not fulfilling the public member role, by far, the most important reason was having very little or no time to devote to board responsibilities. This was a rationale offered by 50 percent of the people in this camp. It must be remembered that most of the public members surveyed were professionally active and engaged in positions, some of which are more demanding than others in terms of time. Thus, such limitations are not surprising. Time is a major barrier to board effectiveness. In presenting board responsibilities to potential governing body members, the presenters must be forthright. Very often realistic time commitments are not presented in the hopes of snaring a recruit. This can complicate matters creating disengagement and low morale.

Thirty percent penned phrases, such as "figuring out still what the public member role is," "trying to understand the role," and "unsure of what is required of me." Such attitudes serve to underscore the significance of orientation and continuing education programs. This lack of clarity concerning expectations of board members is particularly ominous. If enough people hold such an opinion, depending on the overall environment, governing board activities could possibly be driven, in large part, by their personal and social needs.

Other respondents (20 percent) attributed their failure to fulfill the public member role to internal and external political relationships. More specifically, these were related to governing board deference to management and/or the professional associations involved. Typical of such a situation are the comments of one respondent. This person wrote in vivid and bitter fashion:

> What failed me as a public member was that my objective interests were drowned in the politics of the profession involved. I was not empowered nor respected and as an objective minority felt very ineffective. I was on the [name of the board] and completely stifled by the [name of the parent professional association]. I have little respect for the [name of the association] and believe [its] priority is making money and not in the best interests of their constituents or [clients]. They have since reduced the number of public members on the board; so the [public] perspective would not interfere with the business plan.

And another public member indicated: "At first, I felt I was doing the job of a public member. Since the Council has become dominated by the professional association, it has become impossible and therefore causing my resignation." These reasons for not fulfilling the public member role are just as important, and maybe more so, as those for carrying it out.

Although the notion of citizen participation resulted, in part, from the increasingly scientific and technological nature of policy decisions and the resulting power accredited to administrators, it is this very same phenomenon that creates problems for some public members, causing them to believe that they are not successful in their role. Ten percent of the negative respondents declared that they were unable to carry out their responsibilities with success, because their role was compromised due to a lack of expertise. One such respondent asserted: "As a lay person lacking the expertise of the certified members, I don't feel I can contribute significantly to the technical aspects frequently addressed by the board." Such sentiment serves to highlight the need for sound orientation and continuing education programs.

Governing units generate commitment and loyalty when the concerns and opinions of their members are registered by all equally and in the spirit of good faith. All trustees must be treated as equals for this environment to prevail. One respondent correctly affirmed: "The input a public member has to offer can only be valued if the other board members view the input of a public member as equally important as their input." Eighty-five percent of the public member constituency reported being accepted as an equal by other board members. It is noteworthy that several public members reported that their opinions were appreciated and valued by their colleagues who were willing to entertain views on a wide range of subjects. Perhaps with a better understanding of the public member role on all sides this acceptance percentage would be even higher.

Time Commitment

Effective participation on governing boards necessitates time. The responsibilities of the public members require much energy and thought which automatically translates into time, a key element of any governing board service. Earlier, in reference to recruitment of trustees, and the ful-fillment of public member responsibilities, time constraints were noted. These also explain, in part, limitations on board effectiveness (Masaoka & Allison, October 28, 2004). Given the hectic pace of contemporary life, and the significance of issues, such as transparency and the like, the pressures of time are felt in most quarters. Public members surveyed were asked approximately how many hours per week they devoted to their governing board responsibilities. The largest percentage of respondents (48 percent) spent between one and three hours. This group was followed by those persons who gave between four and six hours weekly (25 percent). After the percentages drop significantly. Nine percent of the respondents were involved less than an hour per week. Those spending between ten to 12 hours registered six percent as did the "other" category embracing responses such as several, varies, 60, less than 20, and so forth. Four percent of the public members needed seven to nine hours for their responsibilities and one percent gave between 13 and 15 hours. Two percent opted for a "don't know" response. Some respondents noted these times, in addition to meetings at regular intervals. As in any group, those furnishing more time and effort are much smaller in number.

The average American's investment in organizational activity registered at 2.3 hours per month, having decreased consistently from 1965 (Putnam, 2000). As might be expected, the commitment of public members in terms of hours spent monthly was more and, in some cases, significantly more. Evidently, the amount of free time people have is not correlated with their civic endeavors. The busiest people are those most likely to be deeply involved. And these are the people that give the most time. Organizational involvement is the most consistent predictor of giving time (Putnam) and the public members surveyed, being identified with a galaxy of associations, were definitely "joiners." Also, regardless of their employment situation, historically women have given more time to associational life than their male counterparts. This tendency holds true for the present study. Females, contributing an average of five hours per week, barely surpassed the males who gave four and a half hours. However, this gender difference is not significant.

Time constraints can have a different significance depending on the board constituency involved. For example, as indicated earlier, members of the professions can often count time spent on board responsibilities as working time. This practice does not necessarily apply to public members. Consequently, the burden, even though the number of hours contributed might be the same, could be greater for some public members.

Some studies ("Special Report," 2004) report that directors, and especially, the nonexecutive or outside directors of entities in the private sector, are spending more time than in the past on board matters. In 2001 this contingent spent 13 hours each month on board affairs and within two years this obligation required 19 hours per month. These figures include attending meetings and travel. Thus, the public members surveyed compare favorably to this contingent. British counterparts in comparison spend at least 25 hours a month on board responsibilities. It is noteworthy, however, that all of these noted efforts fail to meet the commitment revealed in research undertaken by the Citizen Advocacy Center and the Council on Licensure, Enforcement, and Regulation. It found that the average board member committed between 21 and 40 days annually to board affairs (*Public Representation*, 1995). Perhaps these more recent studies confirm the decline in citizen engagement. Regardless of specifics, board service is an onerous responsibility in terms of time required.

Relations with Board Colleagues

A governing board has two faces: a public one and a private one. The former depicts the formal role of each member, whereas the latter affords members the opportunity to exhibit the way in which they want to be seen. The effectiveness of this is manifested in the view that trustees have of each other. Being dependent on the attitudes of the people involved and the spirit, competence, and chemistry of the governing unit, this interpersonal assessment varies from individual to individual and from time to time. Sometimes these private and public structures are congruent and at other times they are not. Mueller (1982) explains:

> The roles that members are playing are emotionally charged in accordance with the past individual experiences, and there are various group forces at work. The major internal forces are those of proclivities of individual members versus the forces of board cohesion. There are interactions between individual members, and these tendencies function in various manners (p. 46).

These patterns of interaction and communication are important to overall board operations, including the decision-making process, and to the individual trustee's sense of involvement.

In order to garner a sense of these relationships both the executive directors and public members queried were asked to list up to four words that describe the public members' connections with other members of the board of directors. For the most part, public members were overwhelmingly positive about these relationships. Fifteen percent responded in the negative. The perspective of executive directors was somewhat more reserved, even if only 11 percent used derogatory terms. More specifically, 56 percent of the public members used the word harmonious to describe their relationships as opposed to 47 percent of the executive directors. The words collaborative and cooperative were much more popular in the board constituency, being cited by 50 percent of it, and by only 28 percent of the administrators. Respectful was invoked by 41 percent of the trustees and 25 percent of agency personnel.

There was less disparity between the two camps in reference to the vocable collegial. Twenty-six percent of the executive directors adopted it as opposed to 21 percent of the public members. In terms of utilization of the adjectives informed and informing, the public members slightly surpassed the agency leadership (26 to 25 percent). There were many words that appeared in the executive directors' vocabulary, but not in that of the trustees. These included: honest, insightful, innovative, valuable, egalitarian, responsible, low-key, and nonpartisan, to cite a few.

Public members having negative experiences with their colleagues described these as being guarded, tentative, conflictual, tolerated, controversial, unfocused, challenging, partisan, unequal, and too casual. Many, feeling isolated and only being respected on occasion, their language was much stronger than that of agency personnel who characterized these relationships as provocative, distant, difficult, stressful, cautious, and often sparse and far and few between. Noting that some public members felt the board worked too hard and that they also were willing to take full advantage of the "perks," these officials were more focused in their responses.

It must be remembered that the relationships between governing board constituencies are not firmly established. They are dynamic and have been compared to a choreographed ballet with the dancers constantly changing partners and adopting new policy formations as the setting of the drama changes (Klein & Lewis, 1976). Although, for the most part, relations between public members and their board colleagues seem to be in a healthy state, they do need some preventive medicine. The situation could be worse and it is in the case of interactions between public members and the organizational staff.

Staff-Public Member Relationships

An effective staff is crucial to the performance of governing boards. Comparative studies of these units in the United States and the United Kingdom demonstrate that their role is interlinked and interdependent with the roles of staff members (Harris, 1993). These relationships are important to governance in the broad sense of the term. Staff is primarily responsible for exercising its leadership talents, carrying out responsibilities delegated to it, and offering supportive services required by members of the governing body. Positive board-management relations are important to the health of any organization, its creative potential, and the way in which its trustees, in general, and the public members, in particular, function. In fact, it has been suggested that the commitment of administrators and the nature of their support explain the success of citizen participation endeavors and their quality (Berry, Portney, Bablitch, & Mahoney, 1984; Burke, 1977; Galiher, Needleman, & Rolfe, 1977; Macduff, 2001). This is understandable in light of the fact that public members require staff services more than their colleagues.

Given the often specialized and technical concerns of many nonprofits, public members' dependency on agency staff is accentuated because of their need for information and explanations. Moreover, staff is important to this constituency because it can help it rectify its political imbalance resulting from the expertise of the professional trustees. Knowledge for the latter represents power. Thus, the support of the staff is critical to an active public member role on governing boards. The problem is to find imaginative ways to systematically link the staff's political-balancing potential with public member interests (Morone & Marmor, 1981).

The literature indicates that the board-administration relationship is paradoxical (Masaoka & Allison, October 28, 2004; Middleton, 1987). In many areas, for example, when performing its governing role, the board serves as the final authority. It stands above the staff. It rules. However, when it carries out its supporting role, it acts to support and assist staff-led work. In this role staff takes the lead and has the "upper hand." Often, governing activities become entangled with those related to the control function, resulting in micromanaging, excessive concern for and interference in minor administrative matters. At other times, the directors become so involved in governing that they neglect their supporting role. The challenge is to perceive both functions as complementary and equal, and to perform both, and not treat each one distinctly necessitating an abrupt switch from one to the other. A failure to govern as well as support has been termed "a transgression both against clients and the wider community" (Masaoka & Allison, p. 6).

Also of note is that when governing activities are undertaken, the board, even though it has final authority, is dependent on the executive director for information and policy articulation and implementation. The chief executive officer enjoys emergency powers, but is appointed by and serves at the will of the board. In addition, this official relies on resources of the governing body for many external functions. As with all paradoxes, resolution and disentanglement are difficult, if not impossible.

Such a situation underscores the utility of the governance as leadership model in which lines of authority coalesce.

The board-management relationship is influenced by many factors which include the compositional characteristics of both sectors, organizational arrangements, informal interactions, as well as specific situations or crises that may arise from time to time. Ideally, this relationship should be cemented in a foundation of mutual trust and faith, but this is not the case. It is not permanent, but unstable and dynamic, leading some scholars (Perlmutter, 1977) to argue it must be viewed dialectically. In imaginative fashion, one author has compared it to marriage. He writes: "With a few shining exceptions, [it is] like a marriage that hasn't settled down yet, after twenty-five years! But, for sure, the honeymoon is over" (Scheier, 2001, p. 340).

Executive directors and public members surveyed were asked to choose words to portray the staff's relationship with representatives of the public. Agency personnel gave higher grades to this relationship with 88 percent assigning it a positive evaluation, as opposed to 76 percent of the public members. In this instance, the word harmonious was used much less frequently. It was cited by 32 percent of the public members and 26 percent of the executive directors. Respectful as a descriptor was more important to the public members, being used by 36 percent of that constituency which contrasts with the 26 percent usage of agency leaders. Another key word for the latter contingent was supportive. It was used in 22 percent of the cases, but was scarcely mentioned by public members. For this camp friendly was a label of importance, being alluded to by 21 percent of the sample. These were the major vocables that stood out in the responses. Interspersed among them were a galaxy of adjectives, including many synonyms pointing to the same positive judgement. Cited by agency personnel were such words as helpful, cooperative, collegial, responsive, and encouraging. Public members invoked a different vocabulary which included useful, resourceful, professional, cordial, open, hardworking and congenial.

From the perspective of the trustees, 24 percent described these relations in a negative fashion. A smaller percentage (12 percent) of the chief executive officers had this perception. As with any bureaucracy, governmental or otherwise, part of the negativity of some public members rested on the issue of control. They felt that staff exerted too much control on board affairs and that its members were very partisan. In the board-management relationship power is not distributed equally. Research (Harris, 1993) has demonstrated that the extent of the governing body's role in decision-making results from the latitude allowed by staff. Territoriality is definitely an issue that causes tension between the two camps and these adversarial roles. This animosity was reflected in the public members' negative comments. In the real world of board politics it is noteworthy that staff often perceives boards as a threat, a nuisance, an obstacle to be severely dealt with and controlled, and even an outright enemy. Thus, staff is frequently not interested in having a proactive board of directors. It only gets in their way. It is not surprising that governing bodies have met more organized assertiveness and militancy on the part of staff than in the past (Block, 2001; Houle, 1989; Leduc & Block, 1985; Macduff, 1995; Masaoka & Allison, October 28, 2004). It is noteworthy that recently approximately 50 percent of the 12 million people employed in the nonprofit sector rated the quality of board members as somewhat competent or less ("The age of nonprofits," 2003). This is a harsh judgment.

Frequently public members are caught in the midst of this staff-board friction as evidenced by comments cited earlier in reference to the articulation of opinions not appreciated by staff. Moreover, public members felt that staff did not always give them the same consideration rendered to other board constituencies. They believed that professional members had more credibility with it. Their criticisms were strong and they selected powerful words to express them. Terms, such as biased, cautious, aggressive, difficult, distant, confrontational, controversial, uninformed, unfamiliar, condescending, sinister, and self-serving were used to describe public member-staff relationships.

Executives confirmed these negative sentiments, but in more gentle terms, such as somewhat supportive, overly dependent, and stressful. Like the public member respondents they used the words distant and difficult. Also a few noted the dynamic nature of the relationship and rightly commented that it varies depending on issues and other elements. One of the weapons adopted in the struggle between governing bodies and staff is information. In comments a few agency leaders referred to this arm. They noted that public members are too insistent in their requests for information and they often expect full access to data that is under the purview of the executive director. One wonders if such observations are limited to public members only.

It is quite evident that from both perspectives, that of staff and the public members, that relations between these two camps require attention.

In part, the friction results from the fact that, in comparison with public members, staff enjoy higher status and more legitimacy, originating in its continuous work with the organization and its expertise and, at the same time, less legitimacy, due to the fact its members are employees, not volunteers, thus involving no sacrifice or good will (Pearce, 1993). Efforts must be made to fortify and heal these relationships because they are critical not only to the governing body, but to organizational performance. There is great potential for a wealth of synergy.

Problems: The Perspective of Public Members

The actual state of public participation is very different from that envisioned by the founders. Instituting a practice does not always guarantee the anticipated results. In the case of the public members, as noted, leaders of the movement cited shortcomings in implementation of the project. Whether citizen participation results in the desired redistribution of power in a decision-making arena depends on the nature of this engagement and difficulties encountered by the actual participants and those responsible for managing this participation, all of which are determined by the institution.

To construct a profile of the problems from the perspectives of these constituencies, public members were asked to cite the major problems they confront in carrying out their role and executive directors were also queried as to the principal contentions they have with public members on a board of directors. Thirty-one percent of agency personnel and 20 percent of the public trustees reported that they encountered no major problems. Both groups identified definite areas that from their view needed attention. Even though each contingent, for the most part, experienced different types of difficulties, there was some overlap.

Board Procedures

Problems related to board procedures for the public members prevailed over others in that they were cited by 46 percent of these respondents. This figure is much too high. Effective participation necessitates familiarity with board structure and how it is operationalized. Several trustees noted that they were uncertain as to how the board actually functioned. Having this doubt, they claimed it was difficult to determine their relationship to overall board operations. One public member in a voluntary comment succinctly captured the meaning of the informal as opposed to the formal elements of participation. In a very perceptive statement this person, referring to the practices and routines less formally specified and alluding to the identities, norms, understandings about the nature of things, and values so important to normative institutionalists, noted: "Some things are not always written or can be written. They are discovered by probing and being sensitive to those unstated things one feels. Obviously, this requires time, sensitivity, and a certain astuteness." Unfortunately, not all public members enjoy these advantages.

Time

Once again time, an element manifesting several facets in the responses, entered the picture. Some respondents complained of the pressure of time at board meetings. For them agendas were so overwhelming in terms of their length, they felt that sufficient time and consideration were not devoted to individual items. For other public members time was of a different concern. They referred to the amount of time needed for preparation for meetings and "to keep up to speed." This requisite is cogent for all directors, but, particularly, for public members, many of whom are unfamiliar with the field involved. Time management is an important facet of the efficiency and effectiveness of decision-making institutions. Transparency, in part, accounts for the fact that public trustees spend more time on board matters, in general, and, specifically, on organizational accounts, governance practices, and monitoring financial performance ("Special Report," 2004). These respondents would have preferred that much of the background materials they had to consult be presented at board gatherings so time pressure would be reduced beforehand for them. Also cited in this context was travel time. Often board meetings do not take place in one location, but rotate from city to city. Such a practice often requires more time and energy on the part of individual trustees. Time and effort are definitely costs of participation felt more by the public member and for the health of the institution they must be counterbalanced.

Communications

Communication, a cornerstone of institutional activity, was viewed as a shortcoming in the board process by some respondents. Evidently, this is a common criticism of organizational performance (Panas, 1991). Communications with colleagues were difficult for a few public members who suggested that efforts should be undertaken to open these channels. Others referred to the impact of geography on interactions between directors. One respondent commented: "Distance is a problem. Board members are scattered nation-wide and this is a detriment to timely accomplishments. Follow-through is often a problem with some of the board members. Out of sight. Out of mind?"

Autonomy

An important difficulty related to board operations that was highlighted by some respondents was the effort to remain independent and maintain their own interests throughout board proceedings. "Railroading" or the co-option of public members into following the lead of agency professionals and/or providers of services in decision- making is not uncommon in the history of citizen participation. Various safe participation strategies have been used to achieve this objective. They include selection and socialization of the so-called "right" board members, those that "fit in;" creative differentiation of or dividing the work intelligently by dispersing public representatives on committees controlled by providers, or no committee assignments for these public directors, provision of staff services in such a manner that issues are presented from the technical rather than a social perspective, no specific public member duties, and, lastly, outright management of board gatherings. Status differences are also a factor. Public members, often being assigned lesser status than professional colleagues, are frequently intimidated by the authority this status connotes. They, thus, succumb to their opinions (De Maio & Charles, 1993; Koff, 1988; Mogulof, 1970a, 1970b).

All of these weapons are powerful and have accounted for a generic tendency to deference on the part of public representatives to the professional expertise of agency staff or provider board colleagues. If public members had a constituency, it would be most useful in this context. One purpose of this mechanism is to enrich the power of its representatives. In addition, it provides a stable point of reference for them so that they will not succumb easily to the norms of other groups, but will remain firm in the convictions of their bailiwick. These were the principal irritants related to board procedures that public members cited as barriers to their participation.

The Public Member Role

Next in terms of importance were problems concerning the role of the board vis-à-vis public members. They were noted by 32 percent of the sample. In this context a great deal of uncertainty was attributed to all constituencies, that of the public trustees themselves, the providers, and agency personnel, as to the specific role of the public representatives. Accompanying this uncertainty were diverse perceptions of this role, thus causing, according to some public members, personal attacks on the part of professionals. Comments indicated that public members were an educational and sometimes stressful experience as well as a challenge for all concerned.

In this context, as in others indicated above, sometimes no distinction was made between public and provider representatives, according to some of those surveyed. Consequently, in some instances, other members of the governing body failed to understand why public members were seated at the board table. And, in other cases, the respondents were surprised to find that some board colleagues saw their role as different. Once again it was quite evident that many members of the governing bodies were confused. Obviously, this state of affairs impacts on the nature of citizen engagement. Its quality and impact depend, in part, on the expectations of all participants, citizen and otherwise. Given the situation revealed by this study, cohesive or coherent expectations were absent. As one respondent mentioned: "They weren't sure what to do with me." This was not an uncommon occurrence. Also, several of those surveyed were of the opinion that their talents were not being fully utilized, as noted previously in the case of business professionals. In voluntary comments another public member wrote:

> The organization may have expected me to teach them how to use my public experience as a consumer advocate and officer of several advocacy organizations. I only wish they were clearer in their statement of needs or expectations several years ago. A laissez-faire approach to public members is not the best approach.

This last sentence must be underscored. The lack of clear signals can generate negative consequences.

Approach to Decision-Making and Appropriate Behavior

A few trustees surveyed were confused as well about other matters. They indicated that they were not sure they knew the stance a public member should assume on issues. They claimed they had no idea as to what the public thinks, needs, or how it should be served best. Public members wear many hats and view the substantive area involved from many perspectives, depending on the board function being performed, the issue involved, and individual approach. There is no model public member role, but that representative has to be astute enough to know what

hat to wear and when. Public directors have many different conceptions of the public interest and, as noted elsewhere, interpersonal factors also enter the picture (Koff, 1988).

In addition, these trustees experienced difficulty in determining the appropriate level of involvement in board activities, the exact amount of influence to be exerted, and methods to be used. Stating they had not found a substantial role to play, many also had concerns about their level of contribution. It could be that public members, being uncertain of their role and having diffuse, rather than concentrated interests in a substantive policy area, as opposed to the professional contingent, might not be inclined to demand an active part in decision-making (De Maio & Charles, 1993). This rationale, in turn, could explain their lack of autonomy.

Number of Public Members, Credibility, and Attitude

Moreover, problems related to the size of the public member constituency on individual units were encountered. In many, if not most instances, as noted, it consisted of a single person. Obviously, such a situation makes the task of representation that much more difficult from many perspectives. Mentioned again in this context was the greater credibility the professional members of the board enjoyed with the staff. Problems identified in this category serve to underscore the significance of orientation and continuing education programs for all constituencies involved, a job description for the public member and indications as to how one actually represents the public and what can be expected of a public member.

Another problem area for 29 percent of the public members surveyed related to attitudes. From their perspective they portrayed an environment permeated with hostility and intransigence which is not surprising, given the nature of the cited problems. Environmental characteristics are important to the outcomes of citizen participation and especially to the possibilities for the realization of a redistribution of power in the decision-making process. More specifically, provider attitudes and those of management toward public members' participation determine their repute and the nature and impact of their engagement. New institutionalists believe and research has demonstrated that institutions confer status, authority, power, and legitimacy on some players and deny the same to others. Also within the environmental framework of significance is the amount of conflict that exists. The more conflict and hostility, the less the impact of public representatives on policy outputs and the fewer opportunities for meaningful dialogue (P.A. Hall & Taylor, 1998; Kweit & Kweit, 1981; Metsch & Veney, 1977).

Respondents, having attitudinal concerns, were preoccupied because they felt there was very little receptivity on the part of professional board colleagues to views or analyses other than their own. Thus, discussion was often unpleasant, minimal, and stressful. It was alleged that there was scarce or no interest in attempting to understand an issue from a public member perspective. Again, credibility was a problem and, more specifically, the lack of same for those surveyed. Moreover, it was charged that the professional constituency and officers were wed to notions of control that led to autocratic management of decision-making.

Obviously, the existence of these conditions does not afford an opportunity for the unleashing of positive forces. They are not conducive to the performance of the public member's role or to the expansion of the same. Other studies (Checkoway, 1981), like this one, have found that frequently environmental values, so important to normative institutionalists, are the antithesis of public engagement. More specifically, public representatives are often seen as a nuisance delaying action, often with excessive questions; creating more conflicts than might normally exist, and, in general, not being worth the time and effort involved. Such views only increase the alienation and hostility embedded in the environment.

Circumstances, such as those revealed by these respondents, are of concern. These attitudes are detrimental not only to the decision-making process and the players involved, but also to society at large. Controversy is at the base of quality decision-making as are dialogue and accommodation. Alternative perspectives are critical. However, the reported alienation and hostility must be erased. Needs must be brought into focus in such a way that understanding and response develop. Greer (1976) notes that professional or provider responsibility and consumer or public member trust are both included in a single model, neither side of which is facilely maintained without the other. All constituencies in the spirit of the governance as leadership model must work to develop superior processes of accommodation and to paint an environment free of enmity.

Lack of Knowledge

An essential requirement for effective participation on a governing body is that all of its members be adequately informed. Yet, historically trustees have identified lack of knowledge as a primary problem (Barger & Hadden, 1984; Louden, 1982). In this study 27 percent of public members surveyed listed lack of knowledge and related matters as obstacles to their performance on their board of directors. Comments indicated that this large and multifaceted void related to the substantive area, organization, and profession involved; as well as certification and its procedures, terminology, specific issues and their technical aspects, and the inner politics of institutions, and shifts in their vision. Public members, lacking knowledge, operate with a handicap in comparison to their professional colleagues. This is not easy. And it is this deficit that, in part, attributes a lesser status to them. Attempting to develop and/or maintain a certain expertise is no mean task requiring time. In light of this demand one can appreciate the time pressures indicated earlier by members of this constituency.

Language

Another facet of the respondents' knowledge vacuum and their communication problems concerns learning a new language—that of alphabet soup, jargon, and buzzwords. Vocabulary divides the public member constituency from professional colleagues. Yet, a board, in theory, is a collective and it should manifest a collective welfare and a sense of cohesiveness. It has been suggested that a successful governing body is comparable to a winning football team (Chait et al., 1993). Board members, like football players, must anticipate and react to each other's actions. They undertake diverse, yet related roles. Both are part of interdependent squads whose fortunes are determined by the members' ability to play well as an integral unit. They must play as a group and be able to communicate strategy.

Communication lies at the basis of this integrated group concept. Each field has its own specialized vocabulary and, in addition, it borrows and adapts phrases from others. The use of buzzwords from the management sciences and other disciplines as well as the use of acronyms are two practices that have been standard in the world of organization. They serve a very simple purpose: communication, the key to all board activities. They allow us to communicate rapidly, effectively, and succinctly. They convey in abbreviated form, a concept, an idea, or a reference point that is of significance to board proceedings (Mueller, 1974b). In the long-run, they make communication easier. However, sometimes the alphabet soup and language they produce is very difficult for public members to digest. They become outsiders and intimidated. Not being specialists, and they are not supposed to be, it presents a challenge to them. They have to learn, at worst, a totally new language or, at best, a dialect.

And a significant portion of this challenge is to have to constantly improve one's ability to communicate at board gatherings, with staff, and others external to the organization, using the appropriate jargon and acronyms. As noted, communication with staff is a very sensitive area. In that new concepts are usually expressed in buzzwords and acronyms that are constantly evolving, public members are forced to learn these in order to understand colleagues as well as others in the field, who are usually well-advanced in terms of language usage.

Like street slang, buzzwords and acronyms are mysterious—here to-day and gone tomorrow. They constantly change. Whatever their source and their tenure, they provide wattage to the board meeting and public members must know how to turn on the switch to use them. The rest of the board begins with common professional experience. Thus, even in matters of jargon and acronyms, public members need help and it takes awhile for them to become attuned. Time is of the essence. As long as these trustees are deficient in terms of knowledge and language, the problem appears to be one of asking them in decision-making activities to adopt the approach of staff and professional colleagues on the board without recognizing the public view and thinking independently. Un-fortunately, this often happens. Mueller (1974b) perceptively notes that "anyone can acquire knowledge, but the acquisition of flair in using that knowledge requires a certain talent, particularly with words" (p. 170). That is the test. Moreover, it is the flair that helps guarantee success to the public member.

This lack of knowledge not only relates to these substantive and technical areas and language. It also involves the public member experi-ence in a broad sense. Public members as a group have little or mainly no interaction among themselves. Knowing very little about each other, their experiences and their judgements, they are not able to capitalize on these elements. This is a major void that accounts for difficulties in reaping the fruits of the experiment.

Information

To be productive and active participants, members of governing bodies must be knowledgeable and thus, must enjoy access to the appropriate information sources. Given the nature of problems encountered by the public members surveyed, this need is especially great in their case. One public member respondent pointedly asked: "Can the regulatory board provide the public member with information and assistance specifically related to public board membership? In other words, has the board spelled out its expectations of the public member as related to public responsibilities." This comment, underscoring once more the importance of the job description, rightfully relates information and assistance to the role and tasks to be carried out.

One problem automatically leads to another. It would seem natural to turn to staff for queries and information needed, but relations, in general, and political relations, in particular, with this unit, as noted, are often uneasy. In reality, even though they enjoy less access than other board colleagues, public members are forced to depend on staff, including the executive director, for information. Relying on an "in-house" resource impinges on and often reduces their autonomy and raises questions as to the independent nature of the information provided.

And then there is another danger with the same outcome, but to a larger degree. The situation could develop in which strong staff people nurture and furnish support services to public members and allow their participation to become dependent upon this nurturance and support (Greer, 1976). Frequently, these trustees utilize provider organizations for information purposes and obviously, this raises many of the same questions. A major preoccupation is that ignorance may be the price of independence. Being able to decipher an organization's financial documents, but not being fully acquainted with the industry and specific structure involved, and lacking the appropriate informational resources, it has been found that nonprofessionals might be reluctant to fully discuss strategy, and that they give only superficial attention to the nature of the competition, new products, client satisfaction, and other important matters in the same vein ("Special Report," 2004). The result is that they operate in limited fashion.

It is generally acknowledged that in terms of securing information, professionals have access to more bases not controlled by staff and they turn these into decision-making authority and power. Access to independent resources capable of counterbalancing the force and influence accrued from those of the professional contingent is crucial to public members. And, to a large extent, the latter is not available. Ideally, these points should include not only general information services, but also those related to consultation and technical assistance where public members can seek aid in dealing with a specific problem and/or set of issues.

The inadequacy of resources has not been completely ignored in the nonprofit world. The efforts of the aforementioned Citizen Advocacy Center and Board Source should be singled out for special attention. The latter organization, formerly the National Center for Nonprofit Boards, is a membership organization with the global mission of reinforcing nonprofit governing bodies and thus, improving organizational performance. Board Source offers many products, including board development services, publications, conferences, and the like, focusing on all segments of nonprofit organizations. The Citizen Advocacy Center has a diverse orientation. It offers training and support programs for public members serving on health care regulatory and governing boards. The efforts of these organizations are valiant, but more are needed. Resource inequities prevail, creating an imbalance in favor of the providers. Public representatives must be able to draw on ample, appropriate, and independent information. They must enjoy access to unfiltered information from multiple sources. If public participation is to be practiced in the interests of better decision-making, Brownlea (1987) forcefully and rightly warns that this can only be done

> if sufficient resources of the right kind are at the disposal of potential and actual participants. Participation, if it is to be done well, has to be adequately and appropriately resourced, otherwise it is simply tokenism and does nothing to alter the knowledge balance, the skills balance, and the power balance in the community (p. 607).

Problems: The Perspective of Executive Directors

Lack of Qualifications

From the perspective of the executive directors the major irritants in having public members on their governing boards were slightly different, although many of the same problems were noted. Also, passing from 29 percent to 23 percent, the weights given to the most prevalent problems were in close range. Twenty-nine percent of the agency leaders cited difficulties related to public members' lack of qualifications and understanding of mission, certification, and the profession. Under this rubric several of the respondents expressed concerns with public members' talents or lack of same. They noted that very few were in possession of the talents and time demanded by the role to be able to participate in board activities to the fullest extent possible. Some respondents noted that, due to workload and also demographics, more and more public members are senior citizens. It seems they have more time available to devote to board responsibilities than others. For the respondents these folks somehow presented a problem. In addition, references were made to nonexistent "boardmanship" skills. Many of these deficits can be dealt with in orientation and continuing education sessions. However, they also result from a faulty recruitment and selection process.

Public members were preoccupied with their lack of knowledge which, for the most part, was affiliated with the profession involved and the technical facets of issues discussed at board meetings. Agency personnel recognized unfamiliarity with the profession, but, on the other hand, they stressed the historical dimensions and the politics involved which did not surface in the public members' responses. Executive directors recognized deficits related to issues, but their concern was more general than that of the public members. They also assigned more importance to organizational mission, history and politics, and certification. In addition, they referred to interest, stating that public members demonstrated less interest in mission than professional members. Some bemoaned the fact that public directors failed to understand the nature of the networks that engulf the certification organization and related professional associations. A few respondents confirmed that because of this lack of knowledge at board meetings public members' views were not given a fair hearing.

Orientation and Education

Orientation and education were important problems for 26 percent of the executive directors surveyed. The experience with public members was referred to as a "constant explaining process." This sentiment was echoed in most responses. Respondents referenced the need for orientation and education in the areas cited above. Given the vast deficit of knowledge, this was not viewed as an easy task. To educate people about complex professional issues with which others are familiar is difficult. This disparity, according to some agency personnel, resulted, in part, from the fact that most of the board members were professionals. However, it was also noted that it accrued from the difference in terms of service. Most professionals and thus, most directors, had been involved for years. On the other hand, public members, in comparison, have very short terms. Therefore, the knowledge gap is based also on a continuity-discontinuity dichotomy. It creates a problem for both those having to be taught and those having to teach.

Boardsmanship Skills and Participatation

An equal percentage (26 percent) of agency personnel related their problems with public members to "boardsmanship skills" and participation. More specifically, each respondent in this category mentioned almost a total lack of these elements and thus, of qualified people. Not possessing these skills, some of these trustees did not participate well. It was alleged that many were not prepared for meetings. And, especially, if the board was affiliated with a profession of which these members were not a part, and they should not be, executive directors claimed that it was difficult to get them to feel like they are a valued part of the board. This again draws attention to the importance of social activities for all trustees for purposes of molding a team.

Some of the respondents claimed that public members did not offer their personal perspective. Others, on the other hand, were of the opinion that these directors had to be challenged to set aside their personal or provincial attitudes to work for the good of the association as a whole. Such responses again reflect diverse definitions of the public member and this role. Still others were concerned that public members had difficulty in maintaining the appropriate perspective and were in danger of being co-opted. A significant charge against this constituency was that many of its members do not take the role seriously and do not respect it. Lack of time was bemoaned again and again in this context as well. A few executives once more even worried about trying to remove an unproductive public trustee.

Recruitment, Selection, and Cost

Given these responses, it is not surprising that recruitment and selection were severe problems for 23 percent of the agency personnel. The identification of candidates with the appropriate experiences, personalities to become a team player, and understanding of the public member role presented a major obstacle difficult to surmount. And one respondent even attributed these difficulties to the lack of a good job description.

Costs incurred as a result of public member participation bothered a smaller segment of agency respondents (ten percent). The financial aspect related to the costs of increasing the staff in size and expending more staff time to orient public members and maintain their competency as well as the expenses affiliated with their individual support. Sometimes the public member is financed by the governing body and all other trustees are funded by participating organizations. It is true that public members are costly. However, they are an investment. Many or maybe even most, if used appropriately, would contribute more to the organization than their cost. In light of this investment, agencies should want to review their terms of service and reappointment policies, as well as those concerned with recruitment and selection, so as to be able to derive the greatest returns possible.

The Public Member: Representation and Accountability

Representation as discussed earlier was referred to in the descriptive sense. Arguing that what is important are not ascriptive features of the representatives, but their involvement in the decision-making process, what they do, such as many of the activities cited by the survey participants, and whether these efforts reflect the opinions and desires of those whom they represent, the descriptive approach has been criticized as being less than satisfactory. Adopting this other perspective, representation becomes "a certain characteristic activity, defined by certain behavioral norms or certain things a representative is expected to do" (Pitkin, 1967, p. 112).

The focus is on the nature of the activity, how it is undertaken, and its substance or content. Rather than a mural of social characteristics, representation becomes a system of actions, of endeavors to influence authoritative outputs. In other words, it refers to the particular role of representatives after their selection. The intermediary is no longer a representation, a picture, a portrait, a microcosm, or a mirror. Instead the person is a representative who "literally *acts* for or in the place of the represented" (Diggs, 1968, p. 29). In this notion of representation, labeled substantive representation, the representative is an agent or delegate who is charged with looking after the particular interests of those being represented. Focus is on behavior and the way the person acts in the interests of a particular constituency. The question then becomes: How and on what basis do representatives act? Political philosophers, such as Hobbes, Locke, Rousseau, Burke, and Mill, among others, have wrestled with this matter for centuries. There is no agreement as to what the proper role of representatives should be with regard to those whom they represent. Should they merely register the feelings and desires of those represented? Or should they solicit their opinions and then refine and expand them in view of a more general or national interest? Or, using their personal judgment, should they pursue the best interests of their constituents? A continuing debate concerns the appropriate relationship between representatives and constituents.

Given that activity is the prime concern of substantive representation, representatives establish a relationship or contract with the represented as "another self" as somehow "standing in this person's place" in the practical arena of decision-making (Diggs, 1968). In reference to the public member the question becomes: What interests does the public member look after and from whom does this person take orders? There are diverse connections that representatives can assume vis-à-vis those whom they represent. More specifically, there are four theories related to representatives' obligations. One is based on the notion that they should advocate what they perceive as being the preferences of an effective majority of their constituency. In this sense they are purely and simply delegates. Others believe otherwise. They affirm that they should support positions that they believe are in the represented's interests. Another school argues that representatives should act in support of what they believe the collective unit, all the constituencies involved, or an effective majority of it, wants. And the last asserts that representatives should act in support of what they believe is in the larger general or national interest (Pennock, 1968). From this last perspective representation is identified with independence of thought. Representatives are free to exercise their own judgement on issues. They are like trustees having an obligation to look after their constituents without being obliged to consult or obey them. Obviously, some of these options are more realistic and easier to fulfill than others. Moreover, each one entails a unique method of reasoning and in all accountability is applicable.

In carrying out their governing board activities which alternative serves as a guide for public members' behavior? Which is most plausible? And then what about after-the-fact kinds of activities? Who is most concerned with public members' actions? How and through what mechanisms do public members report to those most concerned with their actions and to the larger community? How do we keep track of their activities? How do we know if public members are doing what those on whose behalf they are acting expect of them? In a truly democratic society no one, especially representatives, should be free from the bonds of obligation and response and reporting to some source outside oneself and to components of the larger community. The search for answers to agonizing questions, such as these, are most difficult in the case of public members and serve to underscore the fact that it is one thing to represent a group and another to be delegated the authority to speak on its behalf and thus, to be held accountable to it. Although accountability is a standard premise of democracy, as it relates to public members' governing board activities, it is a major problem. This sentiment was reflected in many responses offered to survey questions, and especially, in those from public members. The principle that power requires accountability has not been implemented or even given adequate thought with respect to public members. Yet, it is of significance because it signals their institutional purpose, functions, and status.

In truly representative arrangements to ensure that the representative will respond to the needs and desires of constituents and carry out the responsibilities identified with the office, this person is held to account, meaning in one way or another, having to answer to those being served. Norms of appropriate behavior are enforced through expectations of having to provide a rationale for one's actions or inactions as being appropriate to a particular set of circumstances (March & Olsen, 1995).In electoral or political terms, for example, public officials are accountable to the electorate whose support they seek in the form of votes. And the public representative?

Most agencies surveyed adopted some form of both theoretical models of representation, the descriptive and the substantive. The former, for the most part, can be applied to the public members, as noted above, and the latter to professional or provider representatives. It was hoped or assumed that implementation of descriptive representation would achieve the desired ends of substantive representation, such as accountability. Such did not happen. In American history republicanism focused a spotlight on representation. Supporters of citizen participation and public members also found its message attractive. Morone (1990) writes:

> Calling for a "portrait" of the people was an effort to reproduce the communal political process that was capable of ascertaining the public good. The republican image fills in an implicit step in the representational syllogism: if the representatives "think, feel, reason" like the people, they will act like the people: and—furthermore—the people participating in civic affairs is how the public good is discerned (p. 44).

Moreover, it is well-documented that, even if they have similar or identical social characteristics, representatives do not think and act like the groups they supposedly represent (Mick & Thompson, 1984). Morone and Marmor (1981) term these people "not so much representatives as instances of population groups" (p. 32). Accountability is absent. Thus, the extent of descriptive representativeness becomes its substitute (Chesney, 1982). And in discussion of demographics related to the public member contingent it was demonstrated that there was little congruence between this group and the society at large.

Public members have no meaningful constituency. At best, it is a very vague, murky, and nebulous one. They do not have to answer to anybody. In most cases, they are not selected from and held accountable to constituency groups. As a result of not having a well-defined constituency, they act in isolation. This is a major concern. Starr (1980), recognizing that organizational selection is superior to any type of socially descriptive representation, raises the question of which groups are to be responsible for representing the public. In addition, the present situation obliterates completely the notion of a common public member interest. There is little or no connection between this interest and public member representation. Shimberg (1994) refers to this lack of accountability and the situation in general as it relates to public trustees as "not healthy" (p. 9).

On the other hand, the circumstances of the professional or provider board members are the exact opposite. Given the fact that the theory of substantive representation applies to most of the providers, they represent a group of specific interests. Being selected by an organization, accountability is ensured. They are accountable to a particular constituency. Just as in the political world representatives are linked to distinct geographical areas, these providers are identified with a distinct profession. As political representatives are responsible for looking after the desires and interests of those people in their districts, the providers have the same responsibility for those in their profession. In addition to this obligation, there are those to a professional association or associations. Public members have no comparable constituency. As a result of these diverse relationships, on most governing boards, professional members have enjoyed a sense of camaraderie and identification with a common profession and its associations, whereas public members have often been isolated and perceived as outsiders (Shimberg, 1994).

The literature has pointed to this problem of accountability for decades and even though it is recognized in many quarters, solutions have not been realized. It is ironic that public members came into being because decision-making processes were empty of accountability and after institutionalizing public representation, accountability still does not exist. *Plus ça change, plus c'est la même chose* (The more that changes, the more it is the same thing).

Social and Organizational Support

Social support and community organization are closely related to accountability. The lack of a systematic relationship with a constituency indicates an absence of social and organizational support. Representation is more easily sustained when it is substantiated by the latter good. This is available to providers, but not public members. Professionals are able to mobilize more substantial and greater human and physical resources than public members. Their arsenal includes expertise, professional and political skills, great prestige and legitimacy, organizational cohesiveness and assistance, and community organization and support. They are furnished a political base by their professional associations which also provide an identifiable perspective, technical aid, information and consultation from a professional staff, as well as access to various networks and the political arena at different levels of government. Providers enjoy the advantages of these associational interest groups to their fullest. Also, in comparison to public members, professionally they are a homogeneous unit.

Given these circumstances, the marginal costs of political action are reduced. Moreover, they are competitive in a wide variety of scenarios. As noted, a superior comprehension of relevant information is converted into political and decision-making clout. The more technical the subject matter, the greater the advantage. Unequal interests and disproportionate resources combine to imbalance the political market. The significance of provider access to multifaceted and important resources and organizational strength cannot be overemphasized. Professionals are the dominant board members.

Public trustees, on the other hand, are in a very different situation. First and foremost, as noted, they cannot rely on the force of constituency organization. As opposed to professionals, the community or sector they represent does not issue directives or provide a power base. Public members were found to be joiners. Their individual group affiliations, although extensive in nature, are usually not focused on the substantive interest of their governing board, nor do they provide support for their board position. They have a different meaning and perform a diverse role. Lacking connections with other public members and consumer organizations, they do not have access to informational resources not controlled by agency staff as do providers who turn to their professional associations. And, as opposed to their board colleagues, their professions or work situations usually are unrelated to board substance. Thus, their participation on the governing body is of a different character than that of the professional representatives. It is a part-time and often isolated activity (Koff, 1988).

Not being able to enjoy social and organizational support is detrimental to the public trustees' cause. Civic participation, according to Checkoway (1981), must be considered in the context of politics. In addition to requiring a constituency to support their activities, organization is central to public members. In their quest to exert influence and power they must be able to rely on organizational and social support. The extent of their strength is dependent on the nature of this support that is essential to all phases of the decision-making process and to all facets of the public member role. Research efforts (Checkoway & Doyle, 1980) have confirmed this fact. At the moment this assistance is nil. Mobilizing and sustaining a large volume of organizational and social support is critical to the public member constituency, if it is to function correctly and effectively. It is especially significant to its participation, exercise of power, legitimacy, and resource bank. To say the least, to undertake this assignment means assuming a demanding, significant, and mammoth task. However, it is not impossible. A start might be the formation of a general public member caucus or an association.

This chapter has focused on public trustees as team players, their activities in the decision-making game, and their relationships with other members of the team and managers. The analysis has demonstrated that from their perspective and that of their managers, the executive directors, there are severe obstacles to their full participation. Their batting averages are hindered by institutional rules, norms, and administrative obstacles, knowledge deficits, lack of a constituency and community organization, among other cited elements. Moreover, the team chemistry has not been fully developed and there are difficulties concerned with relationships in the organization as well as problems creating interference in public members' play and assessed penalties.

Institutional factors come into play in this context. Being responsible for the organization of governance, they determine how much power any individual or group will have on policy outputs as well as on how and which policies are processed. Survey results indicate they have short shrifted the public member. Institutional purposes, relations, and structures of rules and routines have shaped interactions in such a way that the resulting preferences, interpretations, and outcomes have not met the optimistic aspirations for the public member project. Organizational participation is genuine only if people feel that they can impact outputs and thus, advance their actual felt interests (Pusic, 1998). Survey results indicate this is not the case. Participation is definitely limited and less than ideal.

It is more than the pitcher's mound that interrupts the flatness of the playing field. It might be that, like a pitcher, institutional actors, governing boards, and management, will have to take a step back before going forward. In doing so, they will have an opportunity to reflect on the cited problems and tactics that could create a team in the true sense of the word. The next chapter will explore some game strategies that might serve to help mobilize public members as active, organized, and influential team players. These are necessary because to date they have not realized their potential.

4

Public Members: Maximizing Their Potential

The Challenge

Public members, as demonstrated in the last chapter, have encountered major obstacles to full participation on governing boards. As the fulcrum of nonprofits, members of governing bodies must be provided with the appropriate tools to be able to mature, to satisfy their mandate, and to resolve problems of identity. To date, public members have not enjoyed these instruments. All board members affiliating with a new unit need an appropriate orientation, mentoring, and supervision. However, the needs of the public members are greater and they have not been met.

A board reaches maturity when its members bond as a result of being wed to the institutional mission. This sense is cultivated as people identify with and become fully immersed in the organizational culture and its activities. Once trustees join a board, they enter a double identity situation related to both the institution and their own individual sense of themselves. They must maintain their personal unique identity with its particular sense of responsibility, ethics, and values, while, at the same time, serving the organization and carrying out their responsibilities. They must balance this bifocal identity equation and, depending on how this is done, it can work to the advantage of the institution and enhance their own individual reputations or it can have the opposite effect (Houle, 1989; Mueller, 1974a).

Although these are general problems of board governance, they are especially pertinent to the figure of the public member who is diverse from the rest of the collectivity. What follows is a discussion of some tools that might serve to help public members overcome some of the cited problems and thus, maximize their potential. Some of these suggestions could also apply to governing bodies, in general, and even nonprofit organizations without public members. Moreover, many could be realized in smaller structures with fewer resources.

Beneficial Tools

The Job Description

The process of dealing with responsibilities, maturation, and identity departs immediately from the job description or in normative institutionalists' terms, role definition, the basis of any effort to maximize the potential of public members. Mechanisms to aid them cannot be designed until their responsibilities, authorities, and duties have been detailed along with the purpose of their service and activities. Behaviors are intentional in the aforementioned logic of appropriateness and relate to the fulfillment of obligations affiliated with a specific role in particular circumstances and thus, of attempting to establish the imperative of holding a position (March & Olsen, 1989). Most public members remain without a job description, the key to meeting their needs.

A significant document, it should address many of the questions raised in chapter two concerning representation and the recruitment and selection processes. More specifically, it should deal with items, such as the representative function of the public member with reference to purpose, rationale, and how it is carried out, i.e., the why and how; differences between these directors and their colleagues, general and particular responsibilities of these representatives, specific duties involved, decision-making powers, the relationship of this position to organizational objectives, and expectations as to performance. Each board of directors should take time to reach agreement on this document because without it, services and supports cannot be tailored to public member needs and also, because people acting in this capacity have little notion of how to behave. Moreover, it is these noted elements that suggest appropriate work modes. The roles that institutions assign individuals influence their behavior and define their expectations. In addition, having such a declaration makes it easier to release unproductive people. This statement should be detailed. Having vague ones, based on generalizations, is the same as having no statement at all.

Orientation Program

New institutionalists would assign top priority to orientation programs, simply because propositions related to action begin with rules, identities, roles, and routines, all elements affiliated with these efforts. In fact, March and Olsen (1995) note that when individuals enter institutions they must be taught the rules broadly understood and the closely related logic of appropriateness. In short, institutions mold their participants and orientation programs serve as suitable instruments for the task. Orientation is a, if not the most, significant facet of nonprofit life. It has been labeled "a critical turning point for good or for ill" (C. Oliver, 1999, p. 172). As in this study of public members, most new directors are identified with management, rather than governance, with hands-on as opposed to policy involvement, and often with a parochial and not a general constituency. Without a superior orientation they can have an anemic, undistinguished, and precarious launch into board life that could lead to perilous consequences or they could become easily disengaged or both. Both executive directors and public members, in responding to questionnaires and in unsolicited comments, indicated a galaxy of subjects that would serve their needs and thus, might be included in an orientation program. These responses, as well as other materials, will be utilized in this discussion. However, going beyond the scope of this work, specific detail related to presentation will not be provided for subjects that might be included in training sessions. The discussion is to be considered a suggested outline or format for this important endeavor.

Induction programs are a challenge for all concerned. Given time pressures and the amount of information to be assimilated, it is difficult to learn about the different aspects of large and intricate organizations and their environment. Moreover, a well-structured orientation program must have several facets. In addition to focusing on organizational features, such as leadership, governance, structure, programs, finances, policies, procedures, clientele, and internal and external factors of importance, it must be concerned with organizational culture, traditions, philosophy, and purpose, as well as substantive and technical knowledge and industry-wide trends, among other things. The scope is vast and the task ambitious. Participants must be able to develop a self-concept as part of the organization and hopefully, strong ties amongst themselves. Relationships and interpersonal connections are central to effective governing bodies and the growth of social capital.

Participation in orientation is necessary for all components of the organization. For the public member constituency perhaps there is the most to learn. It must be remembered that, according to the survey, most of these representatives were relatively inexperienced and reported they were swimming in uncharted waters. And even with experience orientation is a must simply because each organization is different. In addition to factual information, there is a definite need to build trust, to develop the processes of accommodation, and often to overcome alienation, suspicion, and hostility. If public members are to participate in a meaningful way, this training is essential to their performance.

Providers of services or professionals require training as well. Their needs, however, are diverse. In addition to the acquisition of knowledge, they must develop a comprehension of and a sensitivity to other constituencies represented on the board, especially that of the public member. It has been argued that for public members to exert greater influence on board activities the perspective of other trustees must be modified. More specifically, some providers admittedly have broad vistas encompassing the public interest, but often this is not the case, given professional and economic interests (*Public Representation*, 1995). Recognizing this, one association's letter of welcome to new board members bluntly states: "The purpose of public protection is foremost; other considerations that come to mind more readily, particularly other professional considerations, have to be put aside." Orientation sessions present an opportunity to underscore the significance of public service over professional loyalty. In addition, providers must grow the skills necessary for resolving the conflicts inherent in intraboard relationships.

Staff profit as well from training sessions. Although many of their needs are technical in nature, they must nurture certain so-called people skills and those skills and attitudes that are conducive to public member participation. They must be familiar with ways to involve all constituencies in organizational activities, to help trustees develop their participatory skills, and to carry out their responsibilities, and to deal with political and personal challenges lodged in the system (Checkoway, O'Rourke, & Bull, 1984; Hochbaum, 1977; Koff, 1988; Kimmey, 1981). Often they must be educated in terms of public participation as well. In other words, they must be prepared for participatory democracy that automatically changes the nature of their work. Participation in orientation gives these people an opportunity to understand materials presented and the reception to them, to witness trustees in action, and to interact with them. Given the often fragile relations between public members and staff, their participation could allow them to buy good will with little effort. Furthermore, attendance better prepares them to confront political and personal challenges, such as differences related to problem solving, professional tendencies to close ranks on some matters and adamantly disagree on others, and external pressures that inevitably arise. Moreover, the fact that they furnish, if not all, most of the information used by the board in decision-making makes their participation mandatory (*Public Representation*, 1995).

It must also be remembered that clients, staff, and trustees all see an organization in a different light. Each sector's perspective is colored by its relationship to and role within the unit (Van Til, 1984). Clients are concerned primarily with the type and quality of services offered. Staff, being employees, view the entity as a business and their eye is focused chiefly on compensation, working conditions, and activities affecting them. The trustees view the organization in a political light, seeing it lodged in a network of competing interests. They are concerned with its position, status, and prestige in the larger organizational world, local, regional, national, and international, and within the specific industry concerned. And the public member's notion could be and often is somewhat different from that of colleagues as evidenced by survey responses cited throughout this work.. These diverse hues must be understood by all. Through the participation of the various sectors involved, except sometimes the clients, exposure to a comprehension of and sensitivity for the various perspectives can be developed. In cases where clients are not participants as trustees, it is assumed that through evaluations and other materials their complexion will emerge. This comprehension is an important element of induction programs.

The specific contents of orientation depend on the nature of the organization and its decision-making body as well as the types of participants involved. In that training has to accommodate organizational requirements and the backgrounds and interests of the attendees, it is essential that an assessment be undertaken prior to designing a program. In some cases, these needs will be congruent and, in other instances, this will not be the case. Given the galaxy of requirements to be recognized in such an activity, the resulting project should be very well-thought-out, focussed, and crisp.

For a full comprehension of their operation, organizations must be seen in a larger social framework. Persons surveyed in this study were all identified with a nonprofit. Thus, for an appropriate understanding of specific associations, it would be natural to view them in the light of the nonprofit sector. It was obvious from executive directors' comments that all trustees, and especially public members, must be educated about the nonprofit world. Providers of services or professionals on governing bodies usually have more knowledge of this area because of their professional affiliation with its inner workings overtime.

A segment of an orientation program could be devoted to the nonprofit sector. More specifically, it could be concerned with its characteristics, dimensions, development, and its role in the United States and elsewhere. Governance and regulation of nonprofits would be appropriate subject matter in that discussion would underscore for public members the importance and role of the individual boards of directors. They would understand that they are responsible for ensuring that their institution follows its mission, that its assets are safeguarded, and that all of its activities should be grounded in the public interest, among other things. It might also be useful to illustrate relationships between the public, private, and nonprofit sectors for comprehension of differences and communalities, as well as the importance of boundary-spanning work. A very brief presentation on the specific profession involved would be helpful as well. Mention might also be made of its development, emerging trends, politics, issues of importance, and future direction. This information might then be related to the organization in question. These introductory materials provide a conceptual framework for participants. The specific association can now be viewed in the light of larger organizational worlds, that of the nonprofit sector and the profession. Attendees' analytic parameters become enlarged as a result of this approach.

This study also revealed that public members were confused about accreditation and certification. Often, they use the two words synonymously. They should know the difference between the terms. In that most of the survey respondents were identified with certification boards or those furnishing services to them, if appropriate, it would be most useful for public members to have a basic knowledge of certification programs prior to becoming fully involved in board activities. A presentation could focus on the origin, purpose, and development of these programs, their scope in terms of occupations and professions covered, and objectives. It might include mention of the different kinds of certification (competency-based, criterion-based, and curriculum-based) and implications of certification for the certificant, the single institution, the profession, and the public. Brief mention of recertification as it relates to the specific field involved would be useful as well. If an organization is affiliated with the National Organization for Competency Assurance, reference should be made to it and its accreditation arm, the National Commission for Certifying Agencies. This information might be of use in any case.

For public members on certification boards the examination process is important. They should have a general understanding of it and its various components. Among other things, they should be familiar with the significance of a common body of knowledge, the job analysis, content outline, item writing and item components (stem, key, distractor), the various cognitive levels (recall, application, analysis), the pretest, the item bank, item validity and reliability, test scoring, and processes related to challenges and appeals.

Knowledge of the nonprofit sector, the profession, certification and accreditation, if appropriate, serves as a backdrop for the public member. Then, moving to concrete matters, first and foremost, public members have to know why they are there. Survey results, as noted, revealed that diverse understandings of the role prevailed along with a great deal of uncertainty. It was clear that many public members themselves, and even board colleagues, and staff did not fully comprehend this position. Many of the questions raised earlier in this work should be addressed in this context. There is a myriad of relevant questions, all of which obviously cannot be given consideration. However, basic ones should be explored.

What is the origin of public members? What is their role and whom do they represent? What interests do they look after and cultivate? How are they different from other trustees? How do they become informed about public needs, opinions, and interests? How do they plant roots in the larger community? What guidelines do they use to develop their position on issues? What methods do they utilize to articulate the public interest? Even summary response to these questions should provide adequate information for all orientation participants to have an understanding, hopefully, a common one, of this unique role. In addition, such a comprehension should serve to help alleviate the reported alienation and other negative attitudes revealed by the survey. Moreover, it should afford an opportunity for board members to not only be imbued with their individual identities vis-à-vis the institution, but also to develop a sensitivity to the disparate identities affiliated with various roles in the organization.

One executive director in comments related to a specific public member asserted: "She is such an asset to our board. Every organization should be as fortunate as we are to have a public member of her caliber. Her contributions exemplify why professional boards need public members." Another wrote: "We have had a public member for many years . . . and the contributions they have made have been great." On the other hand, a third colleague asked for advice on how to get rid of an unproductive public member. How are these conclusions reached? Unfortunately, formal appraisal of public members is not commonplace. If it was done consistently and systematically, much information beneficial to the recruitment, selection, and training processes would result.

Right from the start of their appointment public members must understand how their performance will be evaluated and by whom. They must know what is expected of them as individuals and as members of a collective and how and when they will be judged. Contribution, preparation, participation, initiative, and other factors will enter the picture. Specific criteria for appraisal must be developed and shared with the public member constituency. The entire evaluation process must be made clear to these directors so they know where they stand. How do you measure? What type of measuring stick do you use? Who uses it? Standards of performance must be specified. If executive directors had such an evaluation instrument, they would not have to ask how to release an unsatisfactory public member.

In that every institution is lodged in an environment, the values, norms, and beliefs of which condition its operation, it is imperative that public members be introduced to the organizational culture or those "deeply embedded assumptions and heuristics that define and hold an organization together" (Chait et al., 1993, pp. 9-10). They must be acquainted with these informal rules that govern behavior and the basic assumptions about the operation of the organization that are and have been considered worthy enough to be passed on as applicable to certain circumstances. These cultural elements, recognized as orthodox, in part, prescribe board principles and are binding on the operating process of the body (Mueller, 1982). March and Olsen (2005) observe: "In institutionalized worlds actors are socialized into culturally defined purposes to be sought, as well as modes of appropriate procedures for pursuing the purposes" (p. 10). Trustees unfamiliar with this culture are likely to participate tentatively and automatically isolate themselves by getting off "on the wrong foot." The chances of doing so are greater for the public member and, according to survey responses, it has happened.

Often, the nature of the organizations that boards are supposed to govern are overlooked. Primary core issues confronting public members relate to the purpose or program of the specific agency involved. What is the unit's mission? What is its philosophy? What is its vision? What values does it encompass in its structure? What are the goals that public members are supposed to implement? Relating to the individual and the society at large, goals, especially, are of significance. And, although they are often ignored in the daily operations of an organization, in reality, they are important to professional issues. At many board meetings in which this author has participated they have been displayed in a prominent place as a reminder to all during the decision-making process. This is an indication of their significance. Also, the closer individuals are aligned to the goals of an organization, the greater will be their commitment (Duca, 1986). Unless public members know what the institution is attempting to achieve, the policies they advocate may not be consistent with the objectives they are supposed to be carrying out.

To be effective public members must not only understand the purposes and objectives of the organization. They have to go a step further. To understand the present and to model the future, they must have a clear and precise understanding of the past, knowledge usually possessed by nonpublic board colleagues. They need to be acquainted with the history and position of the enterprise. Board activities are piloted by institutional culture, mission, and history. This must be explained to public members and perhaps, in light of the strategic plan. Moreover, the goals of a program must be related to the specific industry involved. In this manner these directors will develop a notion of how their organization "fits in." They will acquire such knowledge that they will be aware of the institution's shortcomings and its principal accomplishments overtime. This is an essential aid in the decision-making process.

This approach provides critical tools to interpret the meaning of past events in many ways, each one of which might indicate a different future. As Chait et al. (2005) explain: "Power rests with people armed with the knowledge and eloquence to craft an organization's 'dominant narrative' or operative version of 'history' . . . . The power to construct (or reconstruct) the past begets the power to shape the future" (p. 88). For the normative institutionalists the aforementioned accounts which in their theory are so important to an understanding of history perform a function similar to that of the "dominant narrative."

A necessary and significant part of the orientation is that which informs public members of the structure of the organization and its operationalization. It should stress the relationships between the various units so they will understand how they are supposed to relate to them. Obviously, being primarily concerned with the governing body, they should know specific board responsibilities, such as maintaining the enterprise as a legal entity, serving as a trustee to the clients' best interests, planning viewpoints, objectives, goals and policies; providing operating requirements, financial and otherwise; and evaluation or measuring performance against objectives, goals, and plans. Moreover, public members should be given an idea of how the board allocates its time between its various functions or work modes and which are the most important to their role at the present stage of development. They should know exactly what responsibilities are assigned to the board and what it actually does. They will then know what types of assignments are available.

Having this knowledge, they will understand that in their role they wear many hats, that of a member of a legal corporation, a tribunal of last appeal, a board of managers, a board of inquiry, an emergency squad, an underwriter, a society of friends, stabilizer, planner, policy maker, and cheerleader. The important point is the degree of conscious separation between these roles or other categories as the board moves through its agenda. As the process unfolds, one hat is exchanged for a different one. The public member must know what hat to wear and when.

Moreover, having such information provides answers to important questions. How do public members relate to board functions? What are their responsibilities and obligations and at the same time their rights? This facet of the orientation highlights the importance of the job description. One nonprofit's letter of welcome to public members notes the uniqueness of this position. It affirms: "The roles and responsibilities of a board member are very different from those of a member of a profession, or whatever other roles a public member may have." Survey responses from public members showed little sensitivity for governing body functions, their obligations, and the accompanying nuances. This problem could be alleviated in orientation with materials that focus on the nonprofit sector, in general, and on the specific organization involved. This information is of significance because the influence of individual board members depends on their control of needed external resources and their familiarity with the internal operations of the institution (Taylor, 1987).

In some organizations, as noted, the governing body establishes the policies under which the institution is governed and under no circumstances is it to enter into the details of administration. If so, it should be made very clear to public members that others are responsible for the implementation of policy. Policy declarations occasionally will establish the procedure for implementation, but it is not customarily part of policy declaration. At the same time, the role of the board in specific administrative functions and oversight should be detailed. To avoid unpleasant circumstances one organization's commitment to serve document includes a pledge on the part of the public member "to refrain from intruding in administrative matters that are the responsibility of the administration and testing agency, except to monitor the results and prohibit methods incongruent with board policy." This language recognizes the aforementioned nuances.

What is policy and what kinds of policy are unique to the board? What have been its stellar policies? Where has it fallen short? These questions should be answered in detail for the public member and responses should be related to specific and ongoing issues before the board, the organization's current programs and services, and the strategic plan. Without this knowledge the public member could become involved with inappropriate issues in an improper way.

Now that public members know what the board does and what they are supposed to do, they have to know how they are to do it. They must be familiar with how the board carries out its assignments and how it is operationalized. This brings us to board operations and given survey results, they represent a very sensitive and pressing area. Bylaws are intended to specify procedures to be followed by a board, but frequently they are neglected or new practices develop and, consequently, the bylaws that dictate process become obsolete. A current declaration of board-administrative procedures is essential. The development of informal practices, which are of significance to the normative institutionalists, should be clearly explained. Public members, like all directors, need to understand the attributes of membership beyond legal prescription as they relate to board organization and the conduct of business. These are important in shaping identities. In light of an analysis of the data collected in the survey, this is a significant point.

Furthermore, orientation should include a thorough discussion of board organization (officers and their duties and committee structure, etc.), the conduct of business (board meetings, number, type, duration, frequency, attendance policies, total time involvement, recording and reporting decisions), fiduciary and financial responsibilities, and standards of performance. Again, the survey indicates the need for and the importance of this information. Moreover, many public members are not familiar with budgetary materials. They are unable to read and analyze them because they never had the occasion to do so. Remembering that many of the public members surveyed were serving for the first time, they should be "walked through" some financial statements, especially the budget. These documents should be explained in the historical context of the program along with the notions of cash flow, reserves, and other such concepts.

Public members should also have knowledge of the annual organizational timetable so they have an idea of what takes place—when and where. This schedule might include reference to board appointments, conventions, test dates, if applicable; and regularly scheduled organizational events and decisions. Mention should also be made of travel arrangements, expenses incurred, reimbursement policies, dress, and other relevant items. All directors have to do homework, but the load of public members is greater, especially initially, because they are external to the profession and the organization. This responsibility must be highlighted. It should be noted that these representatives have an obligation to be fully prepared for all organizational gatherings, so that the association's business can be carried out with dispatch. Moreover, this responsibility is linked to the aforementioned duty of care. The mechanics of attendance should be explained. A reminder should be issued concerning attendance responsibilities at board meetings and other organizational events. In correspondence related to this project one nonprofit administrator forwarded a copy of a "missed you at the last meeting" letter. It was a unique idea carried out with good taste. Its message was poignant.

Public members, as documented elsewhere, frequently succumb to the wishes of their professional colleagues and/or staff so as not to create difficulties for themselves and the group, in general. They must be reminded that unanimity in decision-making is not a virtue in itself, even though a generally acknowledged index of a governing body's performance is how close it comes to achieving this state in the determination of policy. Issues, complicated or simple, often generate divided perspectives and this is not a bad sign, providing that consensus is eventually reached on most matters. Discussion and disagreement are important components of the decision-making process, in general, and, specifically, of the governance as leadership model. However, a board that is continually divided and, especially, if it is almost always evenly divided, provides evidence of internal problems.

Differences there must be and public members must be made aware of this, but governing units, for the most part, are expected on the basis of dialogue to be able to achieve consensus and find viable solutions to disagreements. When directors continually remain divided the institutional fabric begins to shred. Public members must be impressed with the fact that unanimity in voting is neither essential nor desirable. Moreover, as a support in decision-making, it might be useful to develop a series of questions or criteria tailored to their role that they could use as guidelines in making choices. One public member respondent indicated, as did some others, a recognition of the need for the flow of diverse ideas. This person wrote:

> I take my role pretty seriously, offering input, suggesting ideas and perspectives that the rest of the board may overlook. I really do try to "step back" from the board's technical/professional concerns, and ask myself how "the public" might think about these issues.

This is certainly a start in the right direction that needs development and fine-tuning. The suggested support in decision-making might aid in relieving the feeling of "end running" by professional directors and staff that was noted over and over again in survey responses.

Board meetings require careful preparation and skillful agenda planning to generate enthusiasm. There are many ways to develop workable agendas, to spark interest, and motivate participation in meetings, so as to ensure that business is carried out in a responsible manner. Although the agenda is the purview of the chairperson of the board, any board member is entitled to have important policy issues incorporated into it. Public members must understand this and they should be encouraged to contribute, even if under the rubric of new business. This constituency has failed to make a mark in this area, thus, projecting an image of being a reactor rather than an actor.

In regard to liability issues, it is noteworthy that, in spite of their significance, often they are overlooked by program staff as well as public members. In that so many public members are new to the board world in this capacity, they should have a thorough understanding of exactly what they are liable for and at the same time, specifically, how they are protected. The agency's insurance policy should be available to them, if they so desire.

As far as ethics are concerned, somehow it is assumed that directors act professionally. Would that this were always the case. Ethical behavior is an imperative as part of the board's trusteeship capacity and its moral ties with society at large. Earlier reference was made to fiduciary responsibilities. In this context, the duties of care (the obligation to exercise reasonable care in board decision-making), loyalty (having the responsibility to act at all times in the best interests of the organization), and obedience (the imperative of following in all actions the organization's mission) should be noted for the public member. Once again these duties provide instruments helpful to public members in counteracting "end running" by professional colleagues and/or staff.

Conflict of interest is quite difficult to define and in most situations ethics and public perception are more relevant than legal norms. Public members must be informed of an agency's definition of this concept and its policy on the matter. Not only must they be able to apply the concept to themselves, but they must be able to identify conflict of interest situations and know how to handle them individually. Public members have to make sure there is no compromise in this area that provides a significant reason for their existence. Another matter on which there is no compromise is confidentiality. Even though this is something that seems obvious, many executive directors and governing bodies have had to deal with surprises resulting from the spread of confidential information. This is another concept that must be explored, in general, as well as in specific terms. Many organizations have formal conflict of interest and confidentiality agreements that public members must sign prior to assuming their board positions.

The issue of communication, having internal and external facets, is bidimensional in nature. There is an interpersonal aspect to board membership. The board, as noted above, should nurture the development of its members as a group, attend to its collective welfare, and foster a sense of cohesiveness. Communication lies at the basis of this integrated group concept and thus, importance was assigned earlier in this work to public members' general lack of familiarity with jargon, buzzwords, and acronyms, major communication tools. There are many things that can be done to allow for the construction of a viable, clear, and responsible communication system, an important link between the governing board and management, and a prime feature of effective nonprofit organizations (Light, 2002). On the formal side of the picture, public members must learn the channels of communication within and outside the organization. How do they interface with the chief executive officer? With professional staff? With office personnel? With persons external to the unit?

Closely related is the fact that it is generally assumed that trustees know the limits on their behavior and are astute enough to apply them. Thus, "explicitly stated and reliably enforced norms to govern trustee conduct are rare" (Chait, 2006, p. B6). As a result, frequently the collective welfare and cohesiveness suffer. To avoid freelance governance, specific guidelines pertaining to trustee engagement and its limits should be detailed. Governing board members must know not only how they should interface with other elements, but when and for what reasons. This is the rationale for the new institutionalists' logic of appropriateness discussed above. Any institution needs measures to ensure maintenance of standards of decorum and behavior. They cannot be assumed. Then, in reality, there are informal tools to supplement these formal statements.

Moreover, as participants in diverse types of organizational activities, it is often difficult for public members, in part, due to their status, to ask questions. Nowadays with much board business being carried out by e-mail and conference calls in the interests of economy, it is even harder for them to make inquiries. In this context, it must be impressed on public members that the stupidest question, even in e-mails and conference calls, is the one not asked. This point can never be overemphasized.

For social scientists the dominant vision of human behavior is one of making choices and thus, being involved in decision-making. Theorists concerned with decisions acknowledge that, given human nature, estimates related to decision-making may be biased and not exact. Moreover, the information from which they are derived may be expensive. However, data focusing on the possible effects of decisions is considered significant to making a choice. Therefore, the potency of information and expertise and the importance of reliable and objective information sources merit special attention (March & Olsen, 1984). Information is another matter that also relates to internal communication.

All institutions are information-using and information-processing systems. The flow of information and its nature are pertinent and critical to all governing body endeavors. The board as well as the entire organization must be information-based. In that nonprofits are learning associations, the information flow must be in both directions: top-down and bottom-up. To govern intelligently and to meaningfully participate, board members need information and the ability to use it. To be of value, this information must be unframed, of the right kind, and in the right amount. Furthermore, its flow must be controlled and streamlined (Chait & Taylor, 1989; Drucker, 1990). Unfortunately, these requisites signal problems.

Institutional theories stress the manner in which institutions dictate alternatives and fashion the perception and creation of the framework within which action is realized. More specifically, in reference to information March and Olsen (1995) observe: "Institutional capabilities and structures affect the flow of information, the kinds of search undertaken and the interpretations made of the results" (p. 29). Moreover, they assert that problems have traditionally plagued institutions of information. Knowledge is never neutral and thus, ignorance provides advantages to some institutional actors as opposed to others. Also, many experts are not neutral and they maneuver these same actors by misrepresenting, abusing, and misusing knowledge.

Information is usually not tailored to the needs of board constituencies or board functions. All contingents, in spite of diverse needs, customarily receive the same information that often is not selected with board functions in mind. Thus, trustees might be furnished with management as opposed to governance materials or vice versa. Consequently, notwithstanding sincere motives to share all available data, they are frequently led to excessively meddle in administrative affairs (Chait & Taylor, 1989). Boards are meant to govern and control and not to be involved in micromanagement. More is thought to be better and thus, trustees are swamped with an overabundance of materials, many of which are often irrelevant. Having too much information or information overload is almost as bad as having none at all. Even though board members and staff frequently have more materials than they can use, others are usually requested. Information is generally not selectively distributed and the flow tends to be haphazard. Board members must know what to expect and when. This is especially cogent in the case of public members who, for the most part, not being identified with the industry or the organization, require more and/or special information and therefore, more time to deal with it. They, especially, must pace their learning experience. Information must be matched to the specific needs of a board constituency and it must be congruent with the functions being carried out. Constraints of time and information overload, as noted in survey responses, must be recognized in the preparation of materials for distribution. Appropriate information issued in timely fashion could augment confidence in staff and enhance public member-staff relations (Masaoka, 2001).

Governing bodies must have an effective, crisp, streamlined, and institutionalized governance information system designed to aid the functions and specific activities of an individual board and to fulfill the needs of its various constituencies. For the most part, they require decision information, that which is used in making choices, and performance information, data utilized for monitoring purposes, and interpreting the past in light of the present, and forecasting the future. These are significant to board responsibilities. All other materials, not being used for policy-making or control activities, are incidental. The latter category includes a large quantity of materials that are commonly distributed in abundance. Although they might be of interest, they usually are not focused enough to aid trustees in their primary tasks (Carver, 1990; Carver & Oliver, 2002) and they literally swamp the public member. Given the constraints of time on all concerned and the need to use information efficiently, the appropriate information must be issued according to schedule and it must be concise, correct in quantity, meaningful, timely, relevant to role, duties, and activities; of superior quality, intelligently organized, and in the appropriate format. "An effective board information system should focus decision making, stimulate participation, and support an appropriate balance of responsibility between board and staff" ("How Do," n.d., p. 1). At regular intervals information issued should be evaluated by those for whom it was prepared.

Public members, in particular, need information to be "brought up to speed" and to maintain their competence. Their needs are unique. Unfortunately, inequality among participants in an institution may be caused by the manner in which information is distributed among them in terms of generality and complexity (Pusic, 1998). The key is the right amount of appropriate information at the right time as opposed to inappropriate information and mountains or too little issued haphazardly. McGregor (1984) compares putting large amounts of unintelligible information into the laps of the public to shredding official records. According to him, such an act requires an explanation for contributing to public ignorance. The same applies to these representatives of the public. The "happy medium" has to be found because methods of generating and disseminating information impinge on the quality of discourse.

Collecting information just to collect it seems to assure that decision-making is being approached in the right fashion. Being heavily embedded in social norms, information symbolizes competence, a reaffirmation of social virtue, and confidence. More information becomes a good that is affiliated with better decision-making activities and output. Organizations and decision makers who gather, control, and use more information are deemed better than those who do less of the same. It is through their use of information that organizations create and garner legitimacy (Feldman & March, 1981). However, organizational leaders, working in the interests of effectiveness, would do well to heed the words of Chrislip and Larson (1994). They write: "If you bring the appropriate people together in constructive ways with good information, they will create authentic visions and strategies for addressing the shared concerns of the organization"(p. 14).

Most often governing boards consist of stellar people who are absolute strangers to each other and unfortunately, do not act as a team. Chait (2006) observes: "Most boards are orchestras of soloists" (p. B6). Even though individuals perform specific board tasks, governing responsibilities require cooperative decision-making and joint efforts based on effective communication. Orientation programs, in addition to preparing directors for participation, enhance commitment, enrich the board experience, and forge new relationships. In short, the team chemistry is nurtured. The importance of the social side of orientation is not to be discounted. Social activities do not mean a waste of time and money. It is in this type of more relaxed and less formal setting that communication is extended, bonding takes place, and a sense of inclusiveness and mutual trust are developed. "Difficult to establish and easy to destroy" (Strauss, 1998, p. 211), trust is essential to meaningful participation which cannot prosper in its absence. It is critical to collaborative action, knowledge acquisition, and the contingent use of power. It is also important to the development of solidarity. Elements of trust are influenced by the institutions in which it is embedded. Moreover, normative institutionalists point out that an identity-based theory of politics, such as theirs, incorporates emotions as a foremost ingredient of identity. Thus, friendship, respect, loyalty, and similar feelings are important (Heller, 1998; March & Olsen, 1995; Rothenstein & Stolle, 2002).

Good social and communication relationships are critical to group action and healthy board operations. It is essential that board members be well-acquainted with each other and socially at ease. These relationships impinge on board meetings. Strong social ties among directors provide each individual with "a sharper sense of purpose in that all share a common enterprise, freely undertaken and particularly satisfying" (Naylor, 1967, p. 115). The professional or provider members of the governing body already have a link based on professional interests. Social occasions afford the small public member contingent, lacking numbers and often group ties, an opportunity to become integrated into the board unit.

Due to these social ties directors are more likely to be involved in informal decision-making, an important part of overall governance. Moreover, personal relationships with the leadership and staff, the basis for any strategic partnership, are solidified in these gatherings and enjoying new social relationships, the individual trustee, and especially, the public member, develops an enthusiasm and expects gratification from significant and real accomplishments. The relationships can also aid in tempering some of the attitudinal problems and tensions between board constituencies and between public members and staff identified in survey responses and discussed earlier. Harmonious interpersonal relationships are correlated with effective boards. Moreover, communication is enhanced and the greater the communication among people, the greater the mutual trust, and cooperation becomes that much easier (Chait et al., 1993; Putnam, 1993). Social capital is enhanced as well. These social relationships are turned into productive assets.

It is in this environment that the public member builds communication channels with colleagues and the social contract necessary for effective performance on the governing body. Acceptance in the group is accomplished by this informal social contract between members (Mueller, 1982). The informal facets of the board experience, as noted, are just as significant as the formal ones. These are not learned in regular orientation sessions, but in the confines of social encounters. Here individuals get the low-down of what the membership experience is really like and what is not expected of them as opposed to what is expected. Moreover, the aforementioned unwritten rules of boardroom behavior can be communicated. Like conventions in British politics, these axioms allow for change. Complementing the formal code, they make it flexible and adaptable to new and unforeseen circumstances. It is imperative that board members recognize and comprehend these unwritten laws which "constitute a hierarchy of pragmatism overlaid on the laws and customs which envelop the director" (Mueller, 1974a, p. 130).

It seems self-evident that a governing body is collective in character. However, this often escapes staff and trustees themselves who are oblivious to the nature, norms, and chemistry of a board. Often group dynamics and group processes are overlooked. There is much attention given to how the governance game is organized as far as terms of office, conditions of appointment, and the like are concerned. The same regard is not paid to how this game is actually played and how the team is molded. This can be traumatic for public members as indicated in many of their responses to survey questions. Often they remain in the dark. This is something that can be handled in orientation as well as elsewhere, for example, board meetings which should be viewed as a social instrument so as to be a win situation for all.

It has been noted that governing bodies maintain relationships with units external to their structure. Sometimes directors are responsible for establishing or cultivating these linkages. When orienting public members it must be stressed that the board communicates with the outside world in unison or not at all. This would appear to be another obvious and accepted principle. However, in reality, it has often been violated much to the chagrin of executive directors and boards themselves. Even though unanimity is not required, the board's decision as an entity must be unambiguous. It is easy to appreciate the significance of this point.

Continuing Education Efforts

Participation needs to grow or else it atrophies. Thus, if governing boards are to be equipped to confront the complex issues that continually find a place on their agendas, board education must not end with orientation, as is often the case. The induction program should be perceived as a single component of a learning continuum. Ongoing learning is a requisite for public member board service. Suggested topics for orientation are many and each item cannot be given sufficient attention. Moreover, many more of significance could be added to the list. For public members orientation serves as an introduction. It must be further developed with a galaxy of continuing education programs, tailored to their particular community and held in common with other constituencies or apart, depending on the situation. After all, governing bodies are "communities of practice," that afford particular constituencies, such as that of the public members, the chance to pool usable knowledge. Given the level of specialization in most fields, and the constant generation of new data, and the rapidity and depth of change in contemporary times, many of these efforts should focus on the specific substantive area involved, its development, the technical bases for policies, and those related to the decision-making process, all areas highlighted in survey responses as being worthy of attention. Many of the topics touched upon in orientation can be treated in depth and others can be expanded upon. The possibilities are endless.

Diverse formats and learning materials should be adopted. The former might include seminars, retreats, joint meetings with other governing bodies or groups, lectures, workshops, and conference attendance, among other things, and the latter could consist of printed and audio-visual tools, such as fact sheets, manuals, power point presentations, videos, and DVDs. Variety and flexibility are the keys. Reliance on forums and community resources, if appropriate, might be useful as well. Many associations exclude public members from their own conferences and national and international professional meetings and deny participation in other gatherings that might be relevant to board service. This policy, being most difficult to understand, is open to question. Attendance at any of these activities is an educational experience for the public member and allows an opportunity for networking with other public members, admittedly few in number, which is significant, as well as with other professionals. This policy reflects the old saying "penny wise and pound foolish." For the public member conference attendance may be viewed as a breath of fresh air and as part of the socialization experience. In all of these efforts the scope is to better educate the public member on matters vital to the association and industry involved, so as to enrich board membership. Effective board participation today can mean more of the same for tomorrow, reaping benefits for the individual, an association, the industry, the nonprofit sector, and society at large. It is significant that many public members indicated they would like to sit on other boards in the same capacity. If this is the case, why not help them to broaden their vistas and to become more valuable?

The involvement of all organizational components in orientation and continuing education activities is essential. However, many of the subjects that must be covered in the initial induction program will be viewed as déjà vu and obvious to staff and many of the directors, thus detracting from their interest, motivation, and attention. Due to this attitude, orientation frequently is synthetic and superficial (Werther et al., 2001). In an attempt to avoid this type of situation and to include new actors in the board education process, it might be worthwhile to use some experienced board members and past or present public members, depending on the number involved, as presenters. In the former case, there is a chance that presentations might be less biased because training undertaken by staff alone can be tainted with a single self-interest. Moreover, it is improbable that these contingents will stimulate public member activism. Training that encourages public advocacy should come from outside the institutional establishment or from the constituency itself. This involvement of people, other than staff, might generate more interest, especially in the initial sessions. As a practical matter, to enhance the commitment, enthusiasm, and participation of public members, these non-staff participants should speak to the benefits and rewards of board membership. There is nothing better than to hear these "from the horses' mouths."

The education and development of the public member has an international dimension. The picture now becomes a layer cake. Whereas there is a basic understanding of cultural norms in a domestic context, huge and often cataclysmic changes take place when a program crosses its national boundaries. Globalization and its benefits are a two-way street. This applies to the internationalization of programs as well. Public members frequently have experiences in other cultures and with other languages. This clearly enriches any board. These people can be called on for board development activities and used in program expansion in unique ways. Obviously, inclusion of persons from abroad on a board offers a fruitful resource, but these people require special and diverse preparation, especially, since the notion of the public member has not been firmly cultivated in foreign soil. And, at the same time, it is expected that any governing body to accommodate them would have to have a thorough understanding of their culture, political and otherwise.

All programs, including orientation efforts require evaluation on the part of all participants. Materials utilized should be judged in terms of format and content as should each session provided. In addition, the various presenters should be given a grade as well. All dimensions of educational activities should be appraised. Based on the desired objectives to be achieved, detailed evaluation criteria should be prepared. Only on the basis of generated data can offerings be refined. Continuous self-examination allowing for suggestions by participants is essential.

The significance of orientation and continuing education opportunities for public members must be reiterated. It cannot be overemphasized. Effective board participation requires not only the selection of appropriate people, but also the provision of a stellar development program that allows trustees to uncover the human and material dimensions of the institution. Duca (1986) categorically states: "Any organization stands to lose if its board lacks a program of ongoing board development and education" (p. 83). If orientation and continuing education efforts are not taken seriously, valuable opportunities are lost.

The new institutionalist agenda for governance envisions a reality characterized by a democratic order of rights, rules, and institutions created and sustained by active education and socialization. In this context orientation and other developmental programs become a top priority. Governance relates to the creation of capable institutional actors, who comprehend the operation of their institutions and can deal with them. It involves creating and maintaining cultures, rights, rules, identities, preferences and resources, a system of meaning, as well as a comprehension of history. Development efforts are the foundation of all organizational activities. They are critical for it makes a difference how identity and interactions are organized and how goals are shared (March & Olsen, 1995, 2005). The common knowledge they elicit is ever so critical to the intellectual capital that must be nurtured and harvested. Moreover, if done appropriately, these efforts can spark board members' energy and thus, generate additional institutional inputs that would otherwise be lost.

As far as public members are concerned, research studies have indicated that if they had better preparation for their position and if they were armed with the appropriate information, they could increase their influence on board output (Brownlea, 1987; Chesney, 1984; Graddy & Nichol, 1989; *Public Representation*, 1995; Thain & Haydock, 1983). Board education has been compared to sex education. It is essential. Unfortunately, Ward (1997) poignantly observes that "the training of directors has been handled with the same shoulder shrugging awkwardness our society has shown sex education" (p. 195). This is especially true in the case of public members.

Educational programs are expensive in terms of money and staff time involved because programs must be tailored to the specific needs and backgrounds of all constituencies represented on the board and to those of staff as well. This is particularly true, if new directors are not all seated at the same time. Correspondence with a senior staff member of an agency participating in this study made reference to this problem. She noted the lack of resources to do any kind of large-scale education. Thus, as is common, her organization holds a new member training session of an afternoon's duration. Consisting of several components all of a certain importance, orientation is critical to the performance of a governing board. In addition to preparing members for immediate participation, it institutionalizes the governance process.

Cost is definitely a factor. In terms of nurturing capabilities, the costs are immediate and focused, whereas the returns are diffuse and relate to the long-term. However, these activities must be viewed as a sound investment benefiting the participants, the organization, its stakeholders, the industry, and society at large. Recognizing that it is difficult for any single organization to produce public member training on the scale that is needed, collective thought on the part of a galaxy of associations reflecting disparate interests should be given to the topic. Resources could be pooled in imaginative ways so that the needs of various constituencies could be met and efforts could have a state, regional, or national basis. This is not an easy task, but it is not an impossible one either. Investment in capacity building is a win situation for all, but especially for the public member in terms of support and performance.

Other Aids

It is also beneficial to provide public members with a mentor, hopefully, another public member. Supplementing educational activities as in Greek mythology, this figure serves as a counselor and advisor who can answer questions as they arise and alleviate uncertainties related to the directorship. The one-on-one relationship fosters more open communication and makes it easier to deal with problems in timely fashion. It can also help build confidence and, being a less formal relationship, make it easier to pose those so-called stupid and embarrassing questions and to become integrated into the group.

It must be remembered that initially public members do not enroll in a "crash course" in the field, but only in an intensive one beginning with orientation. Hopefully, their education from this point forward will be continuous and gradual. Thus, it would be useful, as is often the case, to provide them with a manual containing information and documents relevant to their role that can be considered at will. Materials related to many topics referred to in orientation should be included in the volume. Obviously, contents will vary from organization to organization depending on specific needs. However, the following items provide a point of departure.

The first part of the manual might focus on the association involved. Materials would be primarily descriptive and of reference quality. They could include the bylaws and statements related to the organization's mission, vision, values serving as its foundation, and programs. A detailed organizational chart would be useful. This should include a listing of all units, responsibilities affiliated with each one, and individuals assigned to them. Formal external linkages should be noted as well. Detailed governing board structure could be included in this diagram or it could be merely noted and presented separately. Functions and responsibilities of the governing body and its organs should be specified. In addition, serving as an aid to a board constituency of prime importance are job descriptions containing information referred to earlier in this work for public members and other constituencies represented on the governing body. The same should be provided for the board leadership. Guidelines for selecting board members and officers and terms and conditions of office should be set forth. As every board should have a policy related to the appointment and service of board members and leaders and their rights, it should also have one pertaining to their release from membership and/or office in case of a negative report card. Moreover, the evaluation related to this report card should be discussed in a statement listing criteria utilized, the judges, and the time intervals involved, among other elements. Policies relevant to board role should be in the volume. These might include precise statements concerned with confidentiality, conflict of interest, and ethical behavior, to cite a few items. One can never be overreminded of these matters. Also of utility is a roster with contact information for the directors, staff, and other persons involved with the organization on a regular basis. Communication procedures should be specified as well. The roster might also provide a sketch of each person's background and activities. Such information might provide a basis for conversation on initial contact. A calendar, noting regularly scheduled events, such as board meetings, an annual conference, testing dates, workshops, and the like, would be of use as well. As reference materials for public members to help them fulfill their responsibilities, certain background papers, containing historical data that provide a framework for decision-making, if appropriate, should be available along with copies of current policies of relevance. Committee and task force reports and the latest annual report would be helpful. The strategic plan is of utmost importance and pertinent to it and other documents mentioned as well as public member behavior are financial materials. More specifically, members of this constituency should have at hand copies of the annual budget, the audit, and the most recent financial report.

Also, for reference purposes, letters, forms, applications, and the like, used on a regular basis and related to organizational products, might be inserted in the manual, if deemed appropriate. They would serve to indicate types of information requested and distributed. These might also be perceived as micromanagement and information overload and therefore, deemed incidental and unnecessary.

If the organization is involved with certification, a section of the manual might be devoted to this topic. Information could be concerned with the philosophy behind the concept, the process involved, and examination development and practices. Also, it would be fitting to include materials regarding the National Organization for Competency Assurance and the National Commission for Certifying Agencies.

Over and above these formal materials pertaining to the association involved and its activities, information focusing on public member behavior would be suitable. It would be useful to develop materials concerned with how to carry out the public member role. These might address ways to become informed about public needs, opinions, and interests; to plant roots in the larger community, and to seek out public member colleagues. They might also suggest criteria to be used in developing a position on issues, questions to ask, and methods to be invoked in the articulation of the public interest. Mention of sources for obtaining information related to the public member role, in general, and that concerning a specific field, in particular, should be valuable. Groups useful to public members in fulfilling their responsibilities should also be noted.

Given the communication problems and knowledge deficit revealed in survey responses, a list of acronyms and terminology used in the professional field concerned and in certification and accreditation, if appropriate, is essential. Also, in the hope that the public members' interest and curiosity have been sparked and that this person finds some leisure time, reference materials that could be referred to overtime might be suggested. The list could include works concerned with nonprofits, the public member role, the specific industry and organization, as well as accreditation and certification, if fitting. Periodicals, professional journals, books, and internet sources could be referenced.

There are a variety of materials that are eligible for inclusion in such a volume. However, it should be remembered that the contents should meet the aforementioned requirements of a governance information system. Items should consist primarily of items that can be classified as decision and performance information. The manual should be updated as needed, but it should definitely be reviewed every six months.

Public members, according to survey results, very often find themselves swimming in uncharted waters. They, as well as the people with whom they work, frequently encounter frustrating situations that indicate an uneven playing field. This chapter has suggested some efforts that might be undertaken in the context of orientation, continuing education, and reference materials that might help to level the diamond, make play that much easier for all concerned, and generate synergy in the interests of decision- making and bonding and bridging social capital. Many of the suggestions could be undertaken by institutions, regardless of their age, size, or the state of their budget.

The possibilities are many and each organization has to decide what endeavors suit it.

5

Conclusion: The Score and the Standings

Although many forms of democratic participation, such as the electoral, have decreased, other types, such as that related to advocacy democracy, have increased in the interests of extended access to and thus, more control of and influence in decision-making, transparency, and accountability. Although these objectives have been sought after throughout history, each generation that hopes to adapt democracy to a new age, pursues them in its own way. In most recent times public members were part of the response in the context of a growing nonprofit sector that provides new opportunities for action salient to their interests.

This new type of participation has been implemented in diverse structures and with many different intentions, but, nonetheless, it still remains a single phenomenon in spite of murky delineation. Executive directors and public members surveyed were asked if there are advantages in having public members on a board of directors. Although there are a myriad of problems affiliated with the experiment, as noted throughout this work, both camps responded in the affirmative. However, the endorsement of the public members was somewhat more enthusiastic. Ninety-eight percent of the public representatives recognized the benefits as did 94 percent of the management contingent. Although both constituencies supported public representation, they differed slightly in their rationale.

Both camps believed that the external and broader perspective brought to the board by public members was advantageous. It was cited by a majority of both groups: 76 percent of public members and 61 percent of executive respondents. From the view of management it was felt that the presence of public trustees helps to assure that the profession involved does not lose sight of its purpose in the larger world. According to some members of this sector, it helps to keep a board grounded in the "real world" and tempers insularity in its view of issues. It was also noted that public members not only provide a different perspective, theoretically that of the public and along with it fresh viewpoints, but sometimes more informed ones on some issues. A comment from one executive director captures the value of public members in this regard. This person observed:

> They [public members] bring a different perspective to the process, a different understanding of business. They help to broaden our viewpoint away from the mechanics of what we do. This helps us to better serve not only our certificants, but the bigger community we interact with. This has helped us to use our contractors (administrative office, testing company and attorney) more effectively.

Public members tended to echo the sentiments of the executive respondents. They also noted that their view is less myopic than that of their board colleagues and, therefore, tempers the possibilities of parochial thinking. Believing that professionals tend to look after their own kind, they deemed public input a must. Furthermore, many felt their participation was of value because it helped to extend horizons. One public member succinctly summed up these thoughts. "Without them [public members] the group could become victim of tunnel vision, inbreeding, and reluctance to think outside the box."

Also of interest are the comments of two public member respondents. One referred to the value of a different viewpoint, "the views of a non-professional but a professional in another scheme." And the other made reference to experts in finance, educational administration, testing, etc. From such comments it seems that it is assumed a public member is supposed to be a professional. Some executive directors also thought in the same vein. One even proposed that public member board appointments rotate through the professional disciplines. Obviously, this defeats the purpose of this constituency.

There was a consensus that these trustees provided an opportunity for another perspective as well as some very concrete and practical recommendations concerning solutions to complex questions and problems. This external viewpoint was definitely thought to be very helpful. However, in providing a unique and diverse perspective, the only caveat, as indicated by one respondent, is that the relationship of the public member(s) to the other trustees must not become adversarial. Benefits from an external and broader perspective were by far the most popular advantage of public representation in both camps.

It was followed by the significantly less important control function cited by 31 percent of the executives and 24 percent of the public members. Acting in this capacity, these directors provide oversight and balance. They help ensure fewer conflicts of interest and keep boards from becoming embroiled in internal politics, according to survey respondents. It was noted that they keep ideas and processes honest and focussed on a particular goal without being influenced by budget and internal political issues. For example, in the eyes of one executive director respondent: "Public members make a certification process seem less self-serving to a profession or organization and they can deflect fears about a program being put in place for 'cash cow' purposes." These representatives help preclude the profession from becoming self-serving.

In exercising the control function they not only ensure the public's interest is given consideration, but also due process and certificants' rights. It is a two-way street. They have been judged irreplaceable as an assurance that those within the profession always keep the public good at the heart and soul of the decision-making process. One executive director wrote:

> It is reassuring to know that, if the need ever arose, there is someone there who will say "Wait a minute. How does this proposed policy protect the public?" Even though the other board members take their protection of the public role very seriously, it is possible that they could not be able to remove themselves from the subject matter. It could happen without anyone noticing if we had no public member.

Evidently these representatives are seen as being able to raise the important question: Do these requirements serve to protect the public and consumer or do they merely protect or enhance the status of professionals? Also related to the control function is the sensitive issue of ethical questions.

In identifying the advantages of public representation the only elements the two constituencies held in common were: (1) the provision of a diverse perspective and (2) the control function. Then they parted ways. A portion of the public members (21 percent) cited public and/or consumer protection as an important benefit of its participation on boards of directors. It is startling that more respondents did not refer to this advantage. These respondents were of the opinion that decision makers do not intentionally lose sight of the consumer and members of the public. However, often they get overly busy and preoccupied and somehow the public interest is overlooked. Thus, it is beneficial to have representatives for the express purpose of protecting these concerns. Additional responses forthcoming from seven percent of the public trustees were scattered and fell into the "other" category. These included benefits related to advocacy for the profession involved, networking and external linkages, and the fact that the inclusion of public members was a clear statement of the value the governing body places on that constituency.

Another advantage cited by 22 percent of the executive directors surveyed was improvement in decision-making. These respondents felt that the public members challenged the board to articulate needs and concerns in a diverse way, thus enriching the decision-making process along with new views and a broader knowledge base, including skills and expertise. More specifically, it was noted that "public members look at issues, problems and opportunities with a clear eye and they do not carry the baggage of a certificate holder." The value of public members was also attributed to "the fact that they consistently raise new issues that make us think through our policies more carefully and thoroughly." In addition, a few executives indicated that, due to turnover in board composition as a result of elections, the public members' continued involvement makes the decision-making process more stable. Evidently in these cases public representatives must enjoy longer and diverse terms of office.

Credibility was also important to many chief executive officers. It was cited by 20 percent of them. Not carrying the luggage of a certificant, public member involvement, it was argued, enhances defensibility of board decisions, especially in dealing with government agencies or employer groups. It was also deemed useful in the cases of judicial and admissions decisions. Public member participation lends credibility and legitimacy to board output.

Given the nature of the responses noted so far concerning the advantages of having a public member on the governing body, it is not surprising that some executive directors also underscored the significance of the representative function resulting from public involvement. Sixteen percent of the sample was of the opinion that it is important to represent the population that an entity serves. In that programs directly affect the public and ultimately affect it in one way or another, according to one respondent, "it would be a huge oversight not to have the public represented on our board of directors. We need their input and guidance." This representative function was also related in the responses to issues of transparency and accessibility.

The least popular benefit of public involvement in the eyes of agency leaders was the linkage function, i.e., the ability of the representatives to forge relationships between an organization and the public, industry, and various types of other groups. The provision of access to the outside community and its groups was noted by 13 percent of the sample. Some of these persons that assigned importance to this benefit in comments pointed out the enormous potential of public members in this capacity and they coupled such activities with marketing. A very few respondents were quite honest in claiming that public participation was only useful in terms of the aforementioned National Commission for Certifying Agencies' accreditation.

Negative responses to public involvement on governing bodies were issued by six percent of the executives and two percent of the public members. From the executive perspective public trustees were of no value because often they do not participate fully in the board's activities and they manifest little interest in serving after having assumed the commitment. In addition, it was noted that getting public members "up to speed" is an onerous and costly task that is not worth the effort. Not understanding the issues these trustees do not produce meaningful input and, therefore, preference was assigned to people involved in the profession. And one commentator reported that public members were superfluous because expectations for that contingent were the same as any other. Thus, these trustees reaped no special advantage.

Several of these administrators volunteered strong negative reactions to the public member concept. More specifically, several affirmed that the National Commission for Certifying Agencies should dispose of its mandate related to public members. Charging that the accreditation process was convoluted and the requirement of seating a public director on a governing body a burden, a few even declared that they were seeking accreditation outside the constraints of this organization. In the words of one respondent: "In short, public members are just one example of an overly complicated process." Negative comments from the public member contingent were minimal in number. For the most part, they focussed on the lack of expertise and insights that contribute to board deliberations. Another element that was noted was the difficulty in finding appropriate candidates.

In summary and in a positive vein, it is to be noted that public members offer a wealth of opportunities. These trustees and the chief executive officers recognized this in their survey responses, citing, particularly, the availability of an external and broader perspective, oversight, and public/consumer protection, along with an improvement in the decision-making process with the addition of credibility, among other advantages. The fact of the matter is that in commenting on the advantages of having public members on a governing body, in comparison with the executives, public representatives participating in the survey had a very limited notion of the role of the public member and thus, their comments were much more parochial.

In responding to the question one administrator offered thoughtful insight as to the type of unit and the role of the public member involved. This person distinguished the public member sitting on an association's board of directors from one participating in a credentialing entity. The former was judged an asset, but the same evaluation did not apply to the latter. It was explained that in the credentialing arena the work is more mundane and technical discussions are much more frequent. In this specific case, as often occurs in others, a meeting of several days is devoted exclusively to examination development and a public member not in the field is useless and worthless, according to the writer. It is possible to excuse this director from such a meeting, but as the commentator observes: "That would engender mistrust that other business could be undertaken in his/her absence."

The respondent continues: "Such participation in the original development of requirements and the overall credentialing program may have the most utility as the recognition of both professionals in the field and the public recognition of the credential are established." Given that there have been few major changes to the specific program over the years and that any principal modification must receive the approval of the association's governing body that represents the client base and the profession, according to this administrator, it would be more meaningful for a public member to be seated on the association's board of directors as opposed to that of the certification commission. Such an observation definitely provides food for thought.

Those executive respondents, not having public members on their governing bodies, and thus, those who did not complete parts of the survey discussed above, were asked a question in the same vein: Do you think it would be valuable to have public members on boards of directors? In this case responses were not as clear-cut. In fact, they were almost evenly split. Forty-eight percent answered in the affirmative and 47 percent in the negative, leaving five percent in the "don't know" category. These respondents were then asked to explain their position. Often, the rationale echoed opinions offered by colleagues having public members on their governing bodies. By far the most popular reason was the representation function indicated by 29 percent of these administrators. It was followed by enhancement of the decision-making process (14 percent), the importance of accountability and oversight (ten percent), linkage to other communities and contributions to external relations (nine percent), adherence to the standards of the National Commission for Certifying Agencies (three percent), and impact of subject matter on society, in general (three percent). It is noteworthy that a few of these positive responses were qualified. As one executive director wrote: "I have no problem with public members and I would choose to have them on my board—but at a ratio of 1:5 to 1:10." Or another remarked: ". . . if there were no voting rights."

The most important reason (23 percent) for not valuing public members, according to this portion of the executive directors' sample, was that public representation was not pertinent to the constituency or mission of the organization. Focusing on its nature, responses indicated that there was no need for these trustees because the governing body was concerned with organizational issues, or the business of some other limited community, or the organization involved had no or only an indirect impact on the public. In addition, it was affirmed that public members increase the nonindustry bias and detract from the original focus. Moreover, it was also argued that they are not suitable to a young organization. Of significance was the observation that there is no evidence that public members improve the quality of decision-making.

This line of reasoning was followed by arguments advanced by 20 percent of the sample concerned with public members' lack of qualifications, which have been cited throughout this work. One executive director commented: "We had a public member in the past and spent more time educating that person than doing board business." Several respondents noted that it was difficult enough to identify talented individuals in the field as candidates for board membership, much less public members. Thus, they did not want to look for more trouble and voluntarily assume additional responsibilities related to public trustees. In a letter concerned with this project one respondent bluntly noted that the public is not aware of the activities of the profession and, therefore, its representatives serve no purpose on a board.

Some of this constituency (eight percent) reported that it had alternate access to public sentiment and thus, it was not necessary to include public members on governing bodies. The pulse of public opinion was felt through membership in various coalitions, advisory panels, and routine provision of public comment in the policy-making process. Also it was noted that in a few cases the responding constituency, consisting of public servants, was already subject to public demands as mandated through federal, state, and local laws and regulations. And then some respondents felt that having many different fields, such as government, education, and business, represented on boards of directors, it was possible for these trustees to speak as members of the public. In such a view, public members become superfluous another time. Once again cost was cited as a factor, this time by three percent of these respondents.

Persons that opted for a "don't know" response had uncertainties principally because they had never worked with these trustees. They admitted that in theory there were both advantages and disadvantages to the practice, but lacking concrete evidence and direct experience, they were unable to issue a precise judgment. And then in one case past experience with a public member was so negative that the respondent still remained traumatized and uneasy. The responses of these executive directors not having public members on their governing bodies were somewhat different from those of their colleagues having experience with these trustees. They assigned more emphasis to the representative function and gave less importance to the governance, decision-making, control, and linkage roles. Their negative responses had a slightly diverse thrust as well.

The public members surveyed were a satisfied group. Ninety-five percent of them evaluated their board experience as excellent or good (excellent 56 percent and good 39 percent), leaving a small lukewarm contingent (five percent) that issued a rating of fair. No one reported a poor experience. Thus, it was not surprising to find that, as noted, all public members indicated they would serve on another board in the same capacity. This willingness to serve again can be viewed as a sign of satisfaction with the experience and a positive evaluation of the governing body's performance. Obviously, the investment of time and effort was considered worthwhile.

The executives, also, in spite of their reservations and frustrations, were content with public members, but slightly less so than the public members themselves. When asked: "If you had a choice, would you choose to have public members on a board of directors?," 92 percent responded in the affirmative and five percent in the negative. The rest of the respondents (three percent) opted for the "don't know" category.

Great expectations for a reorientation of institutions, diverse output, and a redistribution of power usually accompany attempts at innovations related to citizen participation. In terms of the public member project, optimism was and still is based on expanding access to decision-making, involving new and diverse groups in this process, increasing popular control of elites, and encouraging and realizing more responsive policy output, enhancing organizational accountability to the public, and augmenting the effectiveness and efficiency of the organization in terms of meeting its goals. In this case, entrée to the decision-making arena has been minimally extended in terms of numbers with the addition of public members to governing bodies. However, to exert power more than numbers are necessary. Based on the results of this study, new and diverse groups have not been included in the policy-making process. Rather, existing demographics have been reinforced. Whether the dominance of elites or professionals has been tempered and controlled and whether policies are more in accord with the public interest have not been scientifically confirmed. However, based on comments received from those surveyed, doubt might be raised in both cases.

Research has demonstrated that modifying formal institutions, such as governing bodies, can change practice (Putnam, 1993). Data collected in this study showed that as a result of public member endeavors, some practices were transformed. This result was confirmed by both public members and executive directors. However, not being the central thrust of this project, no concrete and elaborate findings concerning the extent of the impact of public members on board performance and output were identified. This is material for a separate research project. As noted earlier, the contributions of public members were recognized by the constituency itself and by the executive directors. But, the exact extent of these contributions is unknown.

It was assumed that the inclusion of public members on governing bodies would lead to better decision-making. The empirical literature on these matters indicates that the effectiveness and influence of public members is less than positive. It ranges from no noticeable impact on any aspect of board decision-making and thus, no transfer of power (Checkoway, 1982; Cole, 1981; Schneider, 1987; Schutz, 1983), to a very low impact (Public Member Study Subcommittee, 1980), to some influence on certain issues (Grady & Nichol, 1989), and to a much less dramatic effect on output than expected (Thain & Haydock, 1983). From a certain perspective these results are not surprising, given the haphazard implementation of the public member project and the problems raised earlier in this work, especially those related to obstacles to fulfilling public member responsibilities, recruitment and selection, orientation, continuing education, the job description, and support services, to cite a few. If nothing else, the presence of public trustees has served to place and keep, sometimes in tenuous fashion, the public perspective on the table which might not have happened without their creation. Still, this perspective should be much stronger.

Little research has been devoted to this subject and this is definitely a shortcoming. The existing studies are few in number, diverse in scope, and outdated. Analysis and evaluation are of extreme significance. They must be undertaken on a continuous basis, especially since times and experiences constantly change at a rapid pace. The previously mentioned executive director who referred to the lack of solid evidence concerning the public members' value and impact certainly raised a very cogent issue that should be pursued.

Public representatives have been found to be central to decision-making. Research (Riska & Taylor, 1978) comparing their attitudes toward health policy issues with those of professionals on governing boards has shown that on all matters the differences were statistically significant. The significance of including this constituency in the policy-making process to seek a solution-oriented dialogue and to temper the predominance of a provider-based ideology has been established. However, exactly how much and what type of impact these representatives have remains to be determined. This information is of utmost importance because it would aid in dealing with many, if not most, of the problems mentioned in this work. Research of a comparative nature, focusing on diverse types of boards and their public member constituencies, is sorely needed. It would be most valuable to all concerned.

The social value of nonprofits continues to mount in response to the steadily broadening aspirations of society and to the nation's expanding international commitments. Services provided by these organizations are more in demand and the number of units continues to expand. If present trends hold, in the future these organizations will have an even greater role. However, the third sector is, in new institutionalists' terms, at a critical juncture. Public confidence has reached a contemporary low as a result of questions related to how its institutions operate ("The age of nonprofits," 2003). Moreover, the sector is experiencing an image problem along with pressures resulting from a growing gulf between public expectations and the realities of the sector and organizational weaknesses. Consequently, nonprofit boards of directors, in addition to other urgent matters, have to wrestle with these adversities. If their task was a difficult one in the past, it is now more herculean than ever. Effective participation in and stellar decision-making by governing bodies are not automatic. They must be taught, learned, groomed, nurtured, and encouraged, as noted by the new institutionalists. They are dependent on several factors, only some of which can be managed by the people directly involved. The situation indicates the rigor of the task. It is not easy to structure satisfactory public participation (Carson, 2002; Kweit & Kweit, 1981; Werther et al., 2001). However, it is not impossible.

Unfortunately, "institutional layering" was not fully realized as envisioned, given the way in which the public member project grew. Very often with the introduction of new actors into their ranks, as they pursue their own agenda, organizations sometimes experience a modification in their mission. A change in the balance of power toward the direction of new players, thus changing the nature of the playing field, can cause institutional conversion. Such a refashioning of goals and ideas did not take place. The public members are not wholly powerful, but, according to data generated in this study, neither are they wholly powerless. The fact of the matter is that their full potential has not been realized. This situation can be rectified.

The public members' ball game is an exciting one. These players have garnered hits. For example, the notion of the public representative is well-established in many quarters and is becoming more acceptable in others. Positive contributions to board operations and many facets of the governing bodies' output, as noted, have been recognized by both executive directors and public members in responses to survey questions.

The public members have also scored runs as evidenced by their and the agency leaders' acknowledgement of changes in policies, practices, and perspectives due to the efforts of this constituency. Moreover, satisfaction in both camps runs high. However, as in any ball game, some of the action is not within the limits of the established range and thus, the umpire must call a ball. It was noted that the public member is not always used properly. Often, full advantage is not taken of this role and a specific representative's talents and expertise. With repeated instances of this type, an institution walks and does not run. Its pace of play is reduced. Recruitment and selection, orientation, and continuing education receive less attention than they should. They are important to the chemistry of the team. Also staff-public member relations, attitudinal barriers, and problems related to board procedures, as noted in survey responses, require consideration. Often, they too are outside the noted range. These institutional factors have manufactured limited participation.

And there have been strikes as well. One of the scopes of public participation was the injection of new blood into the decision-making process to channel the demands of a broader section of the population to policy makers. In theory, the creation of the public member put a new face on old institutions that was to empower new groups and to facilitate the participation of previously suppressed interests. These "repressed" or "negative" structural interests of the community population, the opposite of the dominant ones, were not served in the past (Alford, 1975) and it might be that they are still not being served. Who actually participates in decision-making is of significance. This is what matters. Data collected in this study have revealed that the institutional landscape of the public members, given their demography, is dominated by professionals. It has changed little or not at all. In this case, as in others throughout history, reform legitimates previously ignored constituencies and at the same time limits them (Morone, 1990). The nonprofit sector continues to be directed by the most privileged of citizens. The so-called "repressed" interests failed to bloom in the organizations surveyed. Professional interests continue in the driver's seat. Innovation, as evidenced by the survey results, has been subverted by professionals. Are the demands they issue and articulate skewed in such a manner as to leave the interests of the ordinary citizens by the wayside? That is a question to be answered in another research project.

Unfortunately, this ball game, like many others, includes errors. The most serious one is the failure to clearly develop, describe, particularize, and appropriately implement the public member project. Nonfulfillment of this task has been underscored several times throughout this work and it has been responsible for disappointing implementation efforts and evaluations as well as the failure of public members to realize their potential. This reform, like others, has been limited because of omissions related to clarification of role, constituencies, responsibilities, and mechanisms of accountability. One observer comments: "Decades of effort to win public member positions will have been in vain if their occupants do not perform effectively" (*Public Representation*, 1995, p. 22). Many of the problem areas revealed in the surveys would be alleviated, if not eliminated, if this error were addressed. Such action would serve to maximize the potential of public members.

Most of these trustees want to be productive and effective directors, but often through no fault of their own, many do not know how to do so or are unable to do so, due to encountered obstacles. Public member participation is an important component of board effectiveness. Galiher et al. (1977), poignantly argue that meaningful public member participation

> can only happen if roles are clearly defined, if orientation to function is a continuing process, if staff have clearly defined roles to nurture it, and if the process is traceable in the activities of the agency at whatever level. What needs to be done to make…[public member] participation fulfill its potential seems clear. Whether it will get done remains to be seen (p. 263).

It has been more than three decades since this statement was penned. Although some action has been taken, these and other prerequisites mentioned have not been met. Thus, the challenge of harnessing the democratic wish to nonprofit institutions with the hope of achieving effective public member participation still remains.

Normative institutionalism is concerned not only with the survival and success of institutions, but also with their ability to correct features that need adjustment (Pai & Sharma, 2005). Representative institutions must be able to respond to changes, including those related to the locus of decision-making, and the identities of the stakeholders and, more specifically, participants. The nonprofit governing boards surveyed did not live up to this challenge. With the birth of the public member project old institutions were supposed to be put in the service of diverse ends as new actors came into play. Institutions empower and control, but, as regards the public members, given the survey results, they were short on empowerment, thus privileging other actors. Institutionalized rules, norms, habits, identities, and standard operating procedures have impacted public member behavior in negative fashion. A principal question about participation focuses on the equality and inequality of participants in their capacity to influence decisions. Public members are definitely limited in this respect. Institutional characteristics are not congruent with their needs.

The institutional community, like the political community, is founded on a shared view of its history and its goals, a common understanding of the logic of appropriateness, or the rights and responsibilities of specific role relationships (March & Olsen, 1989). Unfortunately, the nonprofits studied have not achieved the status of a true community in the spirit of normative institutionalism.

Governance involves the capacity to develop an institutional system that is capable of confronting changing demands and changing environments and thus, "to match 'institutionalized environments,' norms and beliefs about how an organization should be organized and run" (March & Olsen, 1995, p. 41). Formal power is not the same as real power. The potential power of public members has not been translated into real power. There is a significant gap between the hopes for public member participation and actual practice. Full involvement and shared decision-making have not been realized. If the ideal institution is to contain personal power, expert power, and position power, public members' contribution is weak compared to that of other constituencies. This is unfortunate because high-quality public participation impacts participants' belief systems in a positive manner (Halvorsen, 2003).

From the new institutionalist approach, responsibility for this situation lies with the basic nature of the institutions involved. Given the notion of path or historical dependency contained in this perspective, institutions do not undertake and realize change facilely. Instead overtime they have manifested a certain stubbornness or robustness and, according to Morone and Kilbreth (2003), are deaf when it comes to hearing the public's voices. They demonstrate hesitancy towards change because of uncertainty as to what the consequences might be. "The amount of uncertainty implied by the new institutional structures makes actors unwilling to change structure" (Steinmo, 2001, p. 3).

Thus, changes in the eyes of the normative institutionalists are slow to come about. They are often piecemeal and gradual. They evolve and eventually culminate in substantial and significant ones. Those changes that are perceived as being natural, normal, or legitimate are deemed easier to fashion than those that are not (March & Olsen, 1995). There are several of this type relating to public members that could be initiated immediately. Certain measures must be undertaken so that the public member constituency can move up the participation ladder to a rung that represents a higher degree of public power, if not citizen control. The level of decision-making involvement is a key to an understanding of participation. As noted throughout this discussion, as regards the public member constituency, it leaves to be desired.

Institutions adjust to their environments as the environments accommodate them. Institutions and their linkages co-evolve. They are entangled. Often, they are positioned, as in this case, so that the adapting ones, nonprofit governing bodies, are integral parts of other adapting ones, nonprofit organizations (March & Olsen, 1995). Obviously, this situation, creating more than the usual significant lags in the adjustment of institutions to their environment, makes change more complex and less smooth. For normative institutionalists sustained experimentation and exploration are critical to the realization of change. In reference to the public member constituency studied, unfortunately, there has been very little or none. These activities must be stimulated at all costs.

Public members have hit the ball, but they are caught between the bases. With thought and systematization the circumstances can be changed and more runs will be scored. Improvement in the behavior and contribution of public members requires the efforts of all institutional actors—agency chief executive officers, staff, professional board members, and public members themselves—working in unison. In a positive and optimistic vein, March and Olsen (1995) advise that even if early experience with a project might have resulted in failure, future efforts might be more favorable, given that one can only learn by doing. From an institutionalist approach construing a meaningful identity, which has not happened as far as the public member constituency is concerned, and realizing it, require energy, thought, and capability. Fulfilling this identity, "involves matching a changing set of contingent rules to a changing . . . set of situations" (March & Olsen, 1995, p. 32).

Time is of the essence in this era of nonprofit growth, more competition for limited resources, increased calls for transparency and accountability, disaffected citizens, and less stability in the external environment. It is important because, as noted, most institutional history moves slowly and, as Putnam (1993) observes, it is likely to move even more slowly when norms of reciprocity and networks of civic engagement are involved. Maximizing the contribution and effectiveness of public members are not easy tasks, but they are essential and possible ones. The noted advantages of this type of participation far outweigh the disadvantages and, moreover, public members are important to the creation of social capital, a principal determinant of any strong democracy, what goes into the decision-making process, and what evolves from it.

References

Abzug, R., & Galaskiewicz, J. (2001). Nonprofit boards: Crucibles of expertise or symbols of local identities. *Nonprofit and Voluntary Sector Quarterly, 30*(1), 51-73.

Adler, M. W. (1988). Relations between government and nonprofit organizations. In T. D. Connors (Ed.), *The nonprofit organization handbook* (2nd ed.), (pp. 9.1- 9.9). New York: McGraw-Hill.

The age of nonprofits. (2003). Retrieved October 18, 2006, from http://www.brookings.edu/press/books/chapter_1/voicefornonprofits.pdf-2003-07-16

Alford, R. (1975). *Health care politics: Ideological and interest group barriers to reform.* Chicago: University of Chicago Press.

Almond, G. A., & Verba, S. (1965). *The civic culture: Political attitudes and democracy in five nations.* Boston: Little Brown.

Alwin, D. F., & Krosnick, J. A. (1991). Aging, cohorts, and the stability of sociopolitical orientations over the life span. *American Journal of Sociology, 97*(1), 169-195.

Americans are joiners. (2000, February 16). *Board Café.* Retrieved December 4, 2004, from http://www.boardcafe.org

Americans are more spiritual than previously was thought, survey finds. (2006, September 12). *The Post Standard*, p. A-3.

APSA [American Political Science Association] Standing Committee on Civic Education and Engagement. (2003, August). *Report of the working group on the nonprofit, voluntary, and philanthropic sectors.* Paper prepared for delivery at the annual meeting of the American Political Science Association, Philadelphia, PA. Retrieved October 18, 2006, from http://www.politicalscience.org

Arnstein, S. R. (1971). Eight rungs on the ladder of citizen participation. In E.S. Cahn & B.A. Passett (Eds.), *Citizen participation: Effecting community change* (pp. 69-91). New York: Praeger.

Austin, J. E. (1998). Business leaders and nonprofits. *Nonprofit Management and Leadership, 9*(1), 39-51.

Bailey, S. K. (1962). The public interest: Some operational dilemmas. In C.J. Friedrich (Ed.), *The public interest* (pp. 96-106). New York: Atherton Press.

Barger, D., & Hadden, S. G. (1984). Placing citizen members on professional licensing boards. *The Journal of Consumer Affairs, 18*(1), 160-170.

Baumgartner, F. R., & Walker, J. L. (1988). Survey research and membership in voluntary associations. *American Journal of Political Science, 32*(4), 908-928.

Bell, J. (1995). The activist and the alienated: Participation trends in community service. In P.G. Schervish, V.A. Hodgkinson, M. Gates, & Associates (Eds.), *Care and community in modern society: Passing on the tradition of service to future generations* (pp. 441- 458). San Francisco: Jossey-Bass.

Berry, J. M., Portney, K. E., Bablitch, M. B., & Mahoney, R. (1984). Public involvement in administration: The structural determinants of effective citizen participation. *Journal of Voluntary Action Research, 13*(2), 7-23.

Bèteille, A. (2003). The public as a social category. In G. Gurpreet (Ed.), *The public and the private: Issues of democratic citizenship* (pp. 37-55). New Delhi, India: Sage.

Blitz, M. (2001). Public interest. In *International encyclopedia of the social and behavioral sciences* (Vol. 18, pp. 12546-12549). Amsterdam: Elsevier.

Block, S. R. (2001). Board of directors. In J. S. Ott (Ed.), *Understanding nonprofit organizations: Governance, leadership, and management* (pp. 15-24). Boulder, CO: Westview Press.

Board directors: No more Mr. Nice Guy. (2004, March 20). *The Economist*, pp. 16-17.

Bowen, W. G., Nygren, T. I., Turner, S. E., & Duffy, E. A. (1994). *The charitable nonprofits: An analysis of institutional dynamics and characteristics*. San Francisco: Jossey-Bass.

Boyte, H. (1980). *The backyard revolution: Understanding the citizen movement*. Philadelphia: Temple University Press.

Brint, S., & Levy, C. S. (1999). Professions and civic engagement: Trends in rhetoric and practice, 1875-1995. In T. Skocpol & M. P. Fiorina (Eds.), *Civic engagement in American democracy* (pp. 163-210). Washington, DC and New York: Brookings Institution Press and Russell Sage Foundation.

Brooks, Arthur C. (2005). Does social capital make you generous? *Social Science Quarterly*, *86*(1), 1-15.

Brooks, Arthur C. (2006, March 6). Radio broadcast. Syracuse, NY: WAER.

Brownlea, A. (1987). Participation: Myths, realities and prognosis. *Social Science and Medicine*, *25*(6), 605-614.

Brudney, J. L. (2001). Voluntarism. In J. S. Ott (Ed.), *Understanding nonprofit organizations: Governance, leadership and management* (pp. 320-323). Boulder, CO: Westview Press.

Burke, E. M. (1977). Citizen participation strategies. In H. Rosen, J. M. Metsch, & S. Levey (Eds.), *The consumer and the health care system: Social and management perspectives* (pp. 217-233). New York: Spectrum Publications.

Burns, N., Schlozman, K. L., & Verba, S. (2001). *The private roots of public action: Gender, equality and political participation*. Cambridge, MA: Harvard University Press.

Capitalizing on public members to enhance a board's credibility and accountability. (2001). *News & Views: Citizen Advocacy Center*, *13*(4), 21-26.

Carson, E. D. (2002). Public expectations and nonprofit sector realities: A growing divide with disastrous consequences. *Nonprofit and Voluntary Sector Quarterly*, *31*(3), 429-436.

Carver, J. (1990). *Boards that make a difference: A new design for leadership in nonprofit and public organizations*. San Francisco: Jossey-Bass.

Carver, J., & Oliver, C. (2002). *Corporate boards that create value: Governing company performance from the boardroom*. San Francisco: Jossey-Bass.

Cassinelli, C. W. (1958). Some reflections on the concept of the public interest. *Ethics*, *69*(1), 48-61.

Cassinelli, C. W. (1962). The public interest in political ethics. In C. J. Friedrich (Ed.), *The public interest* (pp. 44-53). New York: Atherton Press.

Chait, R. P. (2006, February 17). When trustees blunder. *The Chronicle of Higher Education*, pp. B6-B7.

Chait, R. P., Holland, T. P., & Taylor, B. E. (1993). *The effective board of trustees*. Phoenix, AZ: Oryx Press.

Chait, R. P., Ryan, W. P., & Taylor, B. E. (2005). *Governance as leadership: Reframing the work of nonprofit boards*. Hoboken, NJ: John Wiley & Sons.

Chait, R. P., & Taylor, B. E. (1989). Charting the territory of nonprofit boards. *Harvard Business Review*, 67(1), 44-54.

Charles, C., & De Maio, S. (1993). Lay participation in health care decision making: A conceptual framework. *Journal of Health Politics, Policy and Law*, 18(4), 881-904.

Checkoway, B. (1981). Citizens and health care in perspective: An introduction. In B. Checkoway (Ed.), *Citizens and health care: Participation and planning for social change* (pp. 1-17). New York: Pergamon Press.

Checkoway, B. (1982). Public participation in health planning agencies: Promise and practice. *Journal of Health Politics, Policy and Law*, 7(3), 723-733.

Checkoway, B., & Doyle, M. (1980). Community organizing lessons for health care consumers. *Journal of Health Politics, Policy and Law*, 5(2), 213-226.

Checkoway, B., O'Rourke, T. W., & Bull, D. (1984). Correlates of consumer participation in health planning agencies: Findings and implications from a national survey. *Policy Studies Review*, 3(2), 296-310.

Chesney, J. D. (1982). Strategies for building representative HSAs: The impact of legal structure. *Journal of Health Politics, Policy and Law*, 7(1), 96-110.

Chesney, J. D. (1984). Citizen participation on regulatory boards. *Journal of Health Politics, Policy and Law*, 9(1), 125-135.

Chrislip, D., & Larson, C. E. (1994). *Collaborative leadership: How citizens and civic leaders can make a difference.* San Francisco: Jossey-Bass.

Chrislip, D. D. (2002). *The collaborative leadership fieldbook: A guide for citizens and civic leaders.* San Francisco: Jossey-Bass.

Cohen, P. D. (1982). Community health planning from an interorganizational perspective. *American Journal of Public Health*, 72 (7), 717-721.

Cole, R. L. (1981, September/October). Participation in community service organizations. *Journal of Community Action*, 53-60.

Collins, W. P. (1980). Public participation in bureaucratic decision-making: A reappraisal. *Public Administration*, 58, 465-477.

Colm, G. (1962). The public interest. In C. J. Friedrich (Ed.), *The public interest* (pp. 115-128). New York: Atherton Press.

Commission on Private Philanthropy and Public Needs. (1983). The third sector. In B. O'Connell (Ed.), *America's voluntary spirit: A book of readings* (pp. 299-314). New York: The Foundation Center.

Conger, J. A., Lawler, E. E., III, & Finegold, D. L. (2001). *Corporate boards: Strategies for adding value.* San Francisco: Jossey-Bass.

Connors, T. D. (1988). The board of directors. In T. D. Connors (Ed.), *The nonprofit organization handbook* (2nd ed.), (pp. 10.1-10.27). New York: McGraw-Hill.

Dalton, R. J. (1996). *Citizen politics: Public opinion and political parties in advanced industrial democracies* (2nd ed.). Chatham, NJ: Chatham House.

Dalton, R. J., Scarrow, S. E., & Cain, B. E. (2003). New forms of democracy? Reform and transformation of democratic institutions. In B. E. Cain, R. J. Dalton, & S. E. Scarrow (Eds.), *Democracy transformed?: Expanding political opportunities in advanced industrial democracies* (pp. 1-20). Oxford, England: Oxford University Press.

Daniels, A. K. (1988). *Invisible careers: Women civic leaders from the volunteer world.* Chicago: The University of Chicago Press.

Dawson, R. E., Prewitt, K., & Dawson, K. S. (1977). *Political socialization* (2nd ed.). Boston: Little Brown.

De Maio, S., & Charles, C. (1993). Lay participation in health care decision making: A conceptual framework. *Journal of Health Politics, Policy and Law*, 18(4), 881-904.

DeSario, J., & Langton, S. (1984). Democracy and public policy. *Policy Studies Review*, 3(2), 223-233.

Diggs, B. J. (1968). Practical representation. In J. R. Pennock & J. W. Chapman (Eds.), *Representation* (pp. 28-37). New York: Atherton Press.

Dovi, S. (2002). Preferable descriptive representatives: Will just any woman, black or latino do? *American Political Science Review, 96*(4), 729-743.

Downs, A. (1962). The public interest: Its meaning in a democracy. *Social Research, 29*(1), 1-36.

Drucker, P. F. (1989). What business can learn from nonprofits. *Harvard Business Review, 67*(4), 88-93.

Drucker, P. F. (1990). *Managing the non-profit organization: Practices and principles.* New York: HarperCollins.

Duca, D. J. (1986). *Nonprofit boards: A practical guide to roles, responsibilities, and performance.* Phoenix, AZ: Oryx Press.

Eimicke, W. B. (1974). *Public administration in a democratic context: Theory and practice.* Beverly Hills, CA: Sage.

Eisenberg, P. (1983). The voluntary sector: Problems and challenges. In B. O'Connell (Ed.), *America's voluntary spirit: A book of readings* (pp. 315-329). New York: The Foundation Center.

Fagence, M. (1977). *Citizen participation in planning.* Oxford, England: Pergamon Press.

Feldman, M. S., & March, J. G. (1981). Information as signal and symbol. *Administrative Science Quarterly, 26*(2), 171-186.

Fenn, D. H., Jr. (1971, March-April). Executives as community volunteers. *Harvard Business Review, 49*, 4-9, 12-16, 156-157.

Ferris, J. M., & Graddy, E. (1989). Fading distinctions among the nonprofit, government, and for-profit sectors. In V. A. Hodgkinson, R. W. Lyman, & Associates (Eds.), *The future of the nonprofit sector: Challenges, changes, and policy considerations* (pp. 123-139). San Francisco: Jossey-Bass.

Foley, M. W., & Edwards, B. (1999). Is it time to divest in social capital? *Journal of Public Policy, 19*(2), 141-173.

Freyd, W. P. (1988). The board of directors. In T. D. Connors (Ed.), *The nonprofit organization handbook* (2nd ed.), (pp. 25.1-25.9). New York: McGraw-Hill.

Galiher, C. B., Needleman, J., & Rolfe, A. J. (1977). Consumer participation. In H. Rosen, J. M. Metsch, & S. Levey.(Eds.), *The consumer and the health care system: Social and management perspectives* (pp. 251-265). New York: Spectrum Publications.

Gardner, J. W. (1983). The independent sector. In B. O'Connell (Ed.), *America's voluntary spirit: A book of readings* (pp. ix-xv). New York: The Foundation Center.

Gibelman, M. (2000). The nonprofit sector and gender discrimination: A preliminary investigation into the glass ceiling. *Nonprofit Management & Leadership, 10*(3), 251-269.

Ginsburg, B., Lowi, T. J., & Weir, M. (2003). *We the people: An introduction to American politics* (4th ed.). New York: W. W. Norton.

Gittell, M. (1983). The consequences of mandating citizen participation. *Policy Studies Review, 3*(4), 90-95.

Giving and volunteering in the United States 2001. (n.d.). Retrieved January 7, 2005, from http://www.independentsector.org

Goss, K. A. (1999). Volunteering and the long civic generation. *Nonprofit and Voluntary Sector Quarterly, 28*(4), 378-415.

Graddy, E., & Nichol, M. B. (1989). Public members on occupational licensing boards: Effects on legislative regulatory reforms. *Southern Economic Journal, 55*, 610-625.

Graff, L. L. (1995). Policies for volunteer programs. In T. D. Connors (Ed.), *The volunteer management handbook* (pp. 125-155). New York: John Wiley & Sons.

Greenberg, E. S., & Page, B. I. (1993). *The struggle for democracy*. New York: Harper Collins.

Greer, A. L. (1976). Training board members for health planning agencies. *Public Health Reports*, *91*(1), 58-61.

Griffith, E. S. (1962). The ethical foundations of the public interest. In C.J. Friedrich (Ed.), *The public interest* (pp. 14-25). New York: Atherton Press.

Gupta, L. C. (1989). *Corporate boards and nominee directors*. New Delhi, India: Oxford University Press.

Hage, G. (1998). Reflections on emotional rhetoric and boards for governance of NPOs. In W.W. Powell & E.S. Clemens (Eds.), *Private action and public good* (pp. 291-301). New Haven, CT: Yale University Press.

Hall, P. A., & Taylor, R. C. R. (1996). Political science and the three new institutionalisms. *Political Studies*, *44*, 936-957.

Hall, P. A., & Taylor, R. C. R. (1998). The potential of historical institutionalism: A response to Hay and Wincott. *Political Studies*, *46*, 958-962.

Hall, P. D. (1987). A historical overview of the private nonprofit sector. In W. W. Powell (Ed.), *The nonprofit sector: A research handbook* (pp. 3-26). New Haven, CT: Yale University Press.

Halvorsen, K. (2003). Assessing the effects of public participation. *Public Administration Review*, *63*(5), 535-543.

Hammack, D. C. (2001). Introduction: Growth, transformation, and quiet revolution in the nonprofit sector over two centuries. *Nonprofit and Voluntary Sector Quarterly*, *30*(2), 157-173.

Harris, M. (1993). Clarifying the board role: A total activities approach. In D. R. Young, R. M. Hollister, V. A. Hodgkinson, & Associates (Eds.), *Governing, leading, and managing nonprofit organizations: New insights from research and practice* (pp. 17-31). San Francisco: Jossey-Bass.

Heidrich, K. W. (1990). Volunteers' life-styles: Market segmentation based on volunteers' role choices. *Nonprofit and Voluntary Sector Quarterly*, *19*(1), 21-31.

Heilbron, L. H. (1973). *The college and university trustee*. San Francisco: Jossey-Bass.

Heller, F. (1998). Myth and reality: Valediction. In F. Heller, E.Pusic, G. Strauss, & B. Wilpert, *Organizational participation: Myth and reality* (pp. 220-249). Oxford, England: Oxford University Press.

Herman, R. D., & Renz, D. O. (2000). Board practices of especially effective and less effective local nonprofit organizations. *American Review of Public Administration*, *30*, 146-160.

Herring, P. (1968). Public interest. In *International encyclopedia of the social sciences* (Vol. 13, pp. 170-175). n.p.: Macmillan and The Free Press.

Hochbaum, G. M. (1977). Consumer participation in health planning: Toward conceptual clarification. In H. Rosen, J. M. Metsch, & S. Levey (Eds.), *The consumer and the health care system: Social and managerial perspectives* (pp. 267-277). New York: Spectrum Publications.

Hodgkinson, V. A. (1995). Key factors influencing caring, involvement, and community. In P. G. Schervish, V. A. Hodgkinson, M. Gates, & Associates (Eds.), *Care and community in modern society: Passing on the tradition of service to future generations* (pp. 21-50). San Francisco: Jossey-Bass.

Hodgkinson, V. A., & McCarthy, K. D. (1992). The voluntary sector in international perspective: An overview. In K. D. McCarthy, V. A. Hodgkinson, R. D. Sumariwalla, & Associates (Eds.), *The nonprofit sector in the global community: Voices from many nations* (pp. 1-23). San Francisco: Jossey-Bass.

Hollingsworth, J. R. (2000). Doing institutional analysis: Implications for the study of innovations. *Review of International Political Economy, 7*(4), 595-644.

Hooghe, M. (2003). Participation in voluntary associations and value indicators: The effect of current and previous participation experiences. *Nonprofit and Voluntary Sector Quarterly, 32*(1), 47-69.

Houle, C. O. (1989). *Governing boards: Their nature and nurture.* San Francisco: Jossey-Bass.

How do we keep board members informed? (n.d.). *BoardSource*, pp. 1-3. Retrieved January 7, 2005, from http://www.boardsource.org

Ilsley, P. J. (1990). *Enhancing the volunteer experience: New insights on strengthening volunteer participation, learning, and commitment.* San Francisco: Jossey-Bass.

Inglis, S., Alexander, T., & Weaver, L. (1999). Roles and responsibilities of community nonprofit boards. *Nonprofit Management & Leadership, 10*(2), 153-167.

Joseph, S. (2003). Creating a public: Reinventing democratic citizenship. In G. Mahajan (Ed.), *The public and the private: Issues of democratic citizenship* (pp. 313-323). New Delhi, India: Sage.

Kang, C. H., & Cnaan, R. A. (1995). New findings on large human service organization boards of trustees. *Administration in Social Work, 19*(3), 17-44.

Kimmey, J. R. (1981). Technical assistance and consultation for consumers. In B. Checkoway (Ed.), *Citizens and health care: Participation in planning for social change* (pp. 171-181). New York: Pergamon Press.

Klein, R., & Lewis, J. (1976). *The politics of consumer representation: A study of community health councils.* London: Centre for Studies in Social Policy.

Koff, S. Z. (1988). *Health systems agencies: A comprehensive examination of planning and process.* New York: Human Sciences Press.

Kweit, M. G., & Kweit, R. W. (1981). *Implementing citizen participation in a bureaucratic society: A contingency approach.* New York: Praeger.

Ladd, E. C. (1999). *The Ladd Report.* New York: Free Press.

Ladd, E. C., & Bowman, K. H. (1998). *What's wrong: A survey of American satisfaction and complaint.* Washington, DC: The AEI Press.

Lane, F. S. (1980). Managing not-for-profit organizations. *Public Administration Review, 40*(5), 526-530.

LaPalombara, J., & Weiner, M. (1966). The origin and development of political parties. In J. LaPalombara & M. Weiner (Eds.), *Political parties and political development* (pp. 3-42). Princeton, NJ: Princeton University Press.

Leat, D. (1990). Voluntary organizations and accountability: Theory and practice. In H. K. Anheier & W. Seibel (Eds.), *The third sector: Comparative studies of nonprofit organizations* (pp. 141-153). New York: Walter de Gruyter.

Leduc, R. F., & Block, S. R. (1985). Conjoint directorship: Clarifying management roles between the board of directors and the executive director. *Journal of Voluntary Action Research, 14*(4), 67-76.

Lerner, M. (1983). The joiners. In B. O'Connell (Ed.), *America's voluntary spirit: A book of readings* (pp. 81-89). New York: The Foundation Center.

LeRoux, K. M. (2004, September). *Empowering the disadvantaged: The role of nonprofits in promoting political participation.* Paper prepared for delivery at the annual meeting of the American Political Science Association. Retrieved October 18, 2006, from http://www.politicalscience.org

LeRoux, K. M., & Sneed, B. G. (2005, September). *When public and nonprofit values converge: A research agenda for the bi-sector study of representative bureaucracy.* Paper prepared for delivery at the 2005 annual meeting of the American Political Science Association. Retrieved October 18, 2006, from http://www.politicalscience.org

Levine, C. H. (1984). Citizenship and service delivery: The promise of coproduction. *Public Administration Review, 44*, 178-187.

Levitt, T. (1973). *The third sector.* New York: AMACOM.

Light, P. C. (2002). *Pathways to nonprofit excellence.* Washington, DC: Brookings Institution Press.

Loewenberg, F. M. (1992). Ideology or pragmatism? Further reflections on voluntary and public sector relations in the nineteenth century. *Nonprofit and Voluntary Sector Quarterly, 21*(2), 119-133.

Louden, J. K. (1982). *The director: A professional's guide to effective board work.* New York: AMACOM.

Macduff, N. (1995). Volunteer and staff relations. In T. D. Connors (Ed.), *The volunteer management handbook* (pp. 206-221). New York: John Wiley & Sons.

Macduff, N. (2001). Volunteer and staff relations. In T. D. Connors (Ed.), *The nonprofit handbook: Management* (3rd ed.), (pp. 878-892). New York: John Wiley & Sons.

MacIver, R. M. (1948). *The web of government.* New York: Macmillan.

Mansbridge, J. (1999). Should blacks represent blacks and women represent women? A contingent 'yes'. *Journal of Politics, 61*, 628-657.

March, J., & Olsen, J. (1984). The new institutionalism: Organizational factors in political life. *American Political Science Review, 78*(3), 734-749.

March, J. G., & Olsen, J. P. (1989). *Rediscovering institutions.* New York: The Free Press.

March, J. G., & Olsen, J. P. (1995). *Democratic governance.* New York: The Free Press.

March, J. G., & Olsen, J. P. (2005). *Elaborating the new institutionalism* (Working Paper No. 11). Oslo, Norway: University of Oslo, Center for European Studies. Retrieved October 18, 2006, from http://www.arena.uio.no

Masaoka, J. (2001, January 26). Board meeting packets. *Board Café*, pp. 2-3.

Masaoka, J., & Allison, M. (2004, October 28). Why boards don't govern, part 1. *Board Café*, pp. 3-6.

Masaoka, J., & Allison, M. (2004, November 19). Why boards don't govern, part 2. *Board Café*, pp. 2-3.

Maslow, A. H. (1943). A theory of human motivation. *Psychological Review, 50*, 370-396.

Maslow, A. H. (1954). *Motivation and personality.* New York: Harper & Row.

Mathews, D. (1984). The public in practice and theory. *Public Administration Review, 44*, 120-125.

McFarland, F. W. (1999 November-December). Working on nonprofit boards: Don't assume the shoe fits. *Harvard Business Review, 77*, 65-80.

McGregor, E. B., Jr. (1984). The great paradox of democratic citizenship and public personnel administration. *Public Administration Review, 44*, 126-132.

Meneghetti, M. M. (1995). Motivating people to volunteer their services. In T. D. Connors (Ed.), *The volunteer management handbook* (pp. 12-35). New York: John Wiley & Sons.

Metsch, J. M., & Veney, J. E. (1977). Consumer participation and social accountability. In H. Rosen, J. M. Metsch, & S. Levey (Eds.), *The consumer and the health care system: Social and managerial perspectives* (pp. 83-98). New York: Spectrum Publications.

Mick, S. S., & Thompson, J. D. (1984). Public attitudes toward health planning under the health systems agencies. *Journal of Health Politics, Policy and Law, 8*(4), 782-800.

Middleton, M. (1987). Nonprofit boards of directors: Beyond the governance function. In W. W. Powell (Ed.), *The nonprofit sector: A research handbook* (pp. 141-153). New Haven, CT: Yale University Press.

Milbrath, L. W. (1965). *Political participation: How and why do people get involved in politics?* Chicago: Rand McNally.

Mogulof, M. B. (1970a). *Citizen participation: The local perspective.* Washington, DC: The Urban Institute.

Mogulof, M. B. (1970b). *Citizen participation: A review and commentary on federal policies and practices.* Washington, DC: The Urban Institute.

Morone, J., & Kilbreth, E. H. (2003). Power to the people? Restoring citizen participation. *Journal of Health Politics, Policy and Law, 28*(2-3), 271-288.

Morone, J., & Marmor, T. R. (1981). Representing consumer interests: The case of American health planning. In B. Checkoway (Ed.), *Citizens and health care: Participation and planning for social change* (pp.25-48). New York: Pergamon Press.

Morone, J. A. (1990). *The democratic wish: Popular participation and the limits of American government.* n.p.: Basic Books.

Mueller, R. K. (1974a). *Board life: Realities of being a corporate director.* New York: AMACOM.

Mueller, R. K. (1974b). *Buzzwords: A guide to the language of leadership.* New York: Van Nostrand Reinhold.

Mueller, R. K. (1982). *Board score: How to judge boardworthiness.* Lexington, MA: Lexington Books.

National Commission for Certifying Agencies. (1995, March 27). *Standards for accreditation of national certification organizations.* Washington, DC: National Commission for Certifying Agencies.

Naylor, H. H. (1967). *Volunteers today: Finding, training and working with them.* New York: Association Press.

Nielsen, W. A. (1983). The third sector: Keystone of a caring society. In B. O'Connell (Ed.), *America's voluntary spirit: A book of readings* (pp. 363-369). New York: The Foundation Center.

Nordlinger, E. A. (1968). Representation, governmental stability, and decisional effectiveness. In J. R. Pennock & J. W. Chapman (Eds.), *Representation* (pp. 108-127). New York: Atherton Press.

O'Connell, B. (1983). Introduction. In B. O'Connell (Ed.), *America's voluntary spirit: A book of readings* (pp. xvii-xxi). New York: The Foundation Center.

O'Connell, B. (1985). *The board member's book: Making a difference in voluntary organizations.* New York: The Foundation Center.

O'Connell, B. (1997). *Powered by coalition: The story of INDEPENDENT SECTOR.* San Francisco: Jossey-Bass.

O'Connor, R. J., & Johnson, R. S. (1989). Volunteer demographics and future prospects for volunteering. In V. A. Hodgkinson, R. W. Lyman, & Associates (Eds.), *The future of the nonprofit sector: Challenges, changes and policy considerations* (pp. 403-415). San Francisco: Jossey-Bass.

Odendahl, T., & Youmans, S. (1994). Women on nonprofit boards. In T. Odendahl & M. O'Neill (Eds.), *Women and power in the nonprofit sector* (pp. 183-221). San Francisco: Jossey-Bass.

Oliver, C. (1999). *The policy governance fieldbook: Practical lessons, tips, and tools from the experience of real world boards.* San Francisco: Jossey-Bass.

Oliver, J. E. (2000). City size and civic involvement in metropolitan America. *American Political Science Review, 94*(2), 361-373.

O'Neill, M. (1994). Introduction: The paradox of women and power in the nonprofit sector. In T. Odendahl & M. O'Neill (Eds.), *Women and power in the nonprofit sector* (pp. 1-16). San Francisco: Jossey-Bass.

Organisation for Economic Co-operation and Development. (2003). *The non-profit sector in a changing economy*. Paris: Author.

Outside directors: The fading appeal of the boardroom. (2001, February 10). *The Economist*, pp. 77-79.

Pai, S., & Sharma, P. K. (2005). *New institutionalism and legislative governance in the Indian states: A comparative study of West Bengal and Uttar Pradesh*. (CSLG Working Paper Series CSLG/WP/05-07). New Delhi, India: Jawaharlal Nehru University, Center for the Study of Law and Governance.

Panas, J. (1991). *Boardroom verities: A celebration of trusteeship with some guides and techniques to govern by*. Chicago: Precept Press.

Parkum, K., & Parkum, V. (1973). *Voluntary participation in health planning*. Harrisburg, PA: Pennsylvania Department of Health.

Parkum, K. H. (1984). Dominance and activity trends of consumer and provider volunteers in health planning organizations. *Journal of Voluntary Action Research, 13*(2), 24-36.

Peach, E. B., & Murrell, K. L. (1995). Reward and recognition systems for volunteers. In T. D. Connors (Ed.), *The volunteer management handbook* (pp. 222-243). New York: John Wiley & Sons.

Pearce, J. L. (1993). *Volunteers: The organizational behavior of unpaid workers*. London and New York: Routledge.

Pennock, J. R. (1968). Political representation: An overview. In J. R. Pennock & J. W. Chapman (Eds.), *Representation* (pp. 3-27). New York: Atherton Press.

Perlmutter, F. (1977). Citizen participation and professionalism: A developmental relationship. In H. Rosen, J. M. Metsch, & S. Levey (Eds.), *The consumer and the health care system: Social and managerial perspectives* (pp. 279-286). New York: Spectrum Publications.

Peters, B. G. (2005). *Institutional theory in political science: The 'new institutionalism'* (2nd ed.). London: Continuum.

Peterson, P. E. (1970). Forms of representation: Participation of the poor in the community action program. *American Political Science Review, 64*(2), 491-507.

Phillips, A. (1991). *Engendering democracy*. University Park: The Pennsylvania State University Press.

Phillips, A. (1998). Democracy and representation: Or why should it matter who our representatives are? In A. Phillips (Ed.), *Feminism and politics* (pp. 224-240). Oxford, England: Oxford University Press.

Pitkin, H. F. (1967). *The concept of representation*. Berkeley: University of California.

Pitkin, H. F. (1969). Introduction: The concept of representation. In H. F. Pitkin (Ed.), *Representation* (pp. 1-23). New York: Atherton Press.

Public Member Study Subcommittee. (1980). *A report on the role and effectiveness of public members on licensing boards*. n.p.: Health Occupations Council.

Public representation on health care regulatory, governing, and oversight bodies—Strategies for success. (1995). Proceedings of a workshop convened by the Citizen Advocacy Center December 10-11, 1994. Washington, DC: The Citizen Advocacy Center.

Pusic, E. (1998). Organization theory and participation. In F. Heller, E. Pusic, G. Strauss, & B. Wilpert (Eds.), *Organizational participation: Myth and reality* (pp. 65-96). Oxford, England: Oxford University Press.

Putnam, R. (1995). Tuning in, tuning out: The strange disappearance of social capital in America. *PS: Political Science & Politics, 28*, 664-683.

Putnam, R. D. (1993). *Making democracy work: Civic traditions in modern Italy*. Princeton, NJ: Princeton University Press.

Putnam, R. D. (2000). *Bowling alone: The collapse and revival of American community.* New York: Simon & Schuster.

Putnam, R. D., & Feldstein, L. M. (with Cohen, D.) (2003). *Better together: Restoring the American community.* New York: Simon & Schuster.

Reed, P. B., & Selbee, L. K. (2000). Distinguishing characteristics of active volunteers in Canada. *Nonprofit and Voluntary Sector Quarterly, 29*(4), 571-592.

Reinventing aging: Baby boomers and civic engagement. (2004). Harvard School of Public Health-Metlife Foundation Initiative on Retirement and Civic Engagement. Retrieved December 14, 2004, from http://www.hsph.harvard.edu

Richardson, A. (1983). *Participation.* London: Routledge & Kegan Paul.

Riska, E. & Taylor, J. A. (1978). Consumer attitudes toward health policy and knowledge about health legislation. *Journal of Health Politics, Policy and Law, 3*(1), 112-123.

Rosenblatt, B. (2000, December 21). Nonprofit and corporate boards: Same or different? *Board Café*, pp. 2-3.

Rosenblatt, B. (2001, February 22). New findings on nonprofit CEO pay and board member giving. *Board Café*, pp. 2-3.

Rothenstein, B., & Stolle, D. (2002, August-September). *How political institutions create and destroy social capital: An institutional theory of generalized trust.* Paper prepared for delivery at the 98th meeting of the American Political Science Association, Boston, MA. Retrieved October 18, 2006, from http://www.politicalscience.org

Salamon, L. M. (1990). The nonprofit sector and government: The American experience in theory and practice. In H. K. Anheier & W. Seibel (Eds.), *The third sector: Comparative studies of nonprofit organizations* (pp. 219-240). New York: Walter de Gruyter.

Salamon, L. M., & Anheier, H. K. (1995). Caring sector or caring society: Discovering the nonprofit sector cross-nationally. In P. G. Schervish, V. A. Hodgkinson, M. Gates, & Associates (Eds.), *Care and community in modern society: Passing on the tradition of service to future generations* (pp. 373-402). San Francisco: Jossey-Bass.

Sapiro, V. (1981). When are interests interesting? *American Political Science Review, 75*, 701-721.

Scheier, I. H. (2001). Building staff/volunteer relations. In J. S. Ott (Ed.), *Understanding nonprofit organizations: Governance, leadership, and management* (pp. 339-344). Boulder, CO: Westview Press.

Schervish, P. G. (1995). Introduction: Gentle as doves and wise as serpents: The philosophy of care and the sociology of transmission. In P. G. Schervish, V. A. Hodgkinson, M. Gates, & Associates (Eds.), *Care and community in modern society: Passing on the tradition of service to future generations* (pp. 1-20). San Francisco: Jossey-Bass.

Schindler-Rainman, E. (1988a). Motivating people to volunteer their services. In T. D. Connors (Ed.), *The nonprofit organization handbook* (2nd ed.), (pp. 17.1-17.13). New York: McGraw-Hill.

Schindler-Rainman, E. (1988b). Recruitment, orientation, and retention. In T. D. Connors (Ed.), *The nonprofit organization handbook* (2nd ed.), (pp. 18.1-18.6). New York: McGraw-Hill.

Schlozman, K. L., Verba, S., & Brady, H. E. (1999). Civic participation and the equality problem. In T. Skocpol & M. P. Fiorina (Eds.), *Civic engagement in American democracy* (pp. 427-459). Washington, DC and New York: Brookings Institution Press and Russell Sage Foundation.

Schneider, S. K. (1986). The policy role of state professional licencing agencies: Perceptions of board members. *Public Administration Quarterly, 9*(4), 414-433.

Schneider, S. K. (1987). Influences on state professional licensure policy. *Public Administration Review, 47*(6), 479-484.

Schubert, G. A., Jr. (1957). 'The public interest' in administrative decision-making: Theorem, theosophy, or theory? *American Political Science Review, 51*, 346-368.

Schubert, G. A., Jr. (1960). *The public interest: A critique of the theory of a political concept.* Glencoe, IL: The Free Press.

Schutz, H. G. (1983). Effects of increased citizen membership on occupational licensing boards of California. *Policy Studies Journal, 11*(3), 504-516.

Searing, D. D. (1991). Roles, rules, and rationality in the new institutionalism. *American Political Science Review, 85*(4), 1239-1260.

Sears, D. O., & Valentino, N. A. (1997). Politics matters: Political events as catalysts for preadult socialization. *American Political Science Review, 91*(1), 45-65.

Seel, K., Regel, M. M., & Meneghetti, M. M. (2001). Governance: Creating capable leadership in the nonprofit sector. In T. D. Connors (Ed.), *The nonprofit handbook: Management* (3rd ed.), (pp. 642-662). New York: John Wiley & Sons.

Seibel, W., & Anheier, H. K. (1990). Sociological and political science approaches to the third sector. In H. K. Anheier & W. Seibel (Eds.), *The third sector: Comparative studies of nonprofit organizations* (pp. 7-20). New York: Walter de Gruyter.

Shaiko, R. G. (1996). Female participation in public interest nonprofit governance: Yet another glass ceiling? *Nonprofit and Voluntary Sector Quarterly, 25*(3), 302-320.

Shaiko, R. G. (1997). Female participation in association governance and political representation: Women as executive directors, board members, lobbyists, and political action committee directors. *Nonprofit Management and Leadership, 8*(2), 121-139.

Shimberg, B. (1994, December). *Recruiting public members.* Presentation at a conference on Public Representation on Health Care Regulatory, Governing and Oversight Bodies: Strategies for Success at Airlie House Conference Center, Warrenton, VA.

Skocpol, T. (1999). How Americans became civic. In T. Skocpol & M. P. Fiorina (Eds.), *Civic engagement in American democracy* (pp. 27-80). Washington, DC and New York: Brookings Institution Press and Russell Sage Foundation.

Skocpol, T., & Fiorina, M. P. (1999). Making sense of the civic engagement debate. In T. Skocpol & M. P. Fiorina (Eds.), *Civic engagement in American democracy* (pp. 1-23). Washington, DC and New York: Brookings Institution Press and Russell Sage Foundation.

Skocpol, T., Ganz, M., & Munson, Z. (2000). A nation of organizers: The institutional origins of civic voluntarism in the United States. *American Political Science Review, 94*(3), 527-546.

Smith, B. L. R. (1975). The public use of the private sector. In B. L. R. Smith (Ed.), *The new political economy: The public use of the private sector* (pp. 1-45). New York: John Wiley & Sons.

Smith, D. B. (2004). Volunteering in retirement: Perceptions of midlife workers. *Nonprofit and Voluntary Sector Quarterly, 33*(1), 55-73.

Smith, D. H. (1966). The importance of formal voluntary organizations for society. *Sociology and Social Research, 50*(4), 483-492.

Smith, D. H. (1988). The impact of the nonprofit voluntary sector on society. In T. D. Connors (Ed.), *The nonprofit organization handbook* (2nd ed.), (pp. 2.1-2.12). New York: McGraw-Hill.

Smith, D. H., Baldwin, B. R., & White, E. D. (1988). The nonprofit sector. In T. D. Connors (Ed.), *The nonprofit organization handbook* (2nd ed.), (pp. 1.3-1.15). New York: McGraw-Hill.

Smith, S. R. (2003, August). *NGOs and government: Implications for democracy, citizenship and public administration.* Paper prepared for presentation at the annual meeting of the American Political Science Association, Philadelphia, PA. Retrieved October 18, 2006, from http://www.politicalscience.org

Smith, T. W. (1990). Trends in voluntary group membership: Comments on Baumgartner and Walker. *American Journal of Political Science*, *34*(3), 646-661.

Sorauf, F. J. (1957). The public interest reconsidered. *Journal of Politics*, *19*, 616-639.

Sorauf, F. J. (1962). The conceptual muddle. In C. J. Friedrich (Ed.), *The public interest* (pp. 183-190). New York: Atherton Press.

Special report: Non-executive directors: Where's all the fun gone? (2004, March 20). *The Economist*, pp. 75-77.

Starr, P. (1980). Changing the balance of power in American medicine. *Milbank Memorial Fund Quarterly: Health and Society*, *58*, 166-172.

Steinmo, S. (2001). The new institutionalism. In B. Clarke & J. Foweraker (Eds.), *The encyclopedia of democratic thought*. London: Routledge. Retrieved October 18, 2006, from http://stripe.colorado.edu/~steinmo/foweracker.pdf

Stepputat, A. (1995). Administration of volunteer programs. In T. D. Connors (Ed.), *The volunteer management handbook* (pp. 156-186). New York: John Wiley & Sons.

Story, D. C. (1992). Volunteerism: The 'self-regarding' and 'other-regarding' aspects of the human spirit. *Nonprofit and Voluntary Sector Quarterly*, *21*(1), 3-18.

Strauss, G. (1998). Participation works--If conditions are appropriate. In F. Heller, E. Pusic, G. Strauss, & B. Wilpert (Eds.), *Organizational participation: Myth and reality* (pp. 190-219). Oxford, England: Oxford University Press.

Sundeen, R. A. (1990). Citizens serving government: The extent and distinctiveness of volunteer participation in local public agencies. *Nonprofit and Voluntary Sector Quarterly*, *19*(4), 329-344.

Taylor, B. E. (1987). *Working effectively with trustees: Building cooperative campus leadership* (ASHE-ERIC Higher Education Report No. 2). Washington, DC: Association for the Study of Higher Education.

Thain, G. J., & Haydock, K. (1983, February). *How public and other members of regulation and licensing boards differ: The results of a Wisconsin Survey*. (A Working Paper). n. p.: n.p.

Thelen, K. (draft). How institutions evolve: Insights from comparative-historical analysis. In J. Mahoney & D. Rueschemeyer (Eds.), *Comparative-historical analysis: Innovations in theory and method*. Manuscript in preparation.

Thelen, K., & Steinmo, S. (1992). Historical institutionalism in comparative politics. In S. Steinmo, K. Thelen, & F. Longstreth (Eds.), *Structuring politics: Historical institutionalism in comparative analysis* (pp. 1-32). New York: Cambridge University Press.

Tocqueville, A. de. (1946). *Democracy in America* (H. Reeve, Trans.). London: Oxford University Press. (Original work published in two parts 1835, 1840.)

Van Til, J. (1984). The future of public decisionmaking. *Policy Studies Review*, *3*(2), 311-322.

Van Til, J. (1995). Metaphors and visions for the voluntary sector. In T. D. Connors (Ed.), *The volunteer management handbook* (pp. 3-11). New York: John Wiley & Sons.

Vargo, K. S. (1995). Board member liability and responsibility. In T. D. Connors (Ed.), *The volunteer management handbook* (pp. 309-321). New York: John Wiley & Sons.

Verba, S., & Nie, N. H. (1972). *Participation in America: Political democracy and social equality*. New York: Harper & Row.

Verba, S., Schlozman, K. L., & Brady, H. E. (1995). *Voice and equality: Civic voluntarism in American politics*. Cambridge, MA: Harvard University Press.

Verba, S., Schlozman, K. L., Brady, H., & Nie, N. H. (1993). Citizen activity: Who participates? What do they say? *American Political Science Review*, *87*(2), 303-318.

The voluntary state: Hard at work. (2004, January 10). *The Economist*, p. 26.

Ward, R. (1997). *The 21st century corporate board*. New York: John Wiley & Sons.

Warren, M. E. (2003). A second transformation of democracy? In B. E. Cain, R. J. Dalton, & S. E. Scarrow (Eds.), *Democracy transformed? Expanding political opportunities in advanced industrial democracies* (pp. 223-249). Oxford, England: Oxford University Press.

Werther, W. B., Jr., Berman, W. B., & Berman, E. M. (2001). *Third sector management: The art of managing nonprofit organizations.* Washington, DC: Georgetown University Press.

What are the basic responsibilities of nonprofit boards? (n.d.). Retrieved September 23, 2000, from http://www.ncnb.org

What is the nonprofit sector? (n.d.). Retrieved September 23, 2000, from http://www.ncnb.org

White, I. (1988). Consumer influences: Challenges for the future. In I. Allen (Ed.), *Hearing the voice of the consumer* (pp. 1-12). London: Policy Studies Institute.

Widmer, C. (1985). Why board members participate? *Journal of Voluntary Action Research, 14*(4), 8-23.

W. K. Kellogg Foundation. (2003). *Blurred boundaries and muddled motives: A world of shifting social responsibilities* (A report from the W. K. Kellogg Foundation). Retrieved March 24, 2004, from http://www.wkkf.org

Wolfe, A. (1998). What is altruism? In W. W. Powell & E. S. Clemens (Eds.), *Private action and the public good* (pp. 36-46). New Haven, CT: Yale University Press.

Wolfred, T., & Peters, J. (2001). *Daring to lead: Executive directors and their work experience.* n.p.: CompassPoint Nonprofit Services. Retrieved March 24, 2004, from http://www.compasspoint.org

Wollebaek, D., & Selle, P. (2002). Does participation in voluntary associations contribute to social capital? The impact of intensity, scope and type. *Nonprofit and Voluntary Sector Quarterly, 31*(1), 32-61.

Wuthnow, R. (1999). Mobilizing civic engagement: The changing impact of religious involvement. In T. Skocpol & M. P. Fiorina (Eds.), *Civic engagement in American democracy* (pp. 331-363). Washington, DC and New York: Brookings Institution Press and Russell Sage Foundation.

Young, D. R. (2003). New trends in the US non-profit sector: Towards market integration? In Organisation for Economic Co-operation and Development (Ed.), *The nonprofit sector in a changing economy* (pp. 61-77). Paris: Organisation for Economic Co-operation and Development.

Zwingle, J. L., & Mayville, W. V. (1974). College trustees: A question of legitimacy. Washington, DC: American Association for Higher Education.

Index

For Product Safety Concerns and Information please contact our EU representative GPSR@taylorandfrancis.com Taylor & Francis Verlag GmbH, Kaufingerstraße 24, 80331 München, Germany

Batch number: 08158437

Printed by Printforce, the Netherlands